ENGAGED BUDDHIST READER

ENGAGED BUDDHIST
—————— R E A D E R ——————

*Ten Years of
Engaged Buddhist Publishing*

Edited by
ARNOLD KOTLER

Parallax Press
Berkeley, California

Parallax Press
P.O. Box 7355
Berkeley, California 94707

Cover and book design by Legacy Media, Inc.
Cover photo by Kazuhiro Tsuruta of Sitatara by Zanabazar (1635–1723),
courtesy of the Foreign Ministry and Museum of Fine Arts in Ulan Bator,
Mongolia, and the Asian Art Museum of San Francisco, The Avery
Brundage Collection.
Editorial assistance by Michelle Bernard.

LIBRARY OF CONGRESS CATALOGING-IN-PUBLICATION DATA

Engaged Buddhist reader / edited by Arnold Kotler.
    p. cm.
   ISBN 0-938077-98-8 (pbk.)
    1. Buddhism. 1. Kotler, Arnold, 1946– .
BQ122.E54   1996
294.3—dc20   96-43413
                                      CIP

2 3 4 5 6 7 8 9 10 / 01 00 99 98 97

Contents

ARNOLD KOTLER

Editor's Introduction

"Meditation is not to escape from society, but to come back to ourselves and see what is going on. Once there is seeing, there must be acting. With mindfulness, we know what to do and what not to do to help." —Thich Nhat Hanh

TEN YEARS AGO, Vietnamese Buddhist monk and Nobel Peace Prize nominee Thich Nhat Hanh suggested to several of us, "Why don't we start a press?" Now after a decade of working joyfully together, we present this *Engaged Buddhist Reader*, a collection of essays and poems from the more than sixty books on socially engaged Buddhism we've published. When we began Parallax Press in 1986, there were few books on "engaged Buddhism." Today, there are many, and a worldwide movement is underway. The notion of Buddhism as escapist has to a large extent vanished, and Buddhists fully engaged in their lives and the life of society are visible throughout the world.

The essays in this book present a broad picture of the ideas and insights at the foundation of engaged Buddhism. As you will see, these ideas are nonsectarian and eminently practical. Being peace, touching peace, making peace, and practicing peace are not the domain of just one tradition. These mindfulness-based practices are, as Thich Nhat Hanh has said, "the right medicine for our time."

We offer these essays in the hope that you enjoy reading them and putting them into practice, and that together we can help alleviate some of the suffering in ourselves, our society, and the Earth.

PART I

BEING PEACE

THE DALAI LAMA

Cultivating Altruism

THE BASIC SOURCES OF HAPPINESS are a good heart, compassion, and love. If we have these, even if we are surrounded by hostility, we will feel little disturbance. On the other hand, if we lack compassion and our mental state is filled with anger or hatred, no matter what the situation, we will not have peace. We will feel insecure, and, eventually, afraid and lacking in self-confidence. Then even something small can destabilize our inner world. But if we are calm, even if we are confronted by a serious problem, we will know how to handle it.

To utilize our human intelligence fully, we need calmness. If we become unstable through anger, it is difficult for us to use our intelligence well. When we are overly influenced by negative thoughts, our intelligence becomes tarnished. Looking at human history over the last few thousand years, and particularly in this century, we see that human tragedies like the holocaust arise from negative emotions such as hatred, anger, fear, and suspicion. And we also see that the many positive developments of human history have all come from good mental states, such as compassion.

In economics today, every nation is dependent on every other nation. Even hostile nations have to cooperate in the use of the world's resources. In both the global community and in the family, human beings need harmony and cooperation, which comes through mutual respect. Altruism is the most crucial factor.

If an individual has a sense of responsibility for humanity, he or she will naturally take care of the environment, including slowing down industrial growth and population growth. If we think narrow-mindedly and see only our own surroundings, we will not create a positive future. In the past, when we neglected the long-term effects of our actions, it was less consequential. But today, through science and technology, we can create far greater benefits or much more serious damage. The threat of nuclear weapons and the ability to damage our environment through, for example, deforestation, pollution, and ozone layer depletion, are quite alarming. We can all see the dangers of potential tragedies here. But other, barely noticeable changes, such as the loss of natural resources like topsoil, may be even more dangerous because, by the time they begin to affect us, it will be too late. In all respects, we see that genuine cooperation, the real sense of responsibility based on compassion and altruism, require not only that we respect human beings, but also that we respect, take care of, and refrain from interfering with other species and the environment. On every level of work concerning the happiness or satisfaction of the individual, the family, the nation, and the international community, the key is our altruistic mind.

As I travel around the world and meet people from various walks of life, I see that many are now showing real concern about these matters and agree with these views. The fundamental question is how to develop and maintain compassion. Certain religious beliefs, if you have them, can be very helpful, but if you do not have them, you can also survive quite well. Compassion, love, and forgiveness, however, are not luxuries. They are fundamental for our survival.

Whenever I speak about the importance of compassion and love, people ask me what is the method for developing them? It is not easy. There is no particular package or method that enables you to develop these qualities instantaneously. You cannot just press a button and wait for them to appear. I know that many people expect things like this from a Dalai Lama, but, really, all I have to offer is my own experience. If you find something useful in this, please use it. But if you don't find much of interest, I don't mind if you just leave it.

We must begin by investigating our own daily experience and reading stories about others to see the consequences of anger and the consequences of love and compassion. If we make a comparative study of these two attitudes, we will develop a deeper understanding of the negative results of anger and the positive results of compassion. Once we are convinced of the benefits of compassion and the negative consequences of anger and hatred—that they always cause unhappiness within us—we will make greater efforts to have less anger. We usually think our anger is protecting us from something, but that is a deception. Most important is to realize the negative consequences of anger and hatred. Negative emotions do not help at all.

Sometimes people feel that when there is a natural disaster or a tragedy brought about by human beings, they will have more energy and boldness to fight back if they are angry. But, in my experience, even though anger gives us energy to act or to speak out, it is blind energy and difficult to control. During that moment, we may not care, but, after a few minutes, we will feel much regret. When we are angry, we use nasty or harsh words, which, once spoken, cannot be withdrawn. Afterwards, when our anger has disappeared and we see the other person again, we feel terrible. During that moment, we lost our judgment and became half-mad. There are many different levels and forces of anger. When a small anger is about to arise, it is easy to control. But, if a stronger, more forceful anger comes, we have to try different techniques to handle it. Once we see negative mental states as negative, that alone will reduce their strength. Through my own experience, I am convinced that as a result of less anger, we become happier and healthier, smile and laugh more, and have more friends. Mental tranquility, or calmness, is a very important source of happiness. An external enemy, no matter how powerful, cannot strike directly at our mental calmness, because calmness is formless. Our happiness or joy can only be destroyed by our own anger. The real enemy of joy is anger.

There are many different states of mind, and each directly affects our happiness. When we examine different states of mind within ourselves, we can cultivate and develop those that are positive and beneficial and avoid and eliminate those that are negative and destructive. The basic difference between the investigation of external matter and the investigation of mind is that the former requires large laboratories and a huge budget. In the internal world, you just investigate which thoughts are useful and which ones are harmful, and you keep and develop the ones you like, making constant effort. Over time, your mental state will become much better balanced, and you will find that you are happier and more stable. This is a kind of yoga for the mind.

Each day when we wake up, we can say to ourselves, "Altruistic attitude." If we have an altruistic attitude, many favorable things will come. I practice these things and I know they are helpful. I try to be sincere to everyone, even the Chinese. If I develop some kind of ill-will, anger, or hatred, who will lose? I will lose my happiness, my sleep, and my appetite, but my ill feelings won't hurt the Chinese at all. If I am agitated, my physical condition will become weak, and some people I could make happy will not become happy.

Some people may criticize me, but I try to remain joyful. If we want to work effectively for freedom and justice, it is best to do so without anger or ill-will. If we feel calm and have a sincere motivation, we can work hard for thirty or forty years. I believe that because of my firm commitment to nonviolence, based on a genuine sense of brotherhood and sisterhood, some positive results have been produced.

THICH NHAT HANH

Suffering Is Not Enough

LIFE IS FILLED WITH SUFFERING, but it is also filled with many wonders, like the blue sky, the sunshine, the eyes of a baby. To suffer is not enough. We must also be in touch with the wonders of life. They are within us and all around us, everywhere, any time.

If we are not happy, if we are not peaceful, we cannot share peace and happiness with others, even those we love, those who live under the same roof. If we are peaceful, if we are happy, we can smile and blossom like a flower, and everyone in our family, our entire society, will benefit from our peace. Do we need to make a special effort to enjoy the beauty of the blue sky? Do we have to practice to be able to enjoy it? No, we just enjoy it. Each second, each minute of our lives can be like this. Wherever we are, at any time, we have the capacity to enjoy the sunshine, the presence of each other, even the sensation of our breathing. We don't need to go to China to enjoy the blue sky. We don't have to travel into the future to enjoy our breathing. We can be in touch with these things right now. It would be a pity if we are only aware of suffering.

Meditation is to be aware of what is going on—in our bodies, our feelings, our minds, and the world. Each day 40,000 children die of hunger. The former superpowers still have more than 50,000 nuclear warheads, enough to destroy the Earth many times. Yet the sunrise is beautiful, and the rose that bloomed this morning along the wall is a miracle. Life is both dreadful and wonderful. To practice meditation is to be in touch with both aspects. Don't think you have to be solemn in order to meditate. To meditate well, you have to smile a lot.

Recently I was sitting with a group of children, and a boy named Tim was smiling beautifully. I said, "Tim, you have a beautiful smile," and he said, "Thank you." I told him, "You don't have to thank me, I have to thank you. Because of your smile, you make life more beautiful. Instead of saying, 'Thank you,' you should say 'You're welcome.'"

If a child smiles, if an adult smiles, that is very important. If in our daily life we can smile, if we can be peaceful and happy, not only we, but everyone will profit from it. This is the most basic kind of peace work. When I see Tim smiling, I am so happy. If he is aware that he is making other people happy, he can say, "You are welcome."

Even though life is hard, even though it is sometimes difficult to smile, we have to try. When we wish each other, "Good morning," it must be a real "Good morning." One friend asked me, "How can I force myself to smile when I am filled with sorrow?" I told her to smile to her sorrow. We are more than our sorrow. A human being is like a television set with millions of channels. If we turn the Buddha on, we are the Buddha. If we turn sorrow on, we are sorrow. If we turn a smile on, we are really the smile. We must not let just one channel dominate us. We have the seeds of everything in us, so we have to seize the situation at hand and recover our sovereignty.

We are so busy we hardly have time to look at the people we love, even in our own household, and to look at ourselves. Society is organized in a way that even when we have some leisure time, we don't know how to use it to get back in touch with ourselves. We have millions of ways to lose this precious time—we turn on the TV or pick up the telephone, or start the car and go somewhere. We are not used to being with ourselves, and we act as if we don't like ourselves and are trying to escape from ourselves.

When we sit down peacefully, breathing and smiling, with awareness, we are our true selves. When we open ourselves up to a TV program, we let ourselves be invaded by the program. Sometimes it is a good program, but often it is just noisy. Because we want something other than ourselves to enter us, we sit there and let a noisy television program invade us, assail us, destroy us. Even if our nervous system suffers, we don't have the courage to stand up and turn it off, because if we do that, we will have to return to our self.

Meditation is the opposite. It helps us return to our true self. Practicing meditation in this kind of society is very difficult. Everything seems to work in concert to try to take us away from our true self. We have thousands of things, like videotapes and music, that help us be away from ourselves. Practicing meditation is to be aware, to smile, to breathe. These are on the opposite side. We go back to ourselves in order to see what is going on, because to meditate means to be aware of what is going on. What is going on is very important.

Children understand very well that in each woman, in each man, there is a capacity of waking up, of understanding, and of loving. Many children have told me that they cannot show me anyone who does not have this capacity. Some people allow it to develop and some do not, but everyone has it. This capacity of waking up, of being aware of what is going on in our feelings, our body, our perceptions, and the world is called Buddha nature, the capacity of understanding and loving. We must give the baby of the Buddha in us a chance. Smiling is very important. It is not by going out for a demonstration that we can bring about peace. It is with our capacity of smiling, breathing, and being peace that we make peace.

MAHA GHOSANANDA

Letting Go of Suffering

THE BUDDHA SAID, "I teach only two things—suffering and the end of suffering."

What is the cause of suffering? Suffering arises from clinging. As long as the mind clings, it suffers. When the mind is silent, it becomes peaceful and free.

How can we be free from suffering? The road to peace is called the Middle Path. It is beyond all duality and opposites. Sometimes it is called equanimity. Equanimity harmonizes extremes, like the string of a finely-tuned instrument. Neither too tight nor too loose, it vibrates perfectly and makes beautiful music.

Don't pick or choose. Opposites are endless, and in fact, they produce each other. Day becomes night, light becomes darkness, good luck and bad luck are an endless cycle.

There was once a farmer who lost his mare. When the mare disappeared, the people of the village said, "Bad luck!" But when the mare came home the very next day followed by a good strong horse, the people of the village said, "Good luck!" Yesterday they thought "bad luck," today they think "good luck." Yesterday they said "loss," but today they say "gain." Which is true? Gain and loss are opposites.

When the farmer's son rode the beautiful horse, he fell and broke his leg. Then all of the people said, "Bad luck!" War came, and all of the strong men were drafted. Many men fought and died on the battlefield. Because the farmer's son had broken his leg, he could not go to war. Was this loss or gain? Good luck or bad luck? Who can say?

Life is filled with eating and drinking through our senses, and life is also keeping from being eaten. What eats us? Time! What is time?

Time is living in the past or living in the future, feeding on the emotions. Beings who have been truly mentally healthy for even one minute are rare. Most of us suffer from clinging to pleasant, unpleasant, and neutral feelings, and from hunger and thirst. We eat and drink every second through our eyes, ears, nose, tongue, skin, and nerves, twenty-four hours a day without stopping! We crave food for the body, food for feeling, food for volitional action, and food for rebirth. We are the world, and we eat the world.

When he saw the endless cycle of suffering, the Buddha cried. The fly eats the flower; the frog eats the fly; the snake eats the frog; the bird eats the snake; the tiger eats the bird; the hunter kills the tiger; the tiger's body becomes swollen; flies come and eat the tiger's corpse; the flies lay eggs in the corpse; the eggs become more flies; and the flies eat the flowers....

The Dharma is good in the beginning, good in the middle, and good in the end. Good in the beginning is the goodness of the moral precepts—not to kill, steal, commit adultery, tell lies, or take intoxicants. Good in the middle is concentration. Good in the end is wisdom and nirvana. The Dharma is visible here and now. It is always in the present, the omnipresent. The Dharma is timeless. It offers results at once.

In Buddhism, there are three *yanas*, or vehicles, and none is higher or better than any other. All three carry the same Dharma. There is a fourth vehicle that is even more complete, called Dharmayana. It is the universe itself, and it includes every way that leads to peace and loving kindness. Dharmayana can never be sectarian. It can never divide us from any of our brothers or sisters. Come and experience it for yourself. The Dharma vehicle will bring you to peace right here and now. Step by step, moment by moment, it is comprehensible and can be understood by anyone. This is the kind of Buddhism I love.

The Art of Life

"When you paint spring, do not paint willows, plums, peaches, or apricots—just paint spring." —Dogen

WE USUALLY EVALUATE the creative process in terms of how much feeling or thinking was behind the work, or how well the work was done. What if the standard of excellence was how fully present the artist was during the process? In European traditions, masterpieces are often associated with struggle, suffering, and tragedy. In East Asia, creative people are supposed to be totally relaxed. When you set up an easel in a museum and copy a Western painting, you try to get the composition exactly right, as well as shapes, colors, and textures. You want your product to be as close as possible to the original. When you copy an Oriental piece of art, you attempt to copy the process—the posture, the way of holding the brush, the order of strokes, the way of putting pressure on paper, the brush moving in air, the breathing, feeling, and thinking. In Oriental calligraphy, you are not supposed to touch up or white out a trace of your brush. Every brush stroke must be decisive; there is no going back. It's just like life.

Paintings must have space. A painting without negative space is like music without silence. For music to have intensity, the silent part must be done well: a still moment can be the highlight of a performance. We cannot exactly create space. We can only let it come alive. Space is an extension of our inner force.

To have less control while painting, to allow something unpredictable to happen, try painting without looking. To do it well, you have to concentrate. But don't be too interested in doing well, or your concentration will get in your way. Relaxation may be more helpful.

As soon as you accept accidents, they are no longer accidents. They are just the parts of yourself that you could not expect or design beforehand. This is how the realm of your creativity grows wider. Less judgment, less trying, less improvement, less regret.

There's no need to imagine before you paint. Painting brings forth imagination. Try attentiveness rather than efficiency, gentle flow rather than speed.

You can't hide anything in a line. You are there whatever line you draw. Every line you draw carries your wish for your children and their children. A one-stroke painting leaves little room for thinking. The moment it's started, it's already done. Because one-stroke painting doesn't take much time, you can paint in your friend's studio. Then you have a friend instead of a studio. There is something calming about things you don't have complete control over. That's why a brush is more soothing than a ballpoint pen.

To be thoroughly lazy is a tough job, but somebody has to do it. Industrious people build industry. Lazy people build civilization.

Spiritual Practice and Social Action

HOW CAN WE RECONCILE the question of service and responsibility in the world with the Buddhist concepts of nonattachment, emptiness of self, and non-self? First we must learn to distinguish love, compassion, and equanimity from what might be called their "near-enemies."

The near enemy of love is attachment. It masquerades as love: "I love this person, I love this thing," which usually means, "I want to hold it, I want to keep it, I don't want to let it be." This is not love at all; it is attachment, and they are different. There is a big difference between love, which allows and honors and appreciates, and attachment, which grasps and holds and aims to possess.

The near enemy of compassion is pity. Instead of feeling the openness of compassion, pity says, "Oh, that poor person! They're suffering; they're different from me," and this sets up separation and duality. "That is outside me. I want it. I need it to be complete." I and it are seen as different.

The near enemy of equanimity is indifference. It feels very equanimous to say, "I don't care, I'm not really attached to it," and in a way it is a very peaceful feeling, a great relief. Why is that? Because it is a withdrawal. It is a removal from world and from life. Can you see the difference? Equanimity, like love and compassion, is not a removal. It is being in the middle of the world and opening to it with balance, seeing the unity in things. Compassion is a sense of our shared suffering. Equanimity is a balanced engagement with life. The "near-enemies"—attachment, pity, and indifference—all are ways of backing away or removing ourselves from the things that cause fear. Meditation does not lead to a departure from the world. It leads to a deeper vision of it, one which is not self-centered, which moves from a dualistic way of viewing ("I and other") to a more spontaneous, whole, unified way.

Vimala Thakar has been a meditation teacher in India and Europe for many years. In many ways, she is a Dharma heir to Krishnamurti. After she had been working in rural development for many years, Krishnamurti asked her to begin to teach, and she became a powerful and much-loved meditation teacher. Then she returned to her rural development work, teaching meditation considerably less. I asked her, "Why did you go back to rural development and helping the hungry and homeless after teaching meditation?" and she was insulted by my question. She said, "Sir, I am a lover of life, and I make no distinction between serving people who are starving and have no dignity in their physical lives and serving people who are fearful and closed and have no dignity in their mental lives. I love all of life."

What a wonderful response! There is a Sufi or Islamic phrase that says, "Praise Allah, and tie your camel to the post." It expresses both sides: pray, yes, but also make sure you do what is necessary in the world. It is what Don Juan called "a balance between controlled folly and impeccability." Controlled folly means seeing that all of life is a show of light and sound and that this tiny blue-green planet hangs in space with millions and billions of stars and galaxies, and that people have only been here for one second of world-time compared with millions of years of other changes. This context helps us to laugh more often, to enter into life with joy. The quality of impeccability entails realizing how precious life is, even though it is transient and ephemeral, and how, in fact, each of our actions and words do count, each affects all the beings around us in a very profound way.

If I wanted, I could make a very convincing case for just practicing sitting meditation and doing nothing else; and an equally convincing case for going out and serving the world. Looking at it from the first side, does the world need more oil and energy and food? Actually, no. There are enough resources for all of us. There is starvation, poverty, and disease because of ignorance, prejudice, and fear, because we hoard and create wars over imaginary geographic boundaries and act as if one group of people is different from another. What the world needs is not more oil, but more love and generosity, kindness and understanding. Until those are attained, the other levels will never work. So you really have to sit and meditate and get that understanding in yourself first. Only when you have actually done it yourself can you have the insight to effectively help change the greed in the world and to love. It is not a privilege to meditate, but a responsibility. I will not go any further with this argument, but it is very convincing.

As for the other side, I only have to mention Cambodia or Somalia and the starvation in Central Africa and India, where the enormity of the suffering is beyond comprehension. In India alone, 350 million people live in such poverty that they have to work that day to get enough food to feed themselves that night, when they are lucky. I once interviewed a 64-year-old man in Calcutta who pulled a rickshaw for a living. He had been pulling it for 40 years and had ten people dependent on him for income. He had gotten sick once the year before for ten days, and after a week they ran out of money and had nothing to eat. How can we let this happen? Forty deaths per minute from starvation in the world; $714,000 a minute spent on machines to kill people. We must do something!

Both arguments are totally convincing. The question is how to choose what to do, what path to take, where to put our life energy, even which spiritual path to follow. Spirituality in the West has blossomed and it is exquisite! It is also kind of confusing. There are so many ways to go—how can we choose what to do? For me the answer has been to simply follow the heart. Sometimes it is clear that we must take time to meditate and simplify—to do our inner work. Sometimes it is clear that we must begin to act and give and serve.

I can share my own experience. Ordinarily I spend my year teaching meditation retreats. Some years ago, when war began raging in Cambodia, something in me said, "I'm going." I went, not for very long but long enough to be of some assistance. The following year, feeling a real need to bring a greater marriage of service and formal meditation, I went to India with some friends to collect tapes for radio and television on the relationship between spiritual practice and social responsibility. And now I am back teaching meditation.

I did not think about it much. It just had to be done, and I went and did it. It was immediate and personal. There is not some simple solution, some easy formula for everyone to follow. It is not a matter of imitation. You have to be yourself. That means listening to your heart and knowing the right thing to do, and then doing it in the spirit of growing in awareness and service.

In the face of the tremendous suffering of the world, there is a joy that comes not from denying the pain, but from sitting in meditation, even when it is difficult, and letting our hearts open to the experience. It is the nitty-gritty work of practice to sit here and feel your sadness and my sadness and our fear, desperation, and restlessness, to open to them and begin to learn that to love is to die to how we wanted it to be, and to open more to its truth. To love is to accept. It is not a weakness. It is the most extraordinary power.

True love is really the same as awareness. True love is to see the divine goodness, the Buddha nature, the truth of each moment, and to say, "Yes," to allow ourselves to open, to accept. That is our practice every moment, whether in sitting meditation or action meditation. To be aware, to see the truth, frees us. It opens us to what is now, to what is here, and we see it as it is.

The forces of injustice in the world loom large, and sometimes we feel so tiny. How are we to have an impact? I will leave you with the words of Don Juan: "Only if one loves this Earth with unbending passion can one release one's sadness. A warrior is always joyful because his love is unalterable and his beloved, the Earth, bestows upon him inconceivable gifts....Only the love for this splendorous being can give freedom to a warrior's spirit; and freedom is joy, efficiency, and abandon in the face of any odds."[1]

---

[1] Carlos Castañeda, *Tales of Power* (Cutchogue: Buccaneer Books, January 1991).

PART II

TOUCHING PEACE

Life Is a Miracle

IN VIETNAM WHEN I was a young monk, each village temple had a big bell, like those in Christian churches in Europe and America. Whenever the bell was invited to sound, all the villagers would stop what they were doing and pause for a few moments to breathe in and out in mindfulness. At Plum Village, the community where I live in France, we do the same. Every time we hear the bell, we go back to ourselves and enjoy our breathing. When we breathe in, we say, silently, "Listen, listen," and when we breathe out, we say, "This wonderful sound brings me back to my true home."

Our true home is in the present moment. To live in the present moment is a miracle. The miracle is not to walk on water. The miracle is to walk on the green Earth in the present moment, to appreciate the peace and beauty that are available now. Peace is all around us— in the world and in nature and within us—in our bodies and our spirits. Once we learn to touch this peace, we will be healed and transformed. It is not a matter of faith; it is a matter of practice. We need only to find ways to bring our body and mind back to the present moment so we can touch what is refreshing, healing, and wondrous.

Last year in New York City, I rode in a taxi, and I saw that the driver was not at all happy. He was not in the present moment. There was no peace or joy in him, no capacity of being alive while doing the work of driving, and he expressed it in the way he drove. Many of us do the same. We rush about, but we are not at one with what we are doing; we are not at peace. Our body is here, but our mind is somewhere else—in the past or the future, possessed by anger, frustration, hopes, or dreams. We are not really alive; we are like ghosts. If our beautiful child were to come up to us and offer us a smile, we would miss him completely, and he would miss us. What a pity!

In *The Stranger,* Albert Camus described a man who was going to be executed in a few days. Sitting alone in his cell, he noticed a small patch of blue sky through the skylight, and suddenly he felt deeply in touch with life, deeply in the present moment. He vowed to live his remaining days in mindfulness, in full appreciation of each moment, and he did so for several days. Then, just three hours before the time of his execution, a priest came into the cell to receive a confession and administer the last rites. But the man wanted only to be alone. He tried many ways to get the priest to leave, and when he finally succeeded, he said to himself that that priest lived like a dead man. *"Il vit comme un mort."* He saw that the one who was trying to save him was less alive than he, the one who was about to be executed.

Many of us, although alive, are not really alive, because we are not able to touch life in the present moment. We are like dead people, as Camus says. I would like to share with you a few simple exercises we can practice that can help us reunify our body and mind and get back in touch with life in the present moment. The first is called conscious breathing, and human beings like us have been practicing this for more than three thousand years. As we breathe in, we know we are breathing in, and as we breathe out, we know we are breathing out. As we do this, we observe many elements of happiness inside us and around us. We can really enjoy touching our breathing and our being alive.

Life is found only in the present moment. I think we should have a holiday to celebrate this fact. We have holidays for so many important occasions— Christmas, New Year's, Mother's Day, Father's Day, even Earth Day—why not celebrate a day when we can live happily in the present moment all day long. I would like to declare today "Today's Day," a day dedicated to touching the Earth, touching the sky, touching the trees, and touching the peace that is available in the present moment.

Ten years ago, I planted three beautiful Himalayan cedars outside my hermitage, and now, whenever I walk by one of them, I bow, touch its bark with my cheek, and hug it. As I breathe in and out mindfully, I look up at its branches and beautiful leaves. I receive a lot of peace and sustenance from hugging trees. Touching a tree gives both you and the tree great pleasure. Trees are beautiful, refreshing, and solid. When you want to hug a tree, it will never refuse. You can rely on trees. I have even taught my students the practice of tree-hugging.

At Plum Village, we have a beautiful linden tree that provides shade and joy to hundreds of people every summer. A few years ago during a big storm, many of its branches were broken off, and the tree almost died. When I saw the linden tree after the storm, I wanted to cry. I felt the need to touch it, but I did not get much pleasure from that touching. I saw that the tree was suffering, and I resolved to find ways to help it. Fortunately, our friend Scott Mayer is a doctor for trees, and he took such good care of the linden tree that now it is even stronger and more beautiful than before. Plum Village would not be the same without that tree. Whenever I can, I touch its bark and feel it deeply.

In the same way that we touch trees, we can touch ourselves and others, with compassion. Sometimes, when we try to hammer a nail into a piece of wood, instead of pounding the nail, we pound our finger. Right away we put down the hammer and take care of our wounded finger. We do everything possible to help it, giving first aid and also compassion and concern. We may need a doctor or nurse to help, but we also need compassion and joy for the wound to heal quickly. Whenever we have some pain, it is wonderful to touch it with compassion. Even if the pain is inside—in our liver, our heart, or our lungs—we can touch it with mindfulness.

Our right hand has touched our left hand many times, but it may not have done so with compassion. Let us practice together. Breathing in and out three times, touch your left hand with your right hand and, at the same time, with your compassion. Do you notice that while your left hand is receiving comfort and love, your right hand is also receiving comfort and love? This practice is for both parties, not just one. When we see someone suffering, if we touch her with compassion, she will receive our comfort and love, and we will also receive comfort and love. We can do the same when we ourselves are suffering. Touching in this way, everyone benefits.

The best way to touch is with mindfulness. You know, it is possible to touch without mindfulness. When you wash your face in the morning, you might touch your eyes without being aware that you are touching them. You might be thinking about other things. But if you wash your face in mindfulness, aware that you have eyes that can see, that the water comes from distant sources to make washing your face possible, your washing will be much deeper. As you touch your eyes, you can say, "Breathing in, I am aware of my eyes. Breathing out, I smile to my eyes."

Our eyes are refreshing, healing, and peaceful elements that are available to us. We pay so much attention to what is wrong, why not notice what is wonderful and refreshing? We rarely take the time to appreciate our eyes. When we touch our eyes with our hands and our mindfulness, we notice that our eyes are precious jewels that are fundamental for our happiness. Those who have lost their sight feel that if they could see as well as we do, they would be in paradise. We only need to open our eyes, and we see every kind of form and color—the blue sky, the beautiful hills, the trees, the clouds, the rivers, the children, the butterflies. Just sitting here and enjoying these colors and shapes, we can be extremely happy. Seeing is a miracle, a condition for our happiness, yet most of the time we take it for granted. We don't act as if we are in paradise. When we practice breathing in and becoming aware of our eyes, breathing out and smiling to our eyes, we touch real peace and joy.

We can do the same with our heart. "Breathing in, I am aware of my heart. Breathing out, I smile to my heart." If we practice this a few times, we will realize that our heart has been working hard, day and night, for many years to keep us alive. Our heart pumps thousands of gallons of blood every day, without stopping. Even while we sleep, our heart continues its work to bring us peace and well-being. Our heart is an element of peace and joy, but we don't touch or appreciate it. We only touch the things that make us suffer, and because of that, we give our heart a hard time by our worries and strong emotions, and by what we eat and drink. Doing so, we undermine our own peace and joy. When we practice breathing in and becoming aware of our heart, breathing out and smiling to our heart, we become enlightened. We see our heart so clearly. When we smile to our heart, we are massaging it with our compassion. When we know what to eat and what not to eat, what to drink and what not to drink, what worries and despair we should avoid, we will keep our heart safe.

The same practice can be applied to other organs in our body, for instance our liver. "Breathing in, I know that my liver has been working hard to keep me well. Breathing out, I vow not to harm my liver by drinking too much alcohol." This is love meditation. Our eyes are us. Our heart is us. Our liver is us. If we cannot love our own heart and our own liver, how can we love another person? To practice love is, first of all, to practice love directed toward ourselves taking care of our body, taking care of our heart, taking care of our liver. We are touching ourselves with love and compassion.

When we have a toothache, we know that not having a toothache is a wonderful thing. "Breathing in, I am aware of my non-toothache. Breathing out, I smile at my non-toothache." We can touch our non-toothache with our mindfulness, and even with our hands. When we have asthma and can hardly breathe, we realize that breathing freely is a wonderful thing. Even when we have just a stuffed nose, we know that breathing freely is a wonderful thing.

Every day we touch what is wrong, and, as a result, we are becoming less and less healthy. That is why we have to learn to practice touching what is not wrong—inside us and around us. When we get in touch with our eyes, our heart, our liver, our breathing, and our non-toothache and really enjoy them, we see that the conditions for peace and happiness are already present. When we walk mindfully and touch the Earth with our feet, when we drink tea with friends and touch the tea and our friendship, we get healed, and we can bring this healing to society. The more we have suffered in the past, the stronger a healer we can become. We can learn to transform our suffering into the kind of insight that will help our friends and society.

We do not have to die to enter the Kingdom of Heaven. In fact we have to be fully alive. When we breathe in and out and hug a beautiful tree, we are in Heaven. When we take one conscious breath, aware of our eyes, our heart, our liver, and our non-toothache, we are transported to Paradise right away. Peace is available. We only have to touch it. When we are truly alive, we can see that the tree is part of Heaven, and we are also part of Heaven. The whole universe is conspiring to reveal this to us, but we are so out of touch that we invest our resources in cutting down the trees. If we want to enter Heaven on Earth, we need only one conscious step and one conscious breath.

When we touch peace, everything becomes real. We become ourselves, fully alive in the present moment, and the tree, our child, and everything else reveal themselves to us in their full splendor.

"The miracle is to walk on Earth." This statement was made by Zen Master Lin Chi. The miracle is not to walk on thin air or water, but to walk on Earth. The Earth is so beautiful. We are beautiful also. We can allow ourselves to walk mindfully, touching the Earth, our wonderful mother, with each step. We don't need to wish our friends, "Peace be with you." Peace is already with them. We only need to help them cultivate the habit of touching peace in each moment.

ROBERT AITKEN

The Dragon Who Never Sleeps

THE POEMS THAT FOLLOW set forth occasions for religious practice. Though I made them for modern students, I was inspired by antique antecedents, back to the historical Buddha. My purpose in this essay is to present the ideas and forms of those antecedents. The Buddha's original teaching is essentially a matter of four points—the Four Noble Truths:

1. Anguish is everywhere.
2. We desire permanent existence for ourselves and for our loved ones, and we desire to prove ourselves independent of others and superior to them. These desires conflict with the way things are: nothing abides, and everything and everyone depends upon everything and everyone else. This conflict causes our anguish, and we project this anguish on those we meet.
3. Release from anguish comes with the personal acknowledgment and resolve: we are here together very briefly, so let us accept reality fully and take care of one another while we can.
4. This acknowledgment and resolve are realized by following the Eightfold Path: Right Views, Right Thinking, Right Speech, Right Conduct, Right Livelihood, Right Effort, Right Recollection, and Right Meditation. Here "Right" means "correct" or "accurate"—in keeping with the reality of impermanence and interdependence.[1]

---

[1] Walpola Rahula, *What the Buddha Taught* (New York: Grove Press, 1974), pp. 16-50.

The Four Noble Truths are called "noble" because they present the vocation of wisdom and compassion. They are the foundation of all Buddhism, and form the heart of modern-day Theravada, the Buddhism of South and Southeast Asia. Mahayana, a later tradition that became the Buddhism of East Asia, produced quite radical changes in the way those basic ideas were interpreted and expressed. For example, early emphasis was upon demonstrating the insubstantial nature of the self but in the Mahayana that insubstantial essence itself is given attention:

> It shines everywhere in the daily activities of everyone, appearing in everything. Though you try to grasp it you cannot get it; though you try to abandon it, it always remains. It is vast and unobstructed, utterly empty.[2]

As to interdependence, the Mahayana Buddhist finds that relationships are not just the ordinary activity of giving and receiving support, but in every situation the other person, animal, plant, or thing is experienced as oneself. This is "interbeing," to use Thich Nhat Hanh's felicitous term, and is presented vividly in a multitude of expansive and profound metaphors in *The Avatamsaka Sutra*, translated into Chinese as the *Hua-yen ching*, the last great chronicle of the Mahayana. Central among these metaphors is "The Net of Indra": a multi-dimensional net of all beings (including inanimate things), with each point, each knot, a jewel that perfectly reflects, and indeed contains, all other points.[3] This cosmic, yet intimate perspective is offered again and again throughout the sutra. Thomas Cleary, scholar of Hua-yen philosophy, writes:

> All things [are interdependent, and] therefore imply in their individual being the simultaneous being of all other things. Thus it is said that the existence of each element of the universe includes the existence of the whole universe and hence is as extensive as the universe itself.[4]

---

[2] Christopher Cleary, trans., *Swampland Flowers: The Letters and Lectures of the Zen Master Ta Hui* (New York: Grove Press, 1977), p. 34.

[3] Thomas Cleary, *Entry into the Inconceivable: An Introduction to Hua-yen Buddhism* (Honolulu: University of Hawaii Press, 1983), p. 37.

[4] Ibid., p.7.

This is philosophy at its grandest, and the Buddhist is left with the task of making it personal. Religions with Near Eastern antecedents permit a personal relationship with God, and while many of the metaphorical figures in the *Hua-yen ching* could be called deities, there is no single God ruling all. The Buddha's followers cannot pray, "Thy kingdom come, Thy will be done" but instead they have made such formal promises as, "I will awaken my mind to the teachings of the Buddha for the benefit of all beings." Such vows are found in the very earliest Buddhist writings, and continue to be of primary importance as a way of personalizing the practice in all forms of the religion today.[5] In addition to vows, another way to personalize the Buddha's teaching has been to repeat gathas, four-line verses that sum up important points. Gathas too are found in the earliest Buddhist writings, and commonly have been memorized and used for Right Recollection—guideposts on the Buddha's path. *The Dhammapada*, an anthology drawn from early Buddhist texts, consists entirely of gathas, some of them probably dating from the Buddha's own time. Here is one that is known throughout the various streams of Buddhism today:

> Renounce all evil;
> practice all good;
> keep your mind pure;
> thus all the Buddhas taught.[6]

As Buddhism evolved, we find gathas and vows evolving as well. Early followers vowed to practice wisdom and compassion so that everyone and everything could thereby be freed from anguish. Their successors also vow to engage in wisdom and compassion, but *with*, rather than for, everyone and everything. This is called the way of the Bodhisattva, "The Enlightening Being."[7]

---

[5] Har Dayal, *The Bodhisattva Doctrine in Buddhist Sanskrit Literature* (London: Kegan Paul, 1931), p. 65.

[6] Cf. Irving Babbitt, trans., *The Dhammapada* (New York: New Directions, 1965), p.30.

[7] Thomas Cleary, trans., *The Flower Ornament Scripture: A Translation of the Avatamsaka Sutra*, 3 vols. (Boulder and London: Shambhala, 1984–87), II: 16–17.

Certain traditional Bodhisattvas like Kuan-yin are venerated and even worshipped for the power of the vows they have taken to save everyone and everything. However, Mahayana teachers are clear that the Bodhisattva is an archetype rather than a deity. When I take the noble path of the Buddha, the Bodhisattva is no other than my self-less self. The Bodhisattva-vows are my own.[8]

In the Mahayana the two forms of vows and gathas often converge. The *Hua-yen ching* includes a chapter called "Purifying Practice," consisting of 139 gatha-vows, and I have followed their form in composing the poems in this chapter. The first line establishes the occasion, the second line presents the act of vowing, and the last two lines follow through with the specific conduct that one promises to undertake in these circumstances.

For example, here is a gatha from the "Purifying Practice" chapter:

When I see flowing water
I vow with all beings
to develop a wholesome will
and wash away the stains of delusion.[9]

As always, translation is problematic. Word-for-word the Chinese original reads:

If see flow water
then vow all beings
gain good intention desire
cleanse dispel delusion dirt.[10]

[8] The monk Nyogen Senzaki used to address his American students, "Bodhisattvas," the way speakers of his time would begin their talks, "Ladies and Gentlemen." See also ibid., 1: 312–313.

[9] Cf. ibid., 1: 321.

[10] For the original Chinese see *Flower Adornment Sutra*, ed. by Hsüan Hua, multiple vols. in process, *Chapter 11: Pure Conduct*, trans. by Heng Tsai et al. (Talmage, Calif.: Dharma Realm Buddhist University, 1982), p.171.

The second line is the same in all the *Hua-yen* gathas, and its wording is crucial. The translator must choose a pronoun to indicate who is vowing, and also a word to connect "vow" with the rest of the poem. Cleary translates the line, "They should wish that all beings."[11] "They" are Bodhisattvas, a reference back to the introductory part of the chapter, where Manjushri is asked an elaborate, lengthy question about how Bodhisattvas can attain to wisdom and compassion. He replies with the 139 gathas that set forth occasions to follow the Buddha Way.[12]

We ourselves are Bodhisattvas, so we make these gathas our own. The translation, "They should vow that all beings /develop a wholesome will" becomes "I vow with all beings to develop a wholesome will." I myself follow the Eightfold Path and I join everyone and everything in turning the wheel of the Dharma toward universal understanding. I vow to use the many events of my day as opportunities to fulfill the task I share with all people, animals, plants, and things. Such vows take *ahimsa*, or non-harming, to the most profound level of personal responsibility. I might not realize them completely, but I do the best I can.

Making the vows my own is in keeping with the innermost purpose of Mahayana practice, especially Zen practice. I make the reality of the Buddha's teaching my own. We are here only briefly and we depend on each other—this reality is my own. Even more personally: "This very body is the Buddha," as Hakuin Zenji declared.[13] This is my truth, told of my own body, spoken for me. Everything is affected each time I make a move, here in the grand net of the universe, and as I rediscover my own Buddha nature, my vows are naturally the vows of the Buddha that all beings be freed from their anguish.

"I vow with all beings" is my compassionate vow: "I vow, and I yearn that all beings might vow with me." It is my invitation that we enter the noble way together. It is also my affirmation of the Buddha's

---

[11] Cleary, *The Flower Ornament Scripture:* I, 321.

[12] Ibid., I: 313–329.

[13] Hakuin Ekaku, *Zazen Wasan* (Song of Zazen), Robert Aitken, trans., *Taking the Path of Zen* (San Francisco: North Point Press, 1982), p. 113.

wise teaching of harmony: "I vow, and with universal affinities unit-
ing everyone and everything, all beings are joining me as I vow."
Compassion and wisdom thus blend and are one as I repeat, "I vow
with all beings."

It is a noble, yet everyday-life practice. Events set forth in *Hua-yen*
gathas follow the routine of T'ang period monks and nuns. Each act
in the monastery: washing up, putting on clothes, entering the Buddha hall, sitting down for meditation, getting up from meditation,
receives its Dharma poem. Events on pilgrimage: encountering a tree,
a river, a bridge, a dignitary, a mendicant— likewise offer entries into
the truth. My purpose in this chapter is similar: to show how ordinary occurrences in our modern lay life are in fact the Buddha's own
teachings, and also to show how we can involve ourselves accordingly
in the practice of wisdom and compassion with family and friends—
with everyone and everything.

Of course, monks and nuns of the T'ang period had no gathas for
noticing a billboard advertising Jim Beam Kentucky Sour Mash
Whiskey. As lay Western Buddhists, however, we pick our way daily
through an agglomeration of compelling reminders to pamper ourselves and serve no one else. Our task is harder, it seems, than the one
that faced our ancestors. Somehow we must cultivate methods, perhaps including gathas, to follow the noble path of the Buddha as fellow citizens of Jim Beam and his acquisitive cohorts.

Formal meditation for twenty-five minutes or so per day, meditation meetings once or twice a week, and periodic retreats—all are
helpful methods. Most of us do not, however, live in temples, with
their moment-to-moment invitations to religious practice. We are
caught up in the accelerating tempo of earning a living, and Right
Recollection tends to disappear except during times of formal meditation.

Moreover, we in the modern Western world are children of Freud
as well as of the Buddha. Classical gathas do not deal with human
relationships or emotions, just as the Japanese haiku form of poetry
leaves that side of life alone. I find myself wanting gathas that show
the way to practice and realize interbeing when I am angry with someone. I want gathas of impermanence when my plans don't work out.

What do I do if I am made to wait for someone? How should I respond to an offer of meaningless sex?

Accordingly, I find that many of my gathas are rather like *senryu*, the Japanese poetical form that uses the same syllabic count and line arrangement as haiku. Senryu verses deal with parents, spouses, children, in-laws, neighbors, work supervisors, economies, and politics. The metaphors are as complex as the situations, full of irony and satire.[14] This is human life, which I want my gathas to address.

Finally, gathas must be reckoned as poetry, and in this respect the classical gathas are rather thin. I don't find much ambiguity, irony, paradox, doubt, humor, playfulness, chance, absurdity, frustration, or mystery in them. However, they inspire my practice (including my writing), and for the devotional occasions of stepping into the meditation hall, bowing, reciting sutras, and settling down for zazen, I hope that my gathas will tend for the most part to be as straightforward and simple-hearted as my models.

Waking up in the morning
I vow with all beings
to be ready for sparks of the Dharma
from flowers or children or birds.

Sounding a bell at the temple
I vow with all beings
to ring as true in each moment:
mellow, steady, and clear.

When I bow at the end of zazen
I vow with all beings
to practice this intimate lightness
with family and friends and myself.

---

[14] R. H. Blyth, "Haiku and Senryu" in *Senryu: Japanese Satirical Verses* (Tokyo: Hokuseido Press, 1949), pp. 12–47.

When people show anger and malice
I vow with all beings
to listen for truth in the message,
ignoring the way it is said.

Facing my imminent death
I vow with all beings
to go with the natural process,
at peace with whatever comes.

When my efforts are clearly outclassed
I vow with all beings
to face my own limitations
and bring forth my original self.

When things fall apart on the job
I vow with all beings
to use this regretful energy
and pick up the pieces with care.

When thoughts form an endless procession,
I vow with all beings
to notice the spaces between them
and give the thrushes a chance.

In agony over my koan
I vow with all beings
to give up and refer it along
to the dragon who never sleeps.

When anger or sadness arises
I vow with all beings
to accept my emotional nature—
it's how I embody the Tao.

When I'm left with nothing to say
I vow with all beings
to rest content in the knowledge
there is really nothing to say.

Hearing the crickets at night
I vow with all beings
to find my place in the harmony
crickets enjoy with the stars.

On the shore of the ocean at sunrise
I vow with all beings
to rejoin this enormous power
that rises and falls in great peace.

When green leaves turn in the wind
I vow with all beings
to enjoy the forces that turn me
face up, face down on my stem.

When a train rattles by at the crossing
I vow with all beings
to remember my mother and father
and imagine their thoughts in the night.

When the table is spread for a meal
I vow with all beings
to accept each dish as an offering
that honors my ancient path.

When someone is late for a meeting
I vow with all beings
to give up the past and the future
and relax where nothing begins.

When offered meaningless sex
I vow with all beings
to draw on my store of affection
and grace as I turn it down.

With resources scarcer and scarcer
I vow with all beings
to consider the law of proportion:
my have is another's have-not.

Watching the stars after midnight
I vow with all beings
to remember the point of existence
has no dimension at all.

When roosters crow before dawn
I vow with all beings
to acknowledge each voice in the chorus,
there you are, there you are, friend.

SHUNRYU SUZUKI

Practicing in the World

MUCH OF THE CONFUSION in our society comes from a lack of understanding about the material world. Having labor as the most important element when you determine the value of work is, I think, a kind of arrogance of human beings. Before we count the value of labor, we must think about all of the other things that are given to us and not ignore the Buddha nature that everything has. If we notice this, our system of life will change a lot. Labor only makes sense when we work with respect. That is its true nature. To count only the labor without having a deep respect for what is worked on is a big mistake. When we work with respect, we experience our human life in its truest sense.

So, we pay for the labor, but we also pay for the things that are given to us by God, or by Buddha. When we have this understanding, our economic system will change. I am not an economist, but this is the way I feel. Money should be treated this way also. You pay with respect for the work done, and money is exchanged. Behind the money there is respect—respect for the things that are given to us by Buddha. And there is respect for the labor, the effort someone made.

To exchange is to purify. We may feel that if we have paid for something with money, we don't owe anything else. But something is missing in that idea. Even though we have paid for the labor, there is something we cannot pay for. We cannot pay the true value of what has been given to us by the Buddha. Only when we pay with respect for the things that are given to us, or for the result of someone's labor, can we purify our life within the activities of exchange. Without this, after we pay for the items we have, we still owe something. That is why we must have great respect for things—for money and for labor. This is Dogen Zenji's idea of everyday life. Our money is not ours. It belongs to society.

Because we think the money is ours, we sometimes think that money is dirty. But it is our understanding that is dirty. Money purifies our world. It is important that we take care of it and respect it. It is only when we don't respect money that it becomes dirty. It doesn't matter how much you have. Even if you have very little money, you should respect it and make the best use of it. The best use of it, I think, is to help our society.

Some people are too attached to money. But to accumulate some money can be allowable, for example, to be ready to enter the hospital or prepare for death. A funeral can cost $5,000 or $10,000. But to rely on the power of money is wrong. During the time of the Buddha, the monetary system was not so strong, so he said don't accumulate things—just live on the food that is offered to you and don't beg for more food than will suffice for the next meal. The Buddha understood economics. The reason we have money is for exchange. We should not stop the flow of the money. The Buddha's first principle is that everything changes.

Money is not a symbol. It expresses the value of things that change. If things are valuable because we can eat them or live on them, then the flow of money should not stop. If money stops flowing, that causes a business depression. If money is flowing slowly throughout the society, the society is healthy.

Before we study Buddhism, we should know what we are doing and how we survive. This is a part of our practice. We do not reject people just because they have no money. We are ready to help each other, but each one of us should purify our practice, even with money. That is why each of us must pay something. If you give us some money, someone will take good care of it. We should not accumulate money for Buddhism. Buddha didn't like to accumulate anything.

SAKI F. SANTORELLI

Mindfulness and Mastery in the Workplace:
21 Ways to Reduce Stress during the Workday

THIS ARTICLE EMERGED out of a conversation initiated by Thich Nhat Hanh following the conclusion of a five-day mindfulness retreat in 1987. He had asked the participants to speak together about practical methods they used to integrate mindfulness into everyday life. Most people reported that this was a struggle and that the "how" of doing so was at best, elusive. Since this has been an explicit focus of our approach at the Stress Reduction Clinic, after talking about the clinic work and my own attempts to weave practice into the fabric of my everyday life, Arnie Kotler, who also participated in the discussion and is the editor of Parallax Press, asked me to write this article.

Over the past seventeen years, the Stress Reduction Clinic at the University of Massachusetts Medical Center has introduced more than 8,000 people to mindfulness practice. The clinic is the heart of an over-arching community known as the Center for Mindfulness in Medicine, Health Care, and Society and offers medical patients a substantive, educationally-oriented approach we call *mindfulness-based stress reduction (MBSR)*.

As an instructor, I have had the good fortune of working with several hundred patients/participants each year. In the context of preventive and behavioral medicine, mindfulness practice is a vehicle that assists people in learning to tap deep internal resources for renewal, increase psychosocial hardiness, and make contact with previously unconceived-of possibilities and ways of being. Besides well-documented reductions in both medical and psychological symptoms, participants report an increased sense of self-esteem, shifts in their sense of self that afford them the ability to care for themselves while better understanding their fellow human beings, a palpable deepening of self-trust, and for some, a finer appreciation for the preciousness of every-day life.

In addition to this ongoing clinical work, I have the opportunity to teach in a wide variety of settings in both the public and private sectors. These programs are tailored to individual, corporate, or in-stitutional needs with an underlying emphasis on the cultivation and application of mindfulness and mastery in the workplace. Out of one such program evolved: *21 Ways to Reduce Stress during the Workday*.

During a follow-up program for secretarial staff, I was moved by their struggle to practically integrate the stability and sense of con-nectedness that they sometimes felt during the sitting meditation practice into their daily lives while at work. In response to their struggle, "21 Ways" came into print. In developing these ways, I pro-ceeded by simply asking myself: How do I attempt to handle ongoing stress while at work?—actually from the time I awaken in the morn-ing until I return home at the end of the formal workday. How do I attempt to stitch mindfulness into the cloth of my daily life? What helps me to wake up when I have become intoxicated by the sheer momentum and urgency of living?

Mindfulness harnesses our capacity to be aware of what is going on in our bodies, minds, and hearts in the world—and in the work-place. As we learn to pay closer attention to what is occurring within and around us, one thing we begin to discover is that we are swim-ming in an unavoidable sea of constantly changing events. In the do-main of stress reactivity, the technical term for this fluctuating reality is called a *stressor*. Stressors are ever-present events that we are con-tinually adapting to. Some tend to be met with ease and others draw us away from our sense of stability. The crucial difference in our responses to stressors usually has to do with fear and our perception of feeling threatened or overly taxed by an event, be it either internal or external in origin. Seen from a psychological viewpoint, stress is a relational *transaction* between a person and her environment. From this transactional point of view, our perception and appraisal of the events as either being over-taxing to our inner and outer resources (threatening) or capable of being handled makes a tremendous dif-ference.

Because many of our perceptions and appraisals are operating below the current threshold of our awareness, often we don't even know that our resources are being overly taxed. Conversely, because we have all been conditioned by habit and history, events that are not, or may no longer be threatening are often reacted to as if they are threatening. Therefore, developing our ability to see and understand what is going on inside and around us is an essential skill if we are to be less subject to these unconsciously-driven reactions.

Changing the way we see ourselves in relationship to events actually alters our experience of those events, their impact in our lives, as well as our capacity to maintain our well-being in the midst of such events. Given this viewpoint, the cultivation of mindfulness—our capacity to be aware and to understand ourselves and the world around us—is crucial to our ability to handle stress effectively.

Primarily, what the secretaries were struggling with was the gap between the awareness and stability they were beginning to touch in the domain of formal practice, and the dissipation of awareness and consequent dissonance experienced in the workday environment and their usual "workday mind." What they wanted was a vehicle for integrating "formal practice" into everyday life.

Although this need for integration is the same for all of us, notions about how to work in such a manner remain largely conceptual unless we develop concrete ways of practicing that transform theory into a living reality. This is exactly what the "21 Ways" provided. The participants got enthusiastic about these suggestions because it provided them something solid to work with when attempting to "bridge the gap" and integrate mindfulness into their workplace.

Since then, I have shared these "ways" with many workshop participants and continue to receive letters and telephone calls from people who have either added to the list or posted them as convenient reminders in strategic locations such as office doorways, restroom mirrors, dashboards, and lunch rooms. I've been gladdened to hear from them and happy that by its very nature, the list is incomplete and therefore full of possibility.

Each of these "21 Ways" can be seen as preventive—a strengthening of your stress immunity, or as recuperative—a means of recovering your balance following a difficult experience. Most importantly, they are methods for knowing, and if possible, modifying our habitual reactions in the midst of adversity. As you begin working with this list you'll notice that it includes pre-, during-, and post-work suggestions. Although arbitrary, these distinctions might be initially useful to you. Incorporating awareness practice into your life will necessitate a skillful effort that includes commitment, patience, and repetition. It may be helpful to think of yourself as entering a living laboratory where the elements of your life constitute the ingredients of a lively, educational process. Allowing yourself to be a beginner is refreshing. Give yourself the room to experiment without self-criticism. Allow your curiosity to carry you further into the process.

At the heart of workday practice is the intention to be aware of and connected to whatever is happening inside and around us (mindfulness) as well as the determination to initiate change when called for (mastery). A useful example of this process is revealed in the following story told to me some years ago by a physician friend. I call this story, *Little Green Dots*.

My friend told me that as his practice grew busier and more demanding, he began to develop minor, transient symptoms that included increased neck and shoulder tension, fatigue, and irritability. Initially, these symptom were benign, disappearing after a good night's rest or a relaxing weekend. But as his medical practice continued to grow, the symptoms became persistent and, much to his chagrin, he noticed that he was becoming a "chronic clock-watcher."

One day, while attending to his normal clinical duties, he had a revelation. He walked over to his secretary's supply cabinet and pulled out a package of "little green dots" used for color-coding the files. He placed one on his watch and decided that since he couldn't stop looking at his watch, he'd use the dot as a visual reminder to center himself by taking one conscious breath and dropping his shoulders.

The next day he placed a dot on the wall clock because he realized, "If I'm not looking at the one on my wrist, I'm looking at the one on the wall." He continued this practice and by the end of the week he had placed a green dot on every exam room doorknob. A few weeks after initiating this workday practice, he said that much to his own surprise, he had stopped, taken a conscious breath, and relaxed his shoulders one-hundred times in a single day. This simple, persistent decision to be mindful had been for him, transformative. He felt much better. Most importantly, his patients began telling him that he was "much more like himself." For him, that was the icing on the cake.

The story is simple and direct. Using what is constantly before us as a way of awakening to our innate capacity for stability and calmness is essential if we wish to thrive in the midst of our demanding lives.

Years ago, while working with a group of harried receptionists who described their reaction to the telephone ring as feeling much like Pavlov's dogs, I suggested that they use the first ring of the telephone as a reminder to take one breath, return to themselves, and then pick up the phone. For many, this simple practice became a powerful agent of change. Some said that people they had spoken with for years on the telephone didn't recognize their voices. Clients told them that they were speaking in a more measured pace and their voices had settled into the lower ranges. For the receptionists, the telephone no longer elicited the usual patterned reaction. They had learned to respond to this relentless, invasive, ubiquitous sound rather than to react. Through the action of awareness, the ring of the telephone had shifted from an object of unconscious threat and demand to a vehicle for cultivating greater awareness and skillful action.

Having experimented with the "green dots" on my own watch, I have found, that like any other method, they can quickly sink into the realm of the unconscious. Pretty soon, like the second hand, numbers, or date indicator, the dots become just another part of the watch face, completely unseen, of no help—actually perpetuating more unawareness.

No matter what is chosen as a reminder, our real work is to remember. This remembering is called mindfulness.

The following "21 Ways" are simply a road map. Allow your curiosity and the sense of possibility to unfold as you explore the territory, discovering your own "ways."

21 Ways to Reduce Stress during the Workday

1. Take five to thirty minutes in the morning to be quiet and meditate—sit or lie down and be with yourself...gaze out the window, listen to the sounds of nature, or take a slow quiet walk.

2. While your car is warming up—try taking a minute to quietly pay attention to your breathing.

3. While driving, become aware of body tension, e.g. hands wrapped tightly around the steering wheel, shoulders raised, stomach tight, etc., consciously working at releasing, dissolving that tension.... Does being tense help you to drive better? What does it feel like to relax and drive?

4. Decide not to play the radio and be with your own sound.

5. On the interstate, experiment with riding in the right lane, going five miles below the speed limit.

6. Pay attention to your breathing and to the sky, trees, or quality of your mind, when stopped at a red light or toll plaza.

7. Take a moment to orient yourself to your workday once you park your car at the workplace. Use the walk across the parking lot to step into your life. To know where you are and where you are going.

8. While sitting at your desk, keyboard, etc., pay attention to bodily sensations, again consciously attempting to relax and rid yourself of excess tension.

9. Use your breaks to truly relax rather than simply "pausing." For instance, instead of having coffee, a cigarette, or reading, try taking a short walk—or sitting at your desk and renewing yourself.

10. For lunch, try changing your environment. This can be helpful.

11. Try closing your door (if you have one) and take some time to consciously relax.

12. Decide to stop for one to three minutes every hour during the workday. Become aware of your breathing and bodily sensations, allowing the mind to settle in as a time to regroup and recoup.

13. Use the everyday cues in your environment as reminders to "center" yourself, e.g. the telephone ringing, sitting at the computer terminal, etc.

14. Take some time at lunch or other moments in the day to speak with close associates. Try choosing topics that are not necessarily work related.

15. Choose to eat one or two lunches per week in silence. Use this as a time to eat slowly and be with yourself.

16. At the end of the workday, try retracing today's activities, acknowledging and congratulating yourself for what you've accom-

plished and then make a list *for tomorrow*. You've done enough for today!

17. Pay attention to the short walk to your car—breathing the crisp or warm air. Feel the cold or warmth of your body. What might happen if you open up to and accept these environmental conditions and bodily sensations rather than resist them? Listen to the sounds outside your workplace. Can you walk without feeling rushed? What happens when you slow down?

18. At the end of the workday, while your car is warming up, sit quietly and consciously make the transition from work to home—take a moment to simply *be*—enjoy it for a moment. Like most of us, you're heading into your next full-time job—home!

19. While driving, notice if you are rushing. What does this feel like? What could you do about it? Remember, you've got more control than you might imagine.

20. When you pull into the driveway or park on the street, take a minute to orient yourself to being with your family members or to entering your home.

21. Try changing out of work clothes when you get home. This simple act might help you to make a smoother transition into your next "role"—much of the time you can probably "spare" five minutes to do this. Say hello to each of your family members or to the people you live with. Take a moment to look in their eyes. If possible, make the time to take five to ten minutes to be quiet and still. If you live alone, feel what it is like to enter the quietness of your home, the feeling of entering your own environment.

Walking Meditation

WALKING MEDITATION is meditation while walking. We walk slowly, in a relaxed way, keeping a light smile on our lips. When we practice this way, we feel deeply at ease, and our steps are those of the most secure person on Earth. All our sorrows and anxieties drop away, and peace and joy fill our hearts. Anyone can do it. It takes only a little time, a little mindfulness, and the wish to be happy.

Most of the time, we are lost in the past or carried away by the future. When we are mindful, deeply in touch with the present moment, our understanding of what is going on deepens, and we begin to be filled with acceptance, joy, peace, and love. The seed of mindfulness is in each of us, but we usually forget to water it. We struggle in our mind and body, and we don't touch the peace and joy that are available right now—the blue sky, the green leaves, the eyes of our beloved. To have peace, we can begin by walking peacefully. Everything depends on our steps.

In Buddhism, the word *apranihita* means wishlessness or aimlessness. We do not put anything ahead of ourselves and run after it. We practice walking meditation in this spirit. We just enjoy the walking, with no particular aim or destination. We walk for the sake of walking, and it brings us peace and joy. Why rush? Our final destination will only be the graveyard.

In daily life, there is so much to do and so little time. We feel pressured to run all the time. Just stop! Touch the ground of the present moment deeply, and you will touch real peace and joy.

While walking, practice conscious breathing by counting steps. Notice each breath and the number of steps you take as you breathe in and as you breathe out. If you take three steps during an in-breath, say, silently, "One, two, three," or "In, in, in," one word with each step. As you breathe out, if you take three steps, say, "Out, out, out," with each step. If you take three steps as you breathe in and four steps as you breathe out, you say, "In, in, in. Out, out, out, out," or "One, two, three. One, two, three, four."

Don't try to control your breathing. Allow your lungs as much time and air as they need, and simply notice how many steps you take as your lungs fill up and how many you take as they empty, mindful of both your breath and your steps. The link is the counting. When you walk uphill or downhill, the number of steps per breath will change. Always follow the needs of your lungs. Do not try to control your breathing or your walking. Just observe them deeply.

If you see something along the way that you want to touch with your mindfulness—the blue sky, the hills, a tree, or a bird—just stop, but while you do, continue breathing mindfully. You can keep the object of your contemplation alive by means of mindful breathing. If you don't breathe consciously, sooner or later your thinking will settle back in, and the bird or the tree will disappear. Always stay with your breathing.

You can also practice walking meditation using the lines of a poem, such as the one that follows. In Zen Buddhism, poetry and practice always go together.

> I have arrived, I am home
> in the here, in the now.
> I am solid, I am free.
> In the ultimate I dwell.

When the baby Buddha was born, he took seven steps, and a lotus flower appeared under each step. When you practice walking meditation, you can do the same. Visualize a lotus, a tulip, or a gardenia blooming under each step the moment your foot touches the ground. If you practice beautifully like this, your friends will see fields of flowers everywhere you walk.

Staggering Meditation

IN NOVEMBER 1992, Arnie Kotler, Therese Fitzgerald, and Claude Thomas came to share a Day of Mindfulness with a group of Vietnam veteran ministers. We all could sit, but walking meditation was difficult for a few of us. One man lost his legs in Vietnam; I injured a hip and knee during an incident and cannot walk slowly and deliberately without a cane. I mentioned to Therese that during the walking meditation, as I sat on the porch and watched, I had felt left out and separated from the group; half in jest, I said that what I needed was some form of "staggering meditation." She replied, "It's up to you to invent it."

That day I had left my wooden cane in a corner of my room at the retreat center. For years I have kept it hidden, having learned how to compensate for and disguise my painful problem with walking. That "stick" was a reminder of things I wanted to forget. I did not want to remember "Cripple Corner" in Danang, an intersection near a Vietnamese hospital where maimed Vietnamese soldiers, surrounded by canes, crutches, and makeshift wheelchairs, would gather to wait for an American convoy of large trucks to pass, hoping to be able to throw themselves, or be thrown by friends, under the huge tires so that their families could collect some monetary compensation from the U.S. government. Yet I could not forget, a few years ago, watching a parade in Wheeling, West Virginia. I knelt down beside my young son, and my hip went out and I could not get up, and I was one with the soldiers of years before, a "cripple" by the roadside. Shame, disgust, and despair welled up within me; my helplessness found a focus on that hated cane, and in my anger I would not use it.

When I returned to my room later that afternoon, I sat and thought about inventing "staggering meditation." I decided that I would go for a walk, and rather than take my "stick" along as a necessary evil and out of anxiety over falling, I would "invite" my cane to be my helper. "Please come and be my companion," I said. So we set out to walk into the nearby city center. As we made our way along the sidewalks, I tried being aware not only of my breath but of my feet and of the wooden cane in my hand. Many emotions and thoughts came and I greeted both the pleasant ones and the not-so-pleasant ones and invited them to join us in our walk. After a while, I became less aware of these emotions and thoughts and more aware of the ground on which I was walking, the beauty and gentle warmth of the evening, and the people around me. I even became thankful for the companion which supported me.

As I have continued my "staggering meditation" with my companion, I have tried to think deeply about this practice. For so many years, because of my anger, I deprived myself of support that I needed to be fully mobile. When I did seek that support, I was motivated more by a fear of falling than anything else. I have come to an awareness that my companion is a gift that helps connect me not only with the ground, but also with the many others who for a variety of reasons cannot walk easily, but who also stagger. When I am connected with these brothers and sisters, I no longer feel separated or left out. Rather than a reminder of a terrible past, I have uncovered a deep root of present meaning in this "tree" that I hug in my hand.

THICH NHAT HANH

The Good News

The good news
they do not print.
The good news
we do print.
We have a special edition every moment,
and we need you to read it.
The good news is that you are alive,
that the linden tree is still there,
standing firm in the harsh winter.
The good news is that you have wonderful eyes
to touch the blue sky.
The good news is that your child is there before you,
and your arms are available:
hugging is possible.
They only print what is wrong.
Look at each of our special editions.
We always offer the things that are not wrong.
We want you to benefit from them
and help protect them.
The dandelion is there by the sidewalk,
smiling its wondrous smile,
singing the song of eternity.
Listen. You have ears that can hear it.
Bow your head.

Listen to it.
Leave behind the world of sorrow,
of preoccupation,
and get free.
The latest good news
is that you can do it.

MARCI THURSTON-SHAINE

More Good News

The good news exists,
often twisted and obscure.
We try to print and live it right.
Each of us is a special edition, every moment
new ink wet behind our ears.
The good news is being alive, changing,
knowing the linden tree stands there, changing,
yet strong through many harsh winters.
The good news is your eyes
that touch the blue sky, the cloud.
The good news is the child before me,
my arms available.
Hugging is possible.
So often news is tangled and wrong.
Please look at the special edition
that I offer every moment,
and tell me if I am wrong or hurtful.
The dandelion is there
in a crack in the sidewalk,
smiling her wondrous smile,
singing her song of eternity.
Lo! You have ears capable of hearing
and a voice capable of song.
Bow your head, and listen to her.
Sing to her.

You and I are flowers of a tenacious family.
Breathe slowly and deeply,
free of previous occupation.
The latest good news
is that you can do it,
and that I can take time to do it too, with you.

PART III

COMPASSION IN ACTION

Love in Action

THE ESSENCE OF NONVIOLENCE is love. Out of love and the willing-ness to act selflessly, strategies, tactics, and techniques for a nonvio-lent struggle arise naturally. Nonviolence is not a dogma; it is a process. Other struggles may be fueled by greed, hatred, fear, or ignorance, but a nonviolent one cannot use such blind sources of energy, for they will destroy those involved and also the struggle itself. Nonviolent action, born of the awareness of suffering and nurtured by love, is the most effective way to confront adversity.

The Buddhist struggle for peace in Vietnam in the 1960s and '70s arose from the great suffering inflicted on our nation by international forces. Blood and fire ravaged the countryside, and people everywhere were uprooted. The Vietnam War was, first and foremost, an ideo-logical struggle. To ensure our people's survival, we had to overcome both communist and anticommunist fanaticism and maintain the strictest neutrality. Buddhists tried their best to speak for all the people and not take sides, but we were condemned as "pro-communist neu-tralists." Both warring parties claimed to speak for what the people really wanted, but the North Vietnamese spoke for the communist bloc and the South Vietnamese spoke for the capitalist bloc. The Buddhists only wanted to create a vehicle for the people to be heard—and the people only wanted peace, not a "victory" by either side.

During our struggle, many scenes of love arose spontaneously—a monk sitting calmly before an advancing tank; women and children raising their bare hands against barbed wire; students confronting military police who looked like monsters wearing huge masks and holding bayonets; young women running through clouds of tear gas with babies in their arms; hunger strikes held silently and patiently; monks and nuns burning themselves to death to try to be heard above the raging noise of the war. And all of these efforts bore some fruit.

Any nonviolent action requires a thorough understanding of the situation and of the psychology of the people. In Vietnam, we inherited many ideas from the Buddhist tradition and we learned from our mistakes as we went along. In the late nineteenth and early twentieth centuries, Buddhist monks joined the struggle for independence from the French, and they won the support of their countrymen. When the Vietnam War broke out, they still had that support, as well as the knowledge gained earlier to go beyond passive resistance and undertake positive efforts to overcome the war and the oppression. In 1966, when the people of Huê and Danang learned that Field Marshall Nguyen Cao Ky was about to bring tanks and troops from Saigon to suppress the movement for peace, the people of those cities brought their family altars—the most sacred objects in their homes—onto the streets, relying on their culture and tradition to oppose the forces of destruction. Some people were critical, saying they used religion for political purposes, but I do not agree. They were using their most potent spiritual force to directly confront the violence. This was not a political act; it was an act of love.

Fasting, the method used most by Mahatma Gandhi to help India in its struggle for independence, was also used in Vietnam. Sometimes, thousands of people fasted, and other times, a single person fasted. We fasted as prayer to purify our hearts, consolidate our will, and arouse awareness and compassion in others. When Thich Tri Quang fasted for 100 days, those who passed the Duy Tan Clinic were jarred into awareness, and compassion was born in them. As a result, they felt compelled to meet, talk, and plan, thereby escalating the struggle. Thich Tri Quang had not planned to fast. He had to fast.

We also used literature and the arts as "weapons" to challenge the oppression. Works by antiwar writers, composers, poets, and artists, although illegal, were widely circulated. Antiwar songs were sung in streets and classrooms, and antiwar literature became the largest category of books sold in Vietnam, even infiltrating army units. *Look Back at Your Homeland, Only Death Allows You to Speak Out,* and *Lotus in a Sea of Fire* sold hundreds of thousands of copies. Our literature was considered dangerous by both sides. One book of poems, *Let Us Pray so the White Dove Will Be with Us,* was submitted to the Ministry of Information, and only two of the sixty poems in it were approved. A group of students published it anyway, and within a week, all copies were sold. In Huê, a policeman saw a copy in a bookstore and warned the owner, "Hide this and only bring it out when someone asks for it." Sister Cao Ngoc Phuong was arrested in Huê for transporting antiwar books, and, before I left the country, I was also arrested and imprisoned for a few days in Bao Loc for "antiwar" activities, although I was charged only with the crime of listening to Hanoi Radio.

Folk poetry was used as means of education. This lullaby was sung throughout the country:

> My hand is holding a bowl of ginger and salt.
> Ginger is hot, salt is strong.
> They embrace each other.
> North and South share the same sorrow.
> We love each other,
> why have we abandoned our love?

This "Prayer for Peace" was printed by the tens of thousands and chanted during religious services throughout Vietnam, and its effects were widely felt:

> Homage to all Buddhas in the ten directions.
> Please have compassion for our suffering.
> Our land has been at war for two decades.
> Divided, it is a land of tears,
> and blood and bones of young and old.
> Mothers weep till their tears are dry,
> while their sons on distant fields decay.
> Its beauty now torn apart,
> only blood and tears now flow.
> Brother killing brothers
> for promises from outside.

During the superpower confrontation in Vietnam, while thousands and thousands of peasants and children lost their lives, our land was unmercifully ravaged. Yet we were unable to stop the fighting; we were not able to make ourselves heard or understood. We had little access to the international news media. People thought we Buddhists were trying to seize power, but we had no interest in power. We only wanted to stop the slaughter. The voice of the Vietnamese people—80 percent Buddhists—was lost in the melee of shooting and bombs. But we realized that the means and the end are one, and we never employed any kind of action that betrayed our commitment to nonviolence.

In 1963, Venerable Thich Quang Duc went to the crossroads of Phan Dinh Phung, sat in the lotus position, poured gasoline on himself, and transformed himself into a torch. His disciple read his last words to the press. Madame Nhu described it as a "barbecue." By burning himself, Thich Quang Duc awakened the world to the suffering of the war and the persecution of the Buddhists. When someone stands up to violence in such a courageous way, a force for change is released. Every action for peace requires someone to exhibit the courage to challenge the violence and inspire love. Love and sacrifice always set up a chain reaction of love and sacrifice. Like the crucifixion of Jesus, Thich Quang Duc's act expressed the unconditional willingness to suffer for the awakening of others. Accepting the most extreme kind of pain, he lit a fire in the hearts of people around the world. Self-burning was not a technique or program of action. When anyone wished to burn himself or herself, the Buddhist leaders always tried to prevent it. But many monks, nuns, laymen, and laywomen did sacrifice themselves for peace in this way, including my disciple Nhat Chi Mai, who declared that she wanted to be "a torch in the dark night."

Nhat Chi Mai was one of the first six people ordained into the Tiep Hien Order. In 1966, she placed a statue of Avalokiteshvara, the bodhisattva of compassion, and a statue of the Virgin Mary in front of her, and burned herself alive at the Tu Nghiêm Temple, a nunnery. She left behind letters to the Presidents of North and South Vietnam, imploring them to stop the fighting. She wrote one letter to me: "Thây, don't worry too much. We will have peace soon." Nhat Chi

Mai moved the hearts of millions of her countrymen, evoking the force of love.

I know that the self-immolation of monks and nuns was difficult for Westerners to understand. The Western press called it suicide, but it was not really suicide. It was not even a protest. What the monks wrote in the letters they left behind was intended only to move the hearts of the oppressors and call the world's attention to the suffering of our people. To make a statement while enduring such unspeakable pain is to communicate with tremendous determination, courage, and sincerity. During the ordination ceremony in some Buddhist traditions, the ordainee burns one or more very small spots on his body with moxa incense as he takes the 250 vows of a monk, promising to live a life devoted to helping living beings. If he were to say this while sitting comfortably in an armchair, it would not be the same. When uttered while kneeling before the community of elders and experiencing this kind of pain, his words express the full seriousness of his heart and mind.

The Vietnamese monks, nuns, and laypeople who burned themselves were saying with all their strength and determination that they were willing to endure the greatest of suffering in order to protect their people. But why did they have to burn themselves to death? The difference between burning oneself with incense and burning oneself to death is only a matter of degree. What is important is not to die, but to express courage, determination, and sincerity—not to destroy, but to create. Suicide is an act of self-destruction based on the inability to cope with life's difficulties. In Buddhism, self-destruction is one of the most serious transgressions of the precepts. Those who burned themselves had lost neither courage nor hope, nor did they desire nonexistence. They were extremely courageous and aspired for something good in the future. They sacrificed themselves in order to seek help from the people of the world. I believe with all my heart that those who burned themselves did not aim at the death of the oppressors but only at a change in their policy. Their enemies were not human beings, but the intolerance, fanaticism, oppression, greed, hatred, and discrimination that lay within the hearts of their fellow men and women.

We did not plan self-immolations or any of the other methods that were used. But confronting the situation and having compassion in our hearts, ways of acting came by themselves. You cannot prefabricate techniques of nonviolent action and put them into a book for people to use. That would be naive. If you are alert and creative, you will know what to do and what not to do. The basic requisite is that you have the essence, the substance of nonviolence and compassion in yourself. Then everything you do will be in the direction of nonviolence. Besides self-immolation, fasting, and the use of art, literature, and culture, many other tactics were employed in Vietnam. Foreign Minister Vu Van Mau, for example, resigned in 1963 and shaved his head to protest the violent policies of the Diêm regime, and many professors and students followed suit. There were labor strikes at the harbors and markets, and business owners turned in their licenses. University deans, presidents, and professors resigned, and high school and university students boycotted classes and examinations. Draftees refused to fight. All of these acts were met with atrocious reprisals. The government used unbridled brutality—tear gas, suffocation gas, grenades, prisons, and torture—to obstruct and suppress these nonviolent efforts.

Police agents posed as monks and nuns and infiltrated our movement, damaging our prestige and sowing seeds of fear. They excited extremists and fanatics to overturn and destroy the leadership and members of the movement. No one knows exactly how many Buddhist and non-Buddhist leaders of the nonviolent movement were imprisoned or killed, including professors, students, intellectuals, politicians, workers, and farmers. Even social workers trying to help the peasants were terrorized and murdered. From the School of Youth for Social Service, eight people were kidnapped, six killed, and eleven seriously wounded—all because they refused to take sides in the war. In a memorial service organized for those who were killed, the SYSS students openly affirmed their commitment to nonviolence and neutrality: "Now, in the presence of our dear friends whose bodies are lying here, we solemnly proclaim that we cannot consider you who killed them to be our enemies. Our arms are open wide; we are ready to embrace your ideas and advice to help us continue our nonviolent ways of working for the people of Vietnam."

Despite the results—many years of war followed by years of op-pression and human rights abuse—I cannot say that our struggle was a failure. The conditions for success in terms of a political victory were not present. But the success of a nonviolent struggle can be measured only in terms of the love and nonviolence attained, not whether a political victory was achieved. In our struggle in Vietnam, we did our best to remain true to our principles. We never lost sight that the essence of our struggle was love itself, and that was a real contribution to humanity.

KENNETH KRAFT

Engaged Buddhism

IN THE MID-1960s, as the war in Vietnam escalated, a group of Vietnamese Buddhist monks and nuns began working in a nonviolent and nonpartisan way to aid their suffering countrymen. One spring day a team of eighteen Buddhists attempted to evacuate about 200 civilians trapped in a combat zone. A participant described what happened:

> The idea was to form two lines of Buddhist monks and nuns in yellow robes and lead the civilians out of the war zone. They asked me to carry a big Buddhist flag so that combatants of both sides would not shoot at us.... H. and a nun were quite seriously wounded by stray bullets. The trip lasted terribly long, as we had to stop many times, lying down on the streets and waiting for the shooting to lessen before continuing. We left the district early in the morning, but arrived in Pleiku only after dark. And what a bad time for arrival! It was time for the rockets. Pleiku was shelled. Unfortunately, we were very close to a military camp, and one rocket fell upon us, wounding seven of us. Children and women cried very much. We asked everyone to lie down and tried our best to help those who had been struck by the rocket.
>
> The most wonderful thing that happened that day is that we went through both Saigon and NFL soldiers but none of us was shot at. I must say that they were very thoughtful and kind. Had we not carried the Buddhist symbol I do not know what would have happened. It seemed that as soon as they saw and recognized us, they immediately showed their respect for life.[1]

On that day and on many others, Vietnamese Buddhists parted the red sea of blood that was flooding their land. They displayed the equa-

---

[1] Letter to Chân Không, May 1972, quoted in *Zen Bow* (Rochester: The Zen Center), 5:5, Winter 1973, p. 11.

nimity, the courage, and the selflessness of true peacemakers. Remarkably, the writer of this account even expressed gratitude toward the soldiers on both sides. Rather than feeling rage or outrage, he saw the soldiers as thoughtful and kind, acknowledging them for their ability to respect life even in the midst of war.

The term "engaged Buddhism" refers to this kind of active involvement by Buddhists in society and its problems. Participants in this nascent movement seek to actualize Buddhism's traditional ideals of wisdom and compassion in today's world. In times of war or intense hostility they will place themselves between the factions, literally or figuratively, like the yellow-robed volunteers on the road to Pleiku. Roshi Philip Kapleau, an American Zen teacher, enumerated part of the new agenda:

> A major task for Buddhism in the West, it seems to me, is to ally itself with religious and other concerned organizations to forestall the potential catastrophes facing the human race: nuclear holocaust, irreversible pollution of the world's environment, and the continuing large-scale destruction of non-renewable resources. We also need to lend our physical and moral support to those who are fighting hunger, poverty, and oppression everywhere in the world.[2]

Because Buddhism has been seen as passive, otherworldly, or escapist, an "engaged Buddhism" may initially appear to be a self-contradiction. Isn't one of the distinguishing features of Buddhism its focus on the solitary quest for enlightenment? No enlightenment can be complete as long as others remain trapped in delusion. Genuine wisdom is manifested in compassionate action. When we reexamine Buddhism's 2,500-year-old heritage, we find that the principles and even some of the techniques of an engaged Buddhism have been latent in the tradition since the time of its founder. Qualities that were inhibited in premodern Asian settings can now be actualized through Buddhism's exposure to the West, where ethical sensitivity, social activism, and egalitarianism are emphasized. We can believe that Buddhism may have unique resources to offer the West and the world, and apply ancient Buddhist insights to actual contemporary problems.

---

[2] Philip Kapleau, *A Pilgrimage to the Buddhist Temples and Caves of China* (Rochester: The Zen Center, 1983), p. 26.

Robert Thurman reads the Buddhist philosopher Nagarjuna, active in the second century C.E., "as if he were addressing us today."[3]

The touchstone for engaged Buddhists is a vision of interdependence, in which the universe is experienced as an organic whole, every "part" affecting every other "part." As Joanna Macy writes, "Everything is interdependent and mutually conditioning—each thought, word, and act, and all beings, too, in the web of life."[4] Though classic formulations of this concept push the mind beyond conventional thought, the interconnectedness of things is also evident through ordinary observation. "One sees again and again," says Christopher Titmuss, "the way the mind influences the body, the body influences the mind, the way one influences the world, and the world influences one."[5] On an international level, the interdependence of nations is equally apparent—a Chernobyl meltdown contaminates Polish milk; a Philippine revolution ignites efforts for democratic reform in Korea. In such a world not even the most powerful of nations can solve its problems single-handedly.

For these thinkers, awareness of interconnectedness fosters a sense of universal responsibility. The Dalai Lama states that because the individual and society are interdependent, one's behavior as an individual is inseparable from one's behavior as a participant in society. The darker side of this realization is that each of us contributes in some measure to violence and oppression. The brighter side is that once we recognize our involvement in the conditions we deplore, we become empowered to do something about them. As Thich Nhat Hanh writes:

> We need such a person to inspire us with calm confidence, to tell us what to do. Who is that person? The Mahayana Buddhist sutras tell us that you are that person. If you are yourself, if you are your best, then you are that person. Only with such a person—calm, lucid, aware—will our situation improve.[6]

[3] Robert A. F. Thurman, "Nagarjuna's Guidelines for Buddhist Social Action," p. 80.

[4] Joanna Macy, "In Indra's Net: Sarvodaya & Our Mutual Efforts for Peace," in Fred Eppsteiner, ed., *The Path of Compassion: Writings on Socially Engaged Buddhism*, (Berkeley: Parallax Press, 1988), p. 170.

[5] Christopher Titmuss, "Interactivity: Sitting for Peace & Standing for Parliament," in Eppsteiner, ibid, p. 187.

[6] Thich Nhat Hanh, "Please Call Me by My True Names," p. 109.

Because personal peace is connected with world peace on a fundamental level, we cannot meaningfully "work for peace" as long as we feel upset, angry, or confrontational. "Nonviolence is a day-to-day experience," says Titmuss.[7] The frenzied pace of life in technologically advanced societies exacerbates a tendency to cut oneself off from people and things. That separation is a kind of small-scale violence which breeds violence on a larger scale. Nhat Hanh notes, for example, how rarely we linger over a cup of tea with calm awareness; usually we gulp it down automatically, distracted by conversation, reading, music, or wandering thoughts. We thereby do violence to the tea, to the moment, and to ourselves. This linkage of personal and world peace is one of Buddhism's fresh contributions to politics.

Consistent with Nhat Hanh's gentle way of drinking tea, engaged Buddhist actions reflect a spirit of tolerance and humility rarely encountered among partisan causes. The fourteen precepts of the Order of Interbeing developed by Thich Nhat Hanh begin with three injunctions: avoid dogmatism, remain open, and do not force your views on others. The first reads, "Do not be idolatrous about or bound to any doctrine, theory, or ideology, even Buddhist ones. Buddhist systems of thought are guiding means; they are not absolute truth."[8] Buddhism is not an infallible system that holds all the answers to the problems we face. In the realm of socioeconomic policy, engaged Buddhist thinkers are willing to take points from a variety of other systems and faiths. Nor is any conversion to Buddhism required. The ideas and practices offered are assumed to be effective whether or not a Buddhist label is attached to them. "As part of our planetary heritage," writes Macy, "they belong to us all."[9] Thurman's essay in this book shows that Nagarjuna viewed all belief systems, Buddhist and non-Buddhist alike, as illnesses to be cured. "It does not matter what symbols or ideologies provide the umbrella," Thurman explains, "as long as the function is liberation and enlightenment."

Yet engaged Buddhists refuse to turn away from suffering or sadness. They believe that no one is really able to avoid feeling pain for

---

[7] Titmuss, "Interactivity," *The Path of Compassion*, p. 186.

[8] Fred Eppsteiner, "In the Crucible: The Order of Interbeing," ibid, p. 150.

[9] Macy, "Taking Heart," ibid, p. 204.

what is happening in the world today, try as one might to keep such feelings from coming to consciousness. For centuries Buddhism has focused on suffering as the starting-point of the religious life. Mahayana Buddhism teaches that nirvana is present *within* samsara; that is, awakening or salvation are not separate from suffering and its causes. Engaged Buddhists are updating this mysterious alchemy by transmuting despair into empowerment. A rape victim who practices at a midwestern U.S. Zen center reports, even amidst her lingering fear: "I actually was able to convert this catastrophe into an effective tool for my personal and spiritual growth."[10]

Buddhism has always emphasized that the spiritual path is a way that is "walked, not talked." Scattered throughout the literature of engaged Buddhism are practical insights and specific techniques that one can apply oneself. If you have a hot temper, says the Dalai Lama, try timing the duration of your anger, making each bout a minute or two shorter than the last. Macy offers guided meditations adapted from traditional Buddhist sources on such themes as death, compassion, empowerment, and mutual trust. For example, the media bombard us continually with evidence of the suffering of fellow beings, but before we can get in touch with our feelings of sadness, empathy, or distress, we are hit with the next alarming image or fact (or distracted by a commercial). Macy suggests that such moments are an opportunity to put down the newspaper, turn down the radio or the TV, and focus on breathing:

> Breathe in that pain like a dark stream...let it pass through your heart...surrender it for now to the healing resources of life's vast web.... By breathing through the bad news, rather than bracing ourselves against it, we can let it strengthen our sense of belonging in the larger web of being.[11]

Recently, Buddhists have been seen taking action in widely varying contexts around the globe, sometimes nonviolently and sometimes violently. In certain cases their behavior has been deplored by sensitive observers, and troubling issues have surfaced. Some Buddhists might insist that if the collective karma of a nation is to be invaded, even destroyed, then violent resistance would only create further

---

[10] Judith Ragir, "Rape," ibid, p. 191.

[11] Macy, "Taking Heart," ibid, p. 207.

karmic burdens. There is an incident in the Buddhist scriptures in which Shakyamuni Buddha, after failing twice to turn back an invader nonviolently, stands aside and allows his clan to be massacred.[12] There is also a Jataka story in which the Buddha in a former incarnation sacrifices himself for a starving tigress unable to feed her cubs. Are our only options violent self-defense or genocidal self-sacrifice? Gary Snyder, in his essay for this book, offers support for such means as "civil disobedience, outspoken criticism, protest, pacifism, voluntary poverty, and even gentle violence if it comes to a matter of restraining some impetuous crazy."

Because the implications of an engaged Buddhism are only beginning to be explored in a profound and systematic way within the Buddhist tradition, issues like these remain unresolved. To mention some further questions that have arisen: Are ancient Buddhist teachings adulterated or trivialized when linked to specific social goals? What does it mean to present release from suffering in terms of literacy, irrigation, or marketing cooperatives? What are the actual roots of nonviolence in Buddhism? Does "Buddhist nonviolence" differ in any meaningful way from the nonviolence of other traditions? Can Buddhism offer any guidance in our handling of social organization, economics, or technology? Many formerly Buddhist nations are now under the sway of communism; can some form of Buddhism and some form of communism coexist or even support each other? Further inquiry, reflection, and discussion are needed.

"Compassion" is a pleasant-sounding word, newly fashionable in American campaign rhetoric. As a political buzzword, it implies a rejection of attitudes or policies associated with recent constraints on social services. The compassion valued by Buddhists is something different—a deep sense of oneness with all beings, a spontaneous impulse born of suffering. As the yellow-robed Buddhists of Vietnam demonstrated, at times the path of compassion may even be strafed with bullets. Yet it is also as ordinary as a smile of greeting, as close as the hand that offers help. In simple terms, "The philosophy is kindness."[13]

[12] *Ekottaragama;* Hajime Nakamura, "Violence and Nonviolence in Buddhism," in Philip P. Wiener and John Fisher, eds., *Violence and Aggression in the History of Ideas* (New Brunswick: Rutgers University Press, 1974), p. 176.

[13] The Dalai Lama, "Hope for the Future," p. 252.

Buddhism in a World of Change

WHEN PRINCE SIDDHARTHA saw an old man, a sick man, a dead man, and a wandering monk, he was moved to seek salvation, and eventually he became the Buddha, the Awakened One. The suffering of the present day, such as that brought about at Bhopal and Chernobyl, should move many of us to think together and act together to overcome such death and destruction, to bring about the awakening of humankind.

The origin of Buddhism goes back to the sixth century B.C.E. The founder was an ordinary man, the prince of a small state in Northern India, now Nepal. He was deeply concerned about the problems of life and death and of suffering, and after much effort, he discovered a solution to these deepest of human problems. His solution was universal and radical. It addressed suffering as such, not just this or that sort of suffering. Neither the cause nor the cure of suffering were matters of revelation. The Buddha simply discovered them, as many others could have done before or since. He appeared as a doctor for the ills of humankind. Buddhist liberation—*nibbana*—is accessible to anyone at any time, indifferent to caste or social standing. It requires neither the mastery of an arcane doctrine nor an elaborate regimen of asceticism. In fact, the Buddha condemned extreme austerity, as well as intellectual learning that does not directly address urgent questions of life and death.

The Buddha's original teaching remains a common fund for all branches of Buddhism, and it is expressed in the Four Noble Truths: Suffering; the Cause of Suffering, namely desire or craving; the Cessation of Suffering; and the Way to do so, namely the Eightfold Path.

It is not enough merely to attain an intellectual understanding of these propositions. We have to make them part of our life. Like medicine, they must be taken. It does no good to have aspirins in the bottle; they must be internalized. If we do not regard suffering as something real and threatening, we do not take the message of the Buddha seriously.

The Buddha found that birth is the cause of such suffering as decay and death, and traced the chain back to ignorance. Then he contemplated the way in which ignorance gives rise to karmic formation, which in turn produces consciousness and so on through the twelve-link chain of causation *(paticcasamuppada)*, until he came to birth as the cause of decay and death. Working backward, he saw that cessation of birth is the cause of the cessation of suffering, and finally, he discovered that the cessation of ignorance is the ultimate cause of cessation of the whole chain. He is said to have become the Buddha by means of this contemplation up and down the chain of causation. In other words, he contemplated the way to deliverance from suffering and found that the cause of suffering is ignorance and that by extinguishing ignorance, suffering is extinguished.

The Buddha, having attained the peaceful state of nibbana, is full of compassion. This attitude of compassion or benevolence should be taken as the fundamental principle in our social life. Compassion or love toward one's neighbors is highly esteemed in Buddhism. Compassion is expressed in the Pali word *metta*, which is derived from *mitta* (friend). Compassion therefore means "true friendliness."

Buddhism enters the life of society through the presence of individuals who practice and bear witness to the Way, through their thought, speech, and actions. Anyone who looks at this world and society and sees its tremendous suffering, injustice, and danger, will agree on the necessity to do something, to act in order to change, in order to liberate people. The presence of Buddhist sages—or indeed of any humanist leaders who have attained the Way—means the presence of wisdom, love, and peace. In most societies, the so-called leaders are themselves confused, engrossed in hatred, greed, or delusion, so they become the blind who lead the blind. When they do not have peace of mind, how can they lead others without love or compassion? In Buddhism, we believe that the presence of one such person is very

72 SULAK SIVARAKSA

important, and can have an important influence on society. In Buddhist terminology, we use the term "emptiness of action," or "non-action." To act in a way that arises from non-action is to act in a way that truly influences the situation in a nonviolent way. Naturally, humanists and masters of the Way contribute to the ends to save life, but their most valued contribution is their presence, not their actions. When they act, their actions are filled with the spirit of love, wisdom, and peace. Their actions are their presence, their mindfulness, their own personalities. This non-action, this awakened presence, is their most fundamental contribution.

Since the time of the Buddha there have been many meditation masters. They may appear not to be involved with society, but they contribute greatly. For me, they are the spring of fresh water, living proof that saints are still possible in this world. Without them, religion would be poorer, more shallow. These meditation masters, monks who spend their lives in the forests, are very very important for us and for society. Even those of us who are in society must return to these masters from time to time and look within. We must practice our meditation, our prayer, at least every morning or evening. In the crises of the present day, those of us who work in society, who confront power and injustice daily, often get beaten down and we become tired. At least once a year, we need to go to a retreat center to regain our spiritual strength, so we can return to confront society. Spiritual masters are like springs of fresh water. We who work in society need to carry that pure water to flood the banks, to fertilize the land and the trees, to be of use to the plants and animals, so that they can taste something fresh, and be revitalized. If we do not go back to the spring, our minds get polluted, just as water becomes polluted, and we are not of much use to the plants, the trees, or the earth.

Most of us who are in society must be careful, because we can become polluted very easily, particularly when confronted with so many problems. Sometimes we feel hatred, sometimes greed, sometimes we wish for more power, sometimes for wealth. We must be clear with ourselves that we do not need much wealth or power. It is easy, particularly as we get older, to want softer lives, to want recognition, to want to be on equal terms with those in power. But this is a great danger. Religion means deep commitment, and personal transformation. To be of help we must become more selfless and less selfish. To do this, we have to take more and more moral responsibility in society. This is the essence of religion, from ancient times right up to the present.

Many people, particularly in the West, think that Buddhism is only for deep meditation and personal transformation, that it has nothing to do with society. This is not true. Particularly in South and Southeast Asia, for many centuries Buddhism has been a great strength for society. Until recently, Buddhist values permeated Burma, Siam,[1] Laos, Cambodia, Sri Lanka, and other Buddhist countries. But things have changed, due mainly to colonialism, materialism, and Western education. Many of us who were educated abroad look down on our own cultures, on our own religious values.

Society has become much more complex. Whether we like them or not, industrialization and urbanization have come in, and traditional Buddhism does not know how to cope with them. It did very well in rural, agrarian societies, but in urbanized societies, with the complexities of modern life, Buddhism does not know what to do. The Buddhist university in Siam, for example, is a place where monks read only the scriptures, study only the life of the Buddha in the traditional way. Meanwhile, Bangkok has become like New York or Chicago, but the monks are not aware. They think it is just a big Siamese village, as it was when I was born. They do not realize how complex Bangkok has become. Indeed the monks still have food offered to them in the traditional way, so why should they think things have changed?

They still feel that because we have a king, the government must be just, since the government supports the Sangha. This is the

---

[1] My country has become very Westernized, perhaps more than anywhere else in Southeast Asia. We even changed our name from Siam to Thailand. This kingdom was known as Siam until 1939 when it was changed to Thailand, and it remains so officially. It has been ruled by one dictator after another, and Bangkok has become a kind of second or third rate Western capital. There is not a single Buddhist value left in Bangkok, except as decoration for the tourists, or for mere religious ceremony, and Western urbanization is really beyond our grasp. To me the name Thailand signifies the crisis of traditional Siamese values. Removing from the nation the name it had carried all its life is the first step in the psychic dehumanization of its citizens, especially when its original name was replaced by a hybrid, Anglicized word. This new name also implies chauvinism and irredentism, and I refuse to use it. I prefer to use the name Siam.

Dhammaraja, or "Wheel-Turning King" theory. But in reality the governments have been corrupt in Siam for at least 30 or 40 years. Most came to power through coup d'états, often violent. In the last coup d'état, several hundred people, mostly students, were killed, and several thousand were put in jail. Still, many of the monks feel that the governments are just, so it is the duty of those of us who have a certain spiritual strength and who can see what is going on to tell them that it is otherwise. This is the duty of any religious person. We have to build up political awareness. Politics must be related to religion.

We must also build up economic awareness. Economics also relates to religion. We need what E. F. Schumacher called Buddhist economics—not just Western capitalistic economics, which is unethical and unjust, which only makes the rich richer and the poor poorer. Yes, we also need some socialist economics, but socialist economics makes the state too powerful. We really need Buddhist economics. If we are to be poor, we must be poor together, poor but generous, share our labor, share our thought, share our generosity. We need to build on that. So it is our duty to make economists aware of Buddhist economics.

In *Small Is Beautiful,* Schumacher reminds us that Western economists seek maximization of material gain as if they hardly care for people. He says that in the Buddhist concept of economic development, we should avoid gigantism, especially of machines, which tend to control rather than to serve human beings. With gigantism, we are driven by an excessive greed in violating and raping nature. If bigness and greed can be avoided, the Middle Path of Buddhist development can be achieved, i.e., both the world of industry and agriculture can be converted into a meaningful habitat.[2] I agree with Schumacher that small is beautiful in the Buddhist concept of development, but what he did not stress is that cultivation must first come from within. In the Sinhalese experience, the Sarvodaya Shramadana movement applies Buddhism to the individual first. Through cultivated individuals a village is developed, then several villages, leading to the nation and the world.

---

[2] E. F. Schumacher, *Small Is Beautiful* (London: Blond & Briggs, 1973).

Political awareness and economic awareness are related to ourselves and our society, and very much related to our own culture. To drink Coca Cola, to drink Pepsi Cola, for example, is a great mistake. It is not only junk food, it is exploiting our country economically. Both the Coca Cola Thailand Company and the Pepsi Cola Thailand Company have an ex-prime minister as president. This already makes us suspect something exploitative politically and economically. Culturally, the exploitation is insidious. Pepsi Cola and Coca Cola make the villagers feel ashamed to offer us rainwater to drink. They feel they must offer us something in a bottle. And each bottle costs them one day of their earnings.

For another example, a multinational pineapple company recently expanded its empire into my country. They bought a lot of land from our farmers, who were very proud—poor but proud to be farmers. Now they have become landless. They do not grow rice any more, they just grow pineapples for that company. At first, the company bought at a very good price; later on, they lowered the price; still later on, the farmers just became their employees. In a country without labor unions, without the right to strike, the farmers are at the mercy of the pineapple company (which was started by a missionary).

Some Westerners want to become Buddhist monks only to escape from the world of turmoil, to benefit only themselves. My own experience over the past 30 years clearly indicates that Buddhism in the West has been practiced by many who did not want to get involved with society. However a new generation of Buddhists in England and America have displayed a robust feeling and an inclination to become involved in the spirit of Buddhism.

Phrakru Sakorn is a good example of what I mean by the spirit of Buddhism. He is a Thai monk in his fifties, the abbot of Wat Yokrabat in Samut Sakorn province, a provincial monk who only completed elementary education. Samut Sakorn is only one province away from Bangkok. The people there are mostly impoverished, illiterate farmers. The province is usually flooded with sea water, which perennially destroys the paddies, leaving the people with little or no other means of subsistence.

Most of the people had been driven to gambling, drinking, or playing the lottery. Being fully aware of the people's situation, Phrakru

Sakorn decided to try to help the people before attempting to make any improvements in his own temple or spending a lot of time preaching Buddhist morals. Phrakru organized the people to work together to build dikes, canals, and to some extent, roads. He realized that poverty could not be eradicated unless new crops were introduced, since salt water was ruining the rice fields. He suggested coconut as a substitute, based on the example of a nearby province.

Once the people of Samut Sakorn started growing coconuts, Phrakru advised them not to sell them because middlemen kept the price of coconuts very low. He encouraged them to make coconut sugar, using traditional techniques to do so. With the help of three nearby universities which were interested in the development and promotion of community projects, Phrakru received assistance, and the people of Samut Sakorn began selling their coconut sugar all over the country. He has since encouraged the growing of palm trees for building material, and the planting of herbs to be used as traditional medicine.

Before the end of the Vietnam War, I asked Ven. Thich Nhat Hanh whether he would rather have peace under the communist regime which would mean the end of Buddhism or rather the victory of the democratic Vietnam with the possibility of Buddhist revival, and his answer was to have peace at any price. He argued that Buddhism does not mean that we should sacrifice people's lives in order to preserve the Buddhist hierarchy, the pagodas, the monasteries, the scriptures, the rituals, and the tradition. When human lives are preserved and when human dignity and freedom are cultivated toward peace and lovingkindness, Buddhism can again be reborn in the hearts of men and women.

The presence of Buddhism in society does not mean having a lot of schools, hospitals, cultural institutions, or political parties run by Buddhists. It means that the schools, hospitals, cultural institutions, and political parties are permeated with and administered with humanism, love, tolerance, and enlightenment, characteristics which Buddhism attributes to an opening up, development, and formation of human nature. This is the true spirit of nonviolence.

Having grasped the spirit of Buddhism, we must face the world in full awareness of its condition. In Buddhist terminology, the world is full of *dukkha*, i.e. the dangers of impending world destruction through nuclear weapons, atomic fallout, air, land, and sea pollution, population explosion, exploitation of fellow human beings, denial of basic human rights, and devastating famine. We must realize that if we wish to avoid these catastrophes, humanity must immediately stop all partisan brawls and concentrate all its abilities and energy in the urgent effort to save ourselves.

The struggles of the peoples in the Third World might go on for many more dozens of years. Because of wars, resources are wasted and economies cannot be built up. Third World governments want to spend more and more money to buy weapons from rich countries to fight civil wars, and they fall farther and farther behind on the path of development. The situation grows more and more complex. The fate of humanity is too great a burden. What can we do?

World dukkha is too immense for any country, people, or religion to solve. We can only save ourselves when all humanity recognizes that every problem on earth is our own personal problem and our own personal responsibility. This realization can only occur when the divisions and strife between religions, peoples, and nations cease. We can only serve ourselves when, for example, the rich feel that they should contribute towards alleviating the famine of the world. Unless the rich change their lifestyle considerably, there is no hope of solving this problem. Those in the northern hemisphere must see the difficulties in the Third World as their own problem. They must see the denial of basic human rights in Siam and Chile as their own problem, and the famine in Calcutta as their own agony.

The thoughts and spirit of Buddhism are well suited to the needs of a united world and to the removal of dividing, painful boundaries. The wisdom of Buddhism can provide a shining and illuminating outlook. The language of Buddhism must offer answers which fit our situation. Only then will Buddhism survive, today and tomorrow, as it has in the past, influencing humankind positively and generating love, peace, and nonviolence. The Buddha himself declared:

> All actions, by which one acquires merits are not worth the sixteenth part of friendliness (metta) which is the emancipation of mind; for friendliness radiates, shines and illumines, surpassing those actions as

the emancipation of mind, just as all the lights of the stars are not worth the sixteenth part of the moonlight, for the moonlight, surpassing them all, radiates, shines, and illumines.[3]

In the whole of Buddhist history, there has never been a holy war. Surely Buddhist kings waged war against one another, and they might even have claimed to do so for the benefit of mankind or for the Buddhist religion, but they simply could not quote any saying of the Buddha to support them however just their war might have been. The Buddha said,

> Victory creates hatred. Defeat creates suffering. The wise ones desire neither victory nor defeat.... Anger creates anger.... He who kills will be killed. He who wins will be defeated... Revenge can only be overcome by abandoning revenge.... The wise ones desire neither victory nor defeat.

There is much to be learned from the wisdom and compassion of the Buddha in this pluralistic world.

---

[3] *Anguttara-nikaya.*

ROBERT A. F. THURMAN

Nagarjuna's Guidelines for Buddhist Social Action

[O King!] Just as you love to consider
What to do to help yourself,
So should you love to consider
What to do to help others![1]

NAGARJUNA THUS EXPRESSES the basic principle of Buddhist social action: the universal altruism of "great love" *(mahamaitri)* and "great compassion," or "great empathy" *(mahakaruna)*. The primary Buddhist position on social action is one of total activism, an unswerving commitment to complete self-transformation and complete world-transformation. This activism becomes fully explicit in the Universal Vehicle *(Mahayana)*,[2] with its magnificent literature on the Bodhisattva career. But it is also compellingly implicit in the Individual Vehicle *(Hinayana)* in both the Buddha's actions and his teachings: granted, his attention in the latter was on self-transformation, the pre-

---

[1] All Nagarjuna references are from Nagarjuna, *The Precious Garland*, translated by Jeffrey Hopkins (London: Allen & Unwin, 1975). I have, however, used the Sanskrit original (Vaidya, 1960) in certain places, and on that basis altered the terminology to suit my own preference, thus to maintain coherence between quotes and commentary. [Ed. note: For the verse number of each quote from Nagarjuna, see Professor Thurman's article from which this essay is excerpted, published in *The Eastern Buddhist,* VOL. XVI, NO. 1, Spring 1983.]

[2] I use "Universal" and "Individual" to translate *Maha-* and *Hina-* , based on the fact that the Mahayana is a vehicle designed for riders who wish all other beings to share the ride, and the Hinayana is a vehicle designed for riders who also hope others will get aboard, but who are primarily concerned with hanging on themselves at least. The former thus emphasizes "Universal" liberation, the latter "Individual" liberation. Finally, since universal liberation certainly cannot take place unless it is "universal individual" liberations in totality, these translations also capture the relationship between the two vehicles.

requisite of social transformation. Thus, it is squarely in the center of all Buddhist traditions to bring basic principles to bear on actual contemporary problems to develop ethical, even political, guidelines for action.

This is just what Nagarjuna did during the second century C.E., when he wrote his *Jewel Garland of Royal Counsels* to his friend and disciple, King Udayi of the powerful Satavahana dynasty of south central India. It should thus prove instructive to examine his counsels in some detail. In this essay, I will extrapolate from his specific prescriptions a set of modern "counsels" for today's "kings," in hopes that it will help the buddhistic intellectual clarify his or her own thinking about the emergencies that beset us. I will use these prescriptions as a framework on which to outline guidelines for Buddhist social action in our modern times. The fact that it is counsel to a "king" does not invalidate this approach in the least, for, as R. B. Fuller says, the average citizen of any modern, industrial or post-industrial society lives better in many ways than most kings of bygone eras; indeed is more king of his own fate than they were in many ways.[3] Therefore, everyone can apply these counsels in their own sphere of activity. Political parties could be formed with such principles in their platforms (indeed many parties do have such planks), and Buddhist communities and individuals in particular could work to spread such principles and attitudes. So, let us now read Nagarjuna as if he were addressing us today.

There are 45 verses (#301–345) which contain the whole quintessence of the matter. This section begins with some acknowledgment that good advice is often unpleasant at first hearing, especially to a rich and powerful king who is used to being flattered and having his own way. The king is urged to be tolerant of the "useful but unpleasant" words, and to consider them as true words spoken without anger and from compassion, hence fit to be heard, like water fit for bathing. "Realize that I am telling you what is useful here and later. Act on it so as to help yourself and others."

People in power are still the same. In fact, the entire populations of the "developed" countries are in a way full of people of royal pow-

---

[3] R. B. Fuller is fond of making this point in his essays in *Utopia or Oblivion* (Overlook Press, out of print, 1973).

ers, used to consuming what they want, being flattered and waited upon by people from "underdeveloped" lands, used to having unpleasantly realistic things such as corpses, sicknesses, madnesses, the deformities of poverty, kept out of their sight. They do not want to hear that all is impermanent, that life is essentially painful and fundamentally impure. They do not want to acknowledge that all beings are equal to them and their dear ones, equally lovable and deserving. They do not want to hear that there is no real self and no absolute property and no absolute right. But that they do hear it, and hear it well, is quite the most crucial necessity of our times. The hundreds of millions of "kings" and "queens" living in the developed world must face their obligations to other peoples, to other species, and to nature itself. This is the crisis of our times, the real one, not the supposedly important competitions among the developed powers.

Nagarjuna's first real statement is straight to this most crucial point. "If you do not make contributions of the wealth obtained from former giving, through such ingratitude and attachment you will not gain wealth in the future." There are two beliefs behind this simple yet far-reaching injunction to generosity, an injunction essential today. First, wealth accrues to an individual as the evolutionary effect of generosity in former lives or previously in this life. Second, wealth in this life accrues to one by the generosity of others who give to one, for whatever reason, and therefore one must be grateful to them. Bracketing the question of former lives, which is difficult for modern people, it is a fact that people who are wealthy today usually are so because previous generations worked hard and gave of themselves to the future. Capitalism itself is, in its essence, not a matter of hoarding and attachment, but a matter of ascetic self-restraint, the "investment" of wealth or the giving it up to a larger causality. The more given up from present consumption to productive investment, the more is produced for future consumption. Those who lose sight of the essence of this process and simply consume and hoard, soon lose their wealth, just as Nagarjuna states. It is a fact of economics that the basis of wealth is generosity.

Petty-mindedness, scarcity psychology, short-term profit seeking, destructive rapacity—these are the real enemies. Their opposite is magnanimity, which makes all people friends. In sum, transcendence is the root of generosity. Generosity is the root of evolutionary survival. Evolutionary survival eventually brings forth freedom for the bliss of transcendence. This is a golden three-strand cord more powerful than the usual heap-habit, ego-habit, addiction cycle. The former is a living Nirvana. The latter is the samsara of continual dying.

The foremost type of giving is, interestingly, not just giving of material needs, although that is a natural part of generosity. That of greatest value to beings is freedom and transcendence and enlightenment. These are obtained only through the door of Dharma, Transcendent Truth of Selflessness, Voidness, Openness, and so forth. Therefore, the educational system of a society is not there to "service" the society, to produce its drone-"professionals," its workers, its servants. The educational system is the individual's doorway to liberation, to enlightenment. It is therefore the brain of the body politic. Society has no other purpose than to foster it. It is society's door of liberation. By giving others the gift of education, they gain freedom, self-reliance, understanding, choice, all that is still summed up in the word "enlightenment." Life is for the purpose of enlightenment, not enlightenment for life. The wondrous paradox is, of course, that enlightenment makes life worthwhile: because it makes it less important, it makes it easier to give it away, whereby at last it becomes enjoyable. Therefore, human evolution is consummated in transformative education. Society becomes meaningful when it fosters education. Life is worth living when it values education supremely. And so our "royal" giving should first of all go to support universal, total, unlimited education of all individuals. Nagarjuna is very specific: "Create centers of Teaching, institutions of the Three Jewels, whose name and glory are inconceivable to lesser kings, for fear of their ill-repute after death (if they rule unwisely and selfishly)."

Nagarjuna is not talking about merely creating "religious centers." He is not even talking about creating "Buddhist centers," "Buddhism" understood in its usual sense as one of a number of world religions. It does not matter what symbols or ideologies provide the umbrella, as long as the function is liberation and enlightenment. Clearly Nagarjuna, who proclaims repeatedly that "belief-systems," "dogmatic views," "closed convictions," "fanatic ideologies," and so forth, are sicknesses to be cured by the medicine of emptiness, is not a missionary for any particular "belief-system," even if it is labeled "Buddhism." Rather, he wants the social space filled with doorways to Nirvana, shrines of liberating Truth, facilities for Teaching and Practice, where "things," "duties," "laws," "religions," and "doctrines" can be examined, criticized, refined, used, transcended, and so forth. As already mentioned, these centers are not primarily even for the service of society, although in fact they are essential facilities for the evolutionary betterment of the people. They are the highest product of the society. As society itself has the main function of service to the individual, its highest gift to its individuals is to expose them to the transcendent potential developed by education.

Now these are institutions of the Three Jewels: the Buddha, the Dharma, and the Sangha. And, under the above, critically "dereligionized" interpretation, fully in keeping with Nagarjuna's own Centrist (Madhyamika) critical style, these Three Jewels can demonstrate their value without any sectarian context. In universal social terms, the Buddha is the ideal of the educated person, the full flowering of human potential, the perfectly self-fulfilled and other-fulfilling being. He/she[4] is not a god, not an object of worship, but an object of emulation, a source of enlightenment teaching. He/she is the standard of achievement. The Dharma is his/her Teaching, the Truth and Nirvana he/she realized, which all people can educate themselves to realize, as already explained. The Sangha is the Community of those dedicated to teaching and practicing this Dharma with a view of becoming and helping all become such Buddhas. Very often they are so concentrated on these tasks, they have no time for ordinary social activities, business, professions, family, and so forth, but are specialists in practice and teaching. These become mendicants, identityless, propertyless, selfless monastics, and often in Buddhist history they served as the core staff of Teaching centers. Sometimes, however, part of their Teaching and practice involved, as in the case of Vimalakirti

---

[4] When speaking of Buddha in the context of ideal archetypes, it is important to use the double pronoun, as a modern Buddhist, for males not to monopolize access to religious virtuosity and spiritual perfection. In fact, the 112 superhuman signs of a Buddha contain definite symbols of androgyny, subliminally resonating with the famous pronouncement that "ultimate reality is beyond male and female," found in many Universal Vehicle Scriptures.

and later the Great Adepts *(Mahasiddhas)*, participation in ordinary living patterns, so it is not necessary at all times and places and at all stages of development that they observe the monastic lifestyle.

These institutions will gain fame, as the people come to know that they are verily the gateways to a higher order of living, a higher awareness, a fuller sensibility, a more valid knowledge. They radiate glory as the persons who have developed themselves and have transcended their previous addictive habits naturally and compassionately give invaluable assistance toward the betterment of others according to their capacities and inclinations.

In the second verse, Nagarjuna puts in an important criterion of a genuine institution of Enlightenment Teaching: it must not become a servile establishment in service of the elites of existing societies, there to provide professional training and ideological indoctrination. Its teachers and students must live transcendently, that is, valuing Truth above all personal considerations. They must thus be intensely critical of all falsehood, pretense, delusion, sham. Therefore, their sayings and writings must be so ruthlessly clear and straightforward that inferior persons, elite members as well as kings, must be terrified of being exposed in their pretenses and faults, hence inspired themselves to live and act transcendently. If the institutions are not truly liberal, i.e., liberating in this manner, they had better not be established at all.

To take Nagarjuna's counsel to heart in modern times, this means a drastic revision of our practice nowadays. Liberal education should no longer be seen as an institution necessary for the preservation and enrichment of a free society. Rather liberal education as an institution should represent the fulfillment of the very founding purpose of a free society. Kant's call for enlightenment as the "emergence from the tutelage of others" and Jefferson's call for "universal enlightenment throughout the land" should be seen as expressing the prime priority of the whole nation. Thus it is quite proper that the major expenditure in the national budget should be for education; and it should be offered free to all, regardless of class affiliation, regardless of utilitarian calculations. "If it takes all your wealth, you should disabuse the magnificent elite of their arrogance, inspire the middle classes, and refine the coarse tastes of the lowly."

Nagarjuna seems to have been aware of the economic costliness of his insistence on the priority of education, for he devotes the next five verses to persuading the king that wealth should not be hoarded for lesser necessities, and that he should go the whole way in support of higher education. He harps on the king's death, how such contributions are an investment in his future evolution, how his successor will probably waste it, how happiness comes from the generous use of wealth, not from hoarding and eventual wasting, and how, finally, if he does not do it now while he is young and in control of his ministers, they will not respect his wishes when he sees clearly on his deathbed. In his own words:

> Having let go of all possessions (at death)
> Powerless you must go elsewhere;
> But all that has been used for Dharma
> Precedes you (as positive evolutionary force).
> All the possessions of a previous King come under the control
>   of his successor.
> Of what use are they then to the previous King,
> Either for his practice, happiness, or fame?
> Through using wealth there is happiness in the here and now.
> Through giving there is happiness in the future.
> From wasting it without using it or giving it away there is
>   only misery.
> How could there be happiness?
> Because of impotence while dying,
> You will be unable to make gifts through your ministers.
> Shamelessly they will lose affection for you,
> And will only seek to please the new King.
> Therefore, now while in good health,
> Create Centers of Learning with all your wealth,
> For you are living amid the causes of death
> Like a lamp standing in the breeze.
> Also other Teaching Centers established by the previous kings,
> All temples and so forth should be sustained as before.

From the universalism underlying the educational emphasis of
Buddhist activism, Nagarjuna moves to the principle of pacifism, in
specific application to the appointment of ministers, generals, officials,
administration of justice, and vigilance over the actual conditions in
the nation.

The choice of ministers, generals, and officials is mainly determined by whether or not they practice the Teachings, and manifest this personally by honesty, generosity, kindliness, and intelligent
discrimination. Even with such people, the ruler should be in constant
contact with them, and constantly admonish them to remember the
overall aim and purpose of the nation: namely the Teaching, realization, and practice of the liberating Truth. "If your kingdom exists for
the Truth, and not for fame, wealth, or consumption, then it will be
extremely fruitful; otherwise all will finally be in vain." In modern
terms, this counsel accords well with the experience of successful corporations and government administrations and agencies. They always
choose their leaders from among liberally-educated persons, rather
than from narrow professional circles, as it takes the special "enlightened" ability of clear critical insight to manage large complex affairs
successfully.

In regard to justice, Nagarjuna tells the king to appoint elder
judges, responsible, well-educated, virtuous, and pleasant persons, and
even so he should intervene as much as possible to exercise compassion for criminals. "Even if they (the judges) have rightfully fined,
bound, or punished people, You, being softened with compassion,
should still take care (of the offenders). O King, through compassion
you should always generate an attitude of help, even for all beings who
have committed the most appalling sins. Especially generate compassion for those murderers, whose sins are horrible; those of fallen nature are receptacles of compassion from those whose nature is great."
Nagarjuna goes to the central issue concerning violence and nonviolence in a society, the issue of murder and its retribution. Taking of
life is the worst violence, especially in enlightenment-valuing nations,
where the precious human life, hard won by struggle up from the tor-
mented lower forms of evolution, is the inestimably valuable stage
from which most effectively to attain freedom and enlightenment. But
to take a second life to avenge the first is to add violence to violence,

and hence capital punishment is abolished by Nagarjuna. Punishment must be rehabilitative, and Nagarjuna's formulation of this principle may be the earliest on historical record. "As long as the prisoners are not freed (which, he says, they should be as soon as possible) they should be made comfortable with barbers, baths, food, drink, medicine, and clothing. Just as unworthy sons are punished out of a wish to make them worthy, so punishment should be enforced with compassion and not from hatred or concern for wealth. Once you have examined the fierce murderers and judged them correctly, you should banish them without killing or torturing them." The nonviolent treatment of criminals, even capital offenders, accords with every principle of Buddhist teaching: 1) compassion, of course, in that love must be extended most of all to the undeserving, the difficult to love; further, for society to kill sanctions killing indirectly, setting a bad example; 2) impermanence, in that the minds of beings are changeable, and commission of evil once does not necessarily imply a permanent habit of doing evil; 3) selflessness implies the conditionality of each act, and the reformability of any personality; 4) the preciousness and value of life, especially human life.

In modern times, it is to the great credit of those modern societies founded on enlightenment principles that they finally have abolished capital punishment. By the same token, it is sad that there are strong political pressures to reinstate it. In such a context, it is even more astounding that Nagarjuna should have set forth this clear-cut principle almost two thousand years ago, in such specific, practical terms.

Nagarjuna gives specific advice regarding socialistic universal welfare policy: "Cause the blind, the sick, the humble, the unprotected, the destitute, and the crippled, all equally to attain food and drink without omission." He does not elaborate upon this in specific policy terms. It is perfectly clear that he considers it obvious that the king is obligated to care for everyone in the whole nation as if they were his children. In modern terms, the welfare system created by Roosevelt in the United States, and the welfare socialism the socialist states have implemented, fit extremely well with this policy. But recently, we can observe a trend of assumption that, while any reasonable person would like to give everything to everyone, it is bad for people to get goods for nothing, and it is impossible to support everyone; there is not enough wealth for that purpose. The assumptions underlying this anti-welfare reaction we see around the world are that ɪ) people are inherently lazy, and 2) wealth is inherently insufficient. Indeed, there were certainly such attitudes in Nagarjuna's day and earlier. The central Buddhist story of Prince Vessantara turns on the paradox of generosity and wealth. Everyone loves him because he gives everyone everything they ask for. Yet the nation comes to fear him when it seems he will give away even the very sources of their wealth. So they shrink back in fright, clutch what they have to themselves, and banish their real source of joy, the generous Prince.

Since the welfare system was installed in the United States, that nation has produced the greatest wealth ever produced by any nation in history, including inventions in principle capable of infinite productivity; and this in the midst of a series of disastrous wars, with their aftermaths wherein the nation gave enormous treasure to rebuild the nations it had defeated. Now, the rulers of America confusedly think that their gifts to the people, the real source of their optimism, the energy of real productivity, are exhausting them, and so they want to take it all away. In this confused effort to clutch onto what they see as scarce and shrinking wealth, they will destroy the source of that wealth, the love and optimistic confidence and creativity of the people. Fortunately, this will result in a rapid disaster for all, so the error will soon come to light, and Prince Vessantara will return in triumph from his banishment. Hoarding creates poverty. Giving away creates wealth. Imagination of scarcity is thus the cause of loss. Imagination of abundance creates endless wealth. It is terrible or wonderful, depending on one's tolerance, that life must always be so subtle, so paradoxical, and complex.

Nagarjuna seems to be aware of the charge of "impractical idealism" that tends to be levelled against his *Counsels*, and so his verses closing this passage address the practicality question. "In order to maintain control, oversee your country through the eyes of agents; attentive and mindful, always act in accordance with the principles." An effective intelligence system seems to be necessary! The king must know what is happening throughout his realm to prevent abuses and forestall disasters. In modern terms, Nagarjuna allows for the vital role of "intelligence," the gathering of insightful information about the state of the people. The very mention of an "Intelligence Agency" is so sensitive nowadays, it is hard to remember that it is not the "intelligence" but the stupidity and violence in the paramilitary activities of the CIA, KGB, and their colleagues in other nations that have caused their aura of horror. Theoretically, if the responsible leaders of all nations really had all the information about all consequences of their actions, they surely would desist from the foolish and self-destructive policies they currently espouse.

Nagarjuna sums up his practical counsels with a pleasant metaphor: "The birds of the populace will alight upon the royal tree that gives the cool shade of tolerance, that flourishes with the flowers of honors, and that provides the bounteous fruit of great rewards." That is, an idealistic social policy is realistic. Tolerance, justice, and generosity are not merely lofty ideals, "ultra-obligations" for a few saints and heroes to aspire to embody, but are the essential components of any viable social policy. The ruler or government must manifest them first, and each citizen must strive to cultivate them. Since animals' habits do not automatically tend away from anger, delusion, and greed toward tolerance, justice, and giving, these virtues must gradually be cultivated. As each must do this for himself or herself, individualistic transcendentalism is the foundation of any viable activism. From this basis, pacifism is the social expression of tolerance; educational universalism is the social expression of wise justice; and socialistic sharing of wealth is the social expression of generosity.

These four principles seem to encompass mainstream Buddhist social practice, as counseled by Nagarjuna. These four guidelines should be reliable in choosing a line of action in particular situations. It is always essential to remember, however, the fundamental inconceivability of all things, for which great love seems finally the only adequate response. Nagarjuna insists that "the profound, enlightenment in practice, is emptiness creative as compassion." Jesus Christ's "Love God with all thy heart, and thy neighbor as thyself," and Augustine's "Love God and do what you will"—these two great "pivotal phrases" are very much in the same vein, using of course the theistic term for emptiness. In a culture more used to those great statements, we might express Nagarjuna as follows: "Open thy heart to absolute emptiness, and love all thy neighbors as thyself!" It is such love that is the whole "Law," and is the very body of all Buddhas. Vimalakirti describes it to Manjusri:

The love that is firm, its high resolve unbreakable like a diamond;...the love that is never exhausted because it acknowledges voidness and selflessness; the love that is generosity because it bestows the gift of Truth without the tight fist of bad teachers; the love that is justice because it benefits immoral beings; the love that is tolerance because it protects both self and others; the love that is enterprise because it takes responsibility for all living things; the love that is meditation because it refrains from indulgence in tastes; the love that is wisdom because it causes attainment at the proper time; the love that is liberative technique because it shows the way everywhere; the love that is without formality because it is pure in motivation; the love that is without deviation because it acts decisively; the love that is high resolve because it is free of passions; the love that is without deceit because it is not artificial; the love that is happiness because it introduces living beings to the happiness of a Buddha. Such, Manjusri, is the great love of a bodhisattva.[5]

---

[5] Thurman, *The Holy Teaching of Vimalakirti* (University Park, Pennsylvania: Penn State University Press, 1976), p. 57.

Waking Everybody Up

WE LIVE IN an interdependent world. Whatever we are doing in any part of the world, we have to keep this global perspective in mind. Communications and related technologies are common everywhere, even in places where people have almost nothing to eat. In Japan, the so-called economic miracle of Asia, more than seventy percent of the country's food is imported. It means Japan is dependent upon the rest of the world, mostly on countries where people are starving. If anything happens anywhere, everyone in the world suffers. Many drugs—pesticides and experimental pharmaceuticals—are dumped in our countries from the developed countries. Meanwhile, the industrial countries continue to stockpile nuclear armaments.

In the Sarvodaya Movement,[1] we try to keep this global vision. We know that one of the reasons conditions for the poor are becoming

---

[1] The Sarvodaya Shramadana Movement, founded by A. T. Ariyaratne, spread its influence into hundreds of villages not only in Sri Lanka but in Africa and other parts of Asia. Sarvodaya also began to aim at "world awakening" by convening conferences and offering technical assistance and training to self-help movements in the Third and Fourth Worlds.

With a strong emphasis on decentralization and self-reliance, Sarvodaya has implemented programs in education, health care, transportation facilities, agricultural projects, and a wide range of technologically appropriate energies such as windmills and methane generators which convert human wastes into cooking gas. In a one-year period, Sarvodaya built three times as many roads as did the government, linking for the first time many underdeveloped villages which had been neglected under colonial rule. By the 1970s, Sarvodaya had organized more than a hundred coordinating centers, each serving the needs of twenty to thirty nearby villages. In addition, Sarvodaya now serves a rural awakening program of 3,500 communities.

The movement also has a strong spiritual emphasis. Ariyaratne has organized Sarvodaya's three million members in the practice of "loving kindness" meditation which the members do once or twice daily, all at the same times. Ariyaratne feels that so many loving thought forms being sent out simultaneously have a tangible effect on humankind. The religious philosophy of Sarvodaya prescribes Buddhist ideals of kindness and generosity.

worse is because the international economy is controlled by so few people. Those who are the primary producers of food and labor-intensive products do not receive the fruits of their own labor. In my country, Sri Lanka, a handful of people are benefiting from the economic development and the increased trade with the West, while the poor are becoming poorer and the numbers of poor people are increasing. The same is true in all developing countries. In Sri Lanka, wherever food is processed, we pay more for the processing, the added chemicals and all, than for the food. If there were a direct exchange between people, these expenses would be cut. It is a pyramid, with everything done to satisfy those at the top.

International trade should be restricted, because it produces injustice. It does not satisfy the basic needs of clothing and shelter, but only the greed of rich people in rich countries. When we in the poor countries get cash in return, this cash is spent to buy media-created wants, desires created by advertising. It is a vicious cycle. I advocate totally de-linking from this international economic system—not to disassociate from different peoples in the world, but to strengthen the links that exist between grassroots, nonexploitative groups worldwide that do not support these affluent social systems that direct all our energies.

All of us, whether in rich or poor countries, have our common humanity, our spiritual life. In this, there are no barriers at all. Spiritual life cannot be centralized. If we are to bring about any change at the levels of the individual, the family, or the community, we have to strengthen our spiritual foundation. In the Sarvodaya experience, when several hundred of us meet together, think together, work together, and share our joys and sorrows together, we release certain thought processes that give us a kind of protection, hope, and security. In this way, our communities link together. Despite different economic levels and being in different parts of the world, we who believe in the small community can always get together. In the cases where we stay apart, it is because we allow the technology to be controlled by those who believe in huge systems of power and economic organization. Most of the world's technologies are controlled by a few governments, corporations, and military organizations, those who believe in largeness and centralization. So we, as small communities building on our own spiritual life, need to develop technologies we can use to communicate with each other. We can't launch satellites, but we can use telephones, faxes, e-mail, postal services, printing, and other media. We have to keep in contact.

Western culture has no standard by which to measure good and bad. It is lost in liberal thinking. There is no sin or merit, so Westerners are not accountable. The vast majority of people in the world today, people of all economic classes, belong to the "old society." By this term, I don't mean the societies that existed in the twelfth or thirteenth century. I mean societies in our own time that are steeped in the "old" values, where children have a moral responsibility to look after their parents when they are old, where a family has a responsibility to live in cooperation with the families around it, where the food producer has a moral obligation to produce clean food without destroying the environment or polluting the soil with chemical fertilizers. It is a mistake for us to forget these values, to want just modernization and the accumulation of goods, and to think that this majority should rush to acquire what the minority have. This wealthy minority are not only in the U.S. and Japan; they are in my country, too.

Those of us who belong to the old society must reject this attitude of trying to become an energy-consuming, environment-polluting modern society. We should continue to live in the old ways, satisfying the basic needs of people so that nobody will be poor. We don't need an affluent society, just a no-poverty society. We must make this new society bypassing the modern society in the same way that those who are in the modern society bypass the old society. They have unsuccessfully and, well, dishonorably told the people in the Third World, "Come, you can reach our level. We give you the First Development Decade, the Second Development Decade, the Third. We give you the Year of the Children, Year of the Disabled, Year of the Elderly, of Women." Now after all these beautiful years, are the disabled looked after? Are women liberated? Is every child fed? No. This bluff must stop now.

The poor still cannot find one liter of water to drink while these others have thousands of liters in which to swim. We don't want to reach where they are. Instead we believe in a spiritual foundation, moral relationships, small economic and political organizations in a highly decentralized but highly coordinated way. How can we do it? We must find out. This is why we have to link all these movements around the world and think together.

We in the Sarvodaya Movement are doing our best to help people who have gotten into drugs, prostitution, crimes, or other social evils. There is, for example, a program in the south of Sri Lanka where ex-criminals are being reformed, and at the same time, another program to prevent this from happening in the first place. We need first aid, and we also need prevention. We try to show downtrodden people ways to uplift their conditions and attitudes. However, our social philosophy in the Sarvodaya Movement is that many of these problems are the result of the prevailing unjust economic system.

America must take a substantial share of the responsibility. America was built with very high principles of equality and brotherhood. I remember my parents looking up to America as the country that might liberate the rest of the world. But America and the other great countries are not playing the role that they should. They have no moral right to spend $900 billion a year for armaments when 900 million people are starving. This money is being channeled for the destruction of people, while the economies of poor people are shattered.

International banks set the rules and maintain control. Developing countries have no way out of this situation unless they can gather their courage, educate their people as to what is happening, prepare them to face the worst, and then tell the banks, "We are not going to pay our debt." Right from the beginning when we were given this money, it was obvious that we were not going to be able to pay it back. But to default on these loans will have severe consequences. That is why it can be done only by countries whose leaders have the capacity to show an example of selfless leadership in their own style of life, their own fearlessness, and their own moral integrity. I am speaking about a leader who could say, "Look, here is the reality of the situation: we can go on taking loans and being in debt, but we will never succeed in eradicating poverty in our societies. At most we will only increase the rich by a few more people. To eradicate hunger in our country, therefore, we are going to reject your economic theory, your market economy as it works now, and instead pool all our resources to meet the primary needs of our people."

Basic need is our first economic objective, not growth, not increasing per capita income. Any talk about growth and no-growth is nonsense when there is no value attached to it. The question is not, "How much has our economy grown?" It is, "How many people are getting a balanced meal?" A lot of wealth goes into wasteful consumption. In the old societies, when the primary needs were satisfied, works of art and architecture were built. A Marxist might say that this was from the slave labor of the people, and some societies have been like that, but not Sri Lanka. The samadhi statue of Buddha at Polonaruwa, Sri Lanka, could never have been carved by a slave. It could only have been done by an absolutely free person who got into that stone and carved the serenity of the Buddha. Prime Minister Nehru of India used to come just to look at it for hours on end. Only basic cultures produce great works of art and architecture that last for centuries.

Once basic needs are satisfied, we must satisfy needs at a community level. Every house, for example, does not need a television set. We can have instead a bigger TV for the whole community. I visited one community in Japan where there were only three hundred people, yet they have a day-care center, a preschool, a primary school, a junior secondary school, a senior secondary school, and a university that serve the entire community. They live quite happily without a mass educational system that only prepares people for a society in which competition and individual material advancement are the objectives. By filling educational needs in a cooperative way, their limited resources are more than enough for everyone. Leadership in poor countries has to have the courage to decentralize the economic and political power. In fact, decentralization strengthens the center. Once the country as a whole has that kind of strength, they can say to foreign banks and governments, "Although we customarily pay our debts, we cannot pay you back. In fact, you have already taken it back many times over in other ways."[2]

---

[2] According to a 1988 UNICEF report, Third World debt stood then at more than $1 tril-lion, and debt repayment took one-quarter of the developing world's revenues. Meanwhile, the forty poorest countries in the world have halved health spending over recent years and cut education budgets by one quarter. Lawrence Bruce, president of UNICEF, said, "The mounting debt repayments of so many of these developing countries to Western institutions are quite literally snatching food and medicine out of the mouths of millions of children."

The wave of violence in Sri Lanka was the climax of a breakdown of spiritual, moral, and cultural values that took place over twenty or thirty years. Although it has been described in the press as "communal violence," the communal issue is just an excuse for what happened. People say that Sinhalese Buddhists are killing Tamil Hindus, but that is an absolute lie. No Buddhist killed any Hindu as such. There were gangs of fellows belonging to lawless elements and also to political parties who were waiting for any chance to plunder others and get money. These are the ones who did all this damage—not a single Buddhist monk or what you could call a decent Buddhist.

When this began, none of the leaders came out to stop it. So the Sarvodaya groups appealed to the people to stop the escalation of violence and help those who were affected. We opened up relief camps and did everything possible for relief and reconciliation. I went around the country speaking at public meetings, appealing to both Sinhalese and Tamils not to get trapped in this violence that involved a few hundred people.

We had seventeen Tamil brothers and sisters living in our house. One day a Sinhalese gang came to the door, and my young daughter went out and told them, "My parents' instructions are that if my father is here, he will have to be killed before any Tamil family member is touched. If my mother is here, she will die first. Now, as I am the oldest in the family and my parents are not home, I will have to die before you touch them." Perhaps she didn't realize the gravity of what she was saying, but the people did not harm her. They apologized and went away. Newspapers don't publish this type of thing. Many, many Sinhalese women and children did heroic deeds during that period when insanity prevailed in the country. Buddhists were protecting Tamils.

Sarvodaya will go on. Every village is organized, and our goal is to double the number of places where we work. My dream is to get 16,000 villages in Sri Lanka to build a truly alternative system (without calling it alternative), and then one day declare our freedom. Instead of confronting a government, we confront the whole system. If the spiritual, moral, and cultural value systems of the people are destroyed, everything is lost, and more and more coercive instruments of the

State—the police, the armed forces—are needed to bring about order.

From 1974 to 1984, a frantic attempt was made by the government and the local and multinational economic sectors toward materialistic affluence, which totally ignored the existing value system. Earning and spending money was promoted as the most fundamental value in life. And during that time, the number of liquor shops increased tenfold, gambling and casinos became widespread, and drug addiction became a new and dangerous phenomenon. Pornographic literature fell into the hands of schoolchildren. The bad example set by a very small minority was propagated to the susceptible general public through the media of television, radio, and newspapers. This is the price our country had to pay in this super-speed of economic development.

When all these evils were introduced to our society, violence naturally became part of the structure first, and later it came to the community where not only personal disputes but also political disputes came to be settled by armed power. The materialistic development which was encouraged by the government aggravated the situation. The so-called ethnic conflict was only a symptom. The real causes are ethical, economic, and political. But now it has become a direct violent, political confrontation between power groups. The general public is sandwiched between these groups, and they are helpless. Local and foreign troops control most of the life of the people, and antigovernment armed groups are having a heyday. We have to work very cautiously to keep the people within the nonviolent constructive programs. We are continuing to do this, and in all our Sarvodaya communities our activities are going on despite the prevailing atmosphere. Violence will not take anybody anywhere. When the violent groups have exhausted their energies, they will turn to the nonviolent alternatives offered by the Sarvodaya movement. This is my conviction.

CLAUDE THOMAS

Finding Peace
after a Lifetime of War

I WAS TRAINED to be a soldier from the day I was born, by the way I was brought up and the things I was encouraged to do—hunt, kill, dominate, rule, and control my environment. I was taught not to be mindful, not to be thoughtful.

My father was a schoolteacher. My mother never graduated from school. The environment in my house was not different from most of the houses around me. It was filled with anger and violence, which I did not understand because I did not have the skills to understand.

I went into the military, and then to Vietnam at the age of seventeen. I did not know what else to do, and my father suggested it would make a man out of me. I was a high school athlete, so I was already used to discipline and exerting physical strength. A local journalist said that if he had to charge a hill with anyone, he would want it to be me.

On my second day in the military, I realized it was not a good choice. But I did not know I could get out. So I did the next best thing: I learned to be the best soldier I could. I trained to be a ranger, which meant that I became very skilled in killing. The military is only about killing. It is not about defense. It is about offense.

In my training, I learned to dehumanize the enemy, and in the process, I became dehumanized. I remember a huge drill sergeant standing in my face screaming obscenities, taking out his penis and urinating on me. There was nothing I could do because I did not know I could do anything. And I was unaware at the time how deeply those kinds of actions affect human beings. Experiences like that never go away.

My job in Vietnam was to crew helicopter gunships. Before my eighteenth birthday I had been responsible for the deaths of hundreds of people. This was not my first experience of war. There was the war before the war, and the war after the war, and the war that continues to rage on a daily basis all over the world. My life in high school was one form of war; my family was another form of war. I was prepared to kill before I killed, because I was so filled with anger, resentment, hurt, despair, and suffering. And my story is not unusual. There are similar stories every day all over the world. There will never be peace on Earth until we have peace within ourselves. We have to be able to look deeply into the nature of our suffering—to touch, embrace and hold it—before we can touch peace.

In 1967, when I was shot down for the fifth time, the pilot and the aircraft commander were killed and the gunner was critically wounded. As I lay pinned in the overturned helicopter, I could smell the fuel leaking and I could hear the gunfire hitting the helicopter. I was convinced I would die and believed that I *should* die. I did not want to survive because I hated myself and what I had done. But I did not die. I was hospitalized for nine months, and at the age of twenty I was discharged from the military.

On my way home, as I walked across the airport in Newark to change planes—a highly decorated soldier in uniform—I was approached by a very attractive young woman. I thought she was interested in me or wanted to talk, but when she got within inches of my face, she spit on me. I went to a bar and got drunk, and I stayed drunk and high for the next fifteen years. I needed intoxicants because I had no skills or ability to touch the depth of suffering in my life. By not being able to embrace my suffering, I could not transform it, and it leaked out in indirect ways. My life was full of anger, rage, and violence; it was the only way I knew to be.

I joined in the antiwar movement, not because I believed in peace, but because I believed that if you are going to fight a war, you might as well fight it to win. My thinking has since changed radically: I'm convinced that we *do not need* to fight. It is an insane proposition that because we are human beings it is natural for us to fight and kill. Through mindfulness there are ways to resolve conflicts without violence. I experienced the peace movement as simply another war movement. It was violent and ugly, and Vietnam veterans were a prized possession as long as we could serve their purpose. But when it came to healing, they, like the rest of the country, were not there to help us.

Beginning in 1970, I began to leave the United States on a regular basis. I was embarrassed to be an American, and besides I could not stand to turn on the TV anymore and listen to the talk about the war. In 1974 I bought a one-way ticket from London to Tehran. I did not speak the language, I did not have any idea what went on in Iran, I just knew that it was far away. I thought the insanity of my life rested outside of me. I felt that if I could find the right place or the right teacher, it would heal me. What I was seeking was outside of myself, because I did not have the skills or the encouragement to look inward.

In Iran, it became more and more difficult to keep the lid on the untouched issues of war and violence in my life. I was living in a country where the secret police (the Savak) would come into a family and take away every male person above the age of sixteen and imprison them without a trial for ten years. I saw this happen often, and I reacted to these conditions in the only way I knew, in anger and violence. One taxicab driver stiffed me for fifteen cents, and I totaled his taxi with my bare hands. I continued to put myself at risk, hoping that I would die, because I could not stand to live with what was going on inside me.

One night the police took me away and interrogated me for ten days, trying to get me to sign a paper that I was a spy. During the interrogation, they broke four ribs on one side, five ribs on the other, cracked both my cheekbones, ruptured my spleen, sodomized me, and then just threw me out on the street. I survived, although I did not want to. My response was to act out more violently, and I ended up in jail two more times. I had no other recourse than to act out the anger, to act out in kind, to punish the punisher. I did not know any other way.

I have no idea how or when it began to turn around for me. In 1990, I shut myself in my house, afraid to leave, no longer able to touch society because of all that it represented for me. When I walked outside and heard jets flying overhead, I cringed because I could see treelines going up in napalm and young Vietnamese running from villages. When I walked into the grocery store, I could not take a can of vegetables off the shelf because I was afraid it was booby-trapped. The feelings were vivid, but this time I did not run away. I knew that in order for it to be transformed, I had to stay with my reality.

I heard about Thich Nhat Hanh from a social worker in Cambridge, Massachusetts, who told me about a Zen monk who had had some success helping Vietnam veterans to heal. She did not say that he was Vietnamese. Six months later, someone else told me about a retreat for Vietnam veterans run by this same man. I telephoned the retreat center, not because I wanted to, but because nothing in my life was working and I did not know what else to do. I wanted my life to be different. So, terrified, I went to the retreat.

Part of my military training was to operate in small units of four or five people. We were dropped in to gather information, assassinate, or destroy. If during an operation any of us became wounded and could not continue, our job was to kill them because they would slow us down. I knew how to build walls against terror. I have come in on a helicopter looking at the fifty caliber tracer rounds come at me, glowing as big as softballs, knowing that when you see one, there are five that you do not. I learned ways to deny terror and to just go forward. That is what got me to the retreat. But when this Vietnamese monk walked into the room, sat down, and I looked into his face, I started to cry. I realized in the moment of him sitting there that I did not know the Vietnamese people in any other way than as the enemy. They were the enemy, and if they were the enemy then I did not know how to relate to anyone else in the world other than as the enemy. Everyone was the enemy.

One of the first things this monk said was, "You veterans are the light at the tip of the candle. You burn hot. You have the ability through your experience to help in the transformation of the world, to transform the violence, to transform the hate, to transform the despair. You need to talk." And he said, "The non-veterans need to listen. The veterans deserve to be understood. To understand someone, you need to place yourself in his skin."

All my life when I tried to talk about these things, people always went away. They said, "You're too intense. I can't deal with you. I've got to leave." I have come to understand that what they were really saying is, "In relationship with you, I am touching parts of myself that I do not want to touch."

Thich Nhat Hanh said that the non-veterans were more responsible for the war than the veterans, and I knew the truth in that. He was articulating things I had known all my life. Since the end of the war, more than 58,000 Vietnam vets, young men and women, have killed themselves. In the war, 57,693 Americans died in combat. I can be sure that there are one or two veterans in every group of homeless people I see on the street, and many have ended up in prisons. We have been marginalized.

I did not know what to do. I approached Sister Chân Không after the retreat. I wanted to make amends for the killing, but I did not have the courage to say that. All I said was, "I would really like to go back to Vietnam." And she smiled, "You need to come to Plum Village first. Let us help you." I said, "I cannot afford to come." She said, "We will buy your ticket." This was my enemy. No one in this country had ever offered me an opportunity like that to heal.

In the summers in Plum Village, most of the Vietnamese people live in the Lower Hamlet. When I arrived, Sister Chân Không told me that I would live in the Lower Hamlet. So there I was in a community of 400 Vietnamese, and every place I turned, another terrifying memory would come up from the war. I could not work hard enough, I could not keep busy enough to get away from those memories. When I wanted to talk to somebody, I would approach a monk or a nun and try to explain what was going on, saying, "I see the young Vietnamese women in their *ao-dai* coming into the zendo, and I remember a gun run in a village where I was responsible for killing thirty or forty people." When I would start to talk like that, the monks and nuns would say, "The past is in the past. There is only the present moment, and it is beautiful."

I did not know how to deal with that. So I did not say anything until one day I began to talk about the war and when I got the same spiel from a monk, I turned around in real anger and said, "The past is not in the past for me. It is in the present moment and it is ugly." I talked to Sister Chân Không about this, and she said, "If you are living intensely in the present moment, the past and the future are also there. You just need to be with them like still water." That was all I needed.

I went back to Plum Village the following year, and have since returned twice. On each visit I have to confront myself over and over again. I was victimized, but I cannot continue to maintain the posture of being a victim. I need to heal. I need to transform. I need to challenge the ideas that I have been subjected to throughout my life.

Thich Nhat Hanh always teaches the Five Precepts. The first is: "Aware of the suffering caused by the destruction of life, I vow to cultivate compassion and to learn the ways of protecting the lives of people, animals, plants, and minerals. I am determined not to kill, not to let others kill, and not to condone any act of killing in my thinking and way of life." For me, this is a lifelong practice, and it begins with getting in close touch with the feelings in me and working moment by moment to embrace them and to transform them into love and understanding.

Please Call Me by My True Names

I HAVE A POEM for you. This poem is about three of us. The first is a twelve-year-old girl, one of the boat people crossing the Gulf of Siam. She was raped by a sea pirate, and after that she threw herself into the sea. The second person is the sea pirate, who was born in a remote village in Thailand. And the third person is me. I was very angry, of course. But I could not take sides against the sea pirate. If I could have, it would have been easier, but I couldn't. I realized that if I had been born in his village and had lived a similar life—economic, educational, and so on—it is likely that I would now be that sea pirate. So it is not easy to take sides. Out of suffering, I wrote this poem. It is called "Please Call Me by My True Names," because I have many names, and when you call me by any of them, I have to say, "Yes."

Don't say that I will depart tomorrow—
even today I am still arriving.

Look deeply: every second I am arriving
to be a bud on a Spring branch,
to be a tiny bird, with still-fragile wings,
learning to sing in my new nest,
to be a caterpillar in the heart of a flower,
to be a jewel hiding itself in a stone.

I still arrive, in order to laugh and to cry,
to fear and to hope.

The rhythm of my heart is the birth and death
of all that is alive.

I am the mayfly metamorphosing
on the surface of the river.
And I am the bird
that swoops down to swallow the mayfly.

I am the frog swimming happily
in the clear water of a pond.
And I am the grass-snake
that silently feeds itself on the frog.

I am the child in Uganda, all skin and bones,
my legs as thin as bamboo sticks.
And I am the arms merchant,
selling deadly weapons to Uganda.

I am the twelve-year-old girl,
refugee on a small boat,
who throws herself into the ocean
after being raped by a sea pirate.
And I am the pirate,
my heart not yet capable
of seeing and loving.

I am a member of the politburo,
with plenty of power in my hands.
And I am the man who has to pay
his "debt of blood" to my people,
dying slowly in a forced-labor camp.

My joy is like Spring, so warm
it makes flowers bloom all over the Earth.
My pain is like a river of tears,
so vast it fills the four oceans.

Please call me by my true names,
so I can hear all my cries and my laughter at once,
so I can see that my joy and pain are one.

Please call me by my true names,
so I can wake up,
and so the door of my heart
can be left open,
the door of compassion.

I still have the theme of this poem in my mind. "Where is our enemy?" I ask myself this all the time. Our Earth, our green, beautiful Earth, is in danger and all of us know it. We are not facing a pirate, but we are facing the destruction of the earth where our small boat has been. It will sink if we are not careful. We think that the enemy is the other, and that is why we can never see him. Everyone needs an enemy in order to survive. Russia needs an enemy. The United States needs an enemy. China needs an enemy. Vietnam needs an enemy. Everyone needs an enemy. Without an enemy we cannot survive. In order to rally people, governments need enemies. They want us to be afraid, to hate, so we will rally behind them. And if they do not have a real enemy, they will invent one in order to mobilize us. Yet many people in the United States have gone to Russia and discovered that the Russian people are very nice, and there are Russian citizens who visit the U.S., and when they return home, report that the American people are fine. This after so many decades of both sides telling their own people how evil the other country's people are.

One friend in the peace movement told me, "Every time I see the President on television, I cannot bear it. I have to turn the TV off, or I become livid." He believes that the situation of the world is in the hands of the government, and if only the President would change his policies, we would have peace. I told him that that is not entirely correct. The "President" is in each of us. We always deserve our government. In Buddhism, we speak of interdependent origination. "This is, because that is. This is not, because that is not." Do our daily lives have nothing to do with our government? Please meditate on this question. We seem to believe that our daily lives have nothing to do with the situation of the world. But if we do not change our daily lives, we cannot change the world.

In Japan, in the past, people took three hours to drink one cup of tea. You might think this is a waste of time, because time is money. But two people spending three hours drinking tea, being with each other, has to do with peace. The two men or two women did not speak a lot. They exchanged only a word or two, but they were really there, enjoying the time and the tea. They really knew the tea and the presence of each other.

Nowadays, we allow only a few minutes for tea, or coffee. We go into a cafe and order a cup of tea or coffee and listen to music and other loud noises, thinking about the business we will transact afterwards. In that situation, the tea does not exist. We are violent to the tea. We do not recognize it as living reality, and that it is related to why our situation is as it is. When we pick up a Sunday newspaper, we should know that in order to print that edition, which sometimes weighs 10 or 12 pounds, they had to cut down a whole forest. We are destroying our Earth without knowing it.

Drinking a cup of tea, picking up a newspaper, using toilet paper, all of these things have to do with peace. Nonviolence can be called "awareness." We must be aware of what we are, of who we are, and of what we are doing. When I became a novice in a Buddhist monastery, I was taught to be aware of every act during the day. Since then, I have been practicing mindfulness and awareness. I used to think that practicing like that was only important for beginners, that advanced people did other important things, but now I know that practicing awareness is for everyone, including the abbot. The purpose of Buddhist meditation is to see into your own nature and to become a Buddha. That can be done only through awareness. If you are not aware of what is going on in yourself and in the world, how can you see into your own nature and become a Buddha?

The word "Buddha" comes from the root, buddh, which means "awake." A Buddha is one who is awake. Are we really awake in our daily lives? That is a question I invite you to think about. Are we awake when we drink tea? Are we awake when we pick up the newspaper? Are we awake when we eat ice cream?

Society makes it difficult to be awake. We know that 40,000 children in the Third World die every day of hunger, but we keep forgetting. The kind of society we live in makes us forgetful. That is why we need exercises for mindfulness. For example, a number of Buddhists I know refrain from eating a few times a week in order to remember the situation in the Third World.

One day I asked a Vietnamese refugee boy who was eating a bowl of rice, whether children in his country eat such high quality rice. He said, "No," because he knows the situation. He experienced hunger in Vietnam—he only ate dry potatoes and he longed for a bowl of rice. In France, he has been eating rice for a year, and sometimes he begins to forget. But when I ask him, he remembers. I cannot ask the same question of a French or American child, because they have not had that kind of experience. They cannot understand. I realize how difficult it is for the people who live in Western countries to know what the situation in the Third World really is. It seems to have nothing to do with the situation here. I told the Vietnamese boy that his rice comes from Thailand, and that most Thai children do not have this rice to eat. They eat rice of a poor quality, because the best rice is for export. Their government needs foreign currency, and they reserve the best rice for Westerners and not them.

In Vietnam we have a delicious banana called *due duja*, but now children and adults in Vietnam do not have the right to eat these bananas because they are all for export. And what do we get in return? Guns. Some of us practice this exercise of mindfulness: We sponsor a child in the Third World in order to get news from him or her, thus keeping in touch with the reality outside. We try many ways to be awake, but society keeps us forgetful. It is so difficult to practice awareness in this society.

A French economist named Perrault, who is the head of the Institute of Mathematics and Economics in Paris, said that if Western countries would reduce the consumption of meat and alcohol by 50%, that would be enough to change the fate of the Third World. How can we do it when we do not remember to be aware? We are intelligent people, but we keep forgetting. Meditation is to help us remember.

There are means for us to nourish awareness, to enjoy silence, to enjoy the world. There was a thirteen-year-old boy from Holland who came to our Center and ate lunch with us in silence. It was the first time he had eaten a silent meal, and he was embarrassed. The silence was quite heavy. After the meal, I asked whether he felt uneasy, and he said, "Yes." So I explained that the reason we eat in silence is in order to enjoy the food and the presence of each other. If we talk a lot we cannot enjoy these things. I asked him if there was some time when he turned off the TV in order to better enjoy his dinner or the conversation with friends, and he said, "Yes." I invited him to join us for another meal, and he ate with us in silence and enjoyed it very much.

We have lost our taste for silence. Every time we have a few minutes, we pick up a book to read, or make a telephone call, or turn on the TV. We do not know how to be ourselves without something else to accompany us. We have lost our taste for being alone. Society takes many things from us and destroys us with noises, smells, and so many distractions. The first thing for us to do is to return to ourselves in order to recover ourselves, to be our best. This is very important. We need to reorganize our daily lives so that we do not allow society to colonize us. We have to be independent. We have to be real persons and not just the victim of society and other people.

The boat people said that every time their small boats were caught in storms, they knew their lives were in danger. But if one person on the boat could keep calm and not panic, that was a great help for everyone. People would listen to him or her and keep serene, and there was a chance for the boat to survive the danger. Our Earth is like a small boat. Compared with the rest of the cosmos, it is a very small boat, and it is in danger of sinking. We need such a person to inspire us with calm confidence, to tell us what to do. Who is that person? The Mahayana Buddhist sutras tell us that you are that person. If you are yourself, if you are your best, then you are that person. Only with such a person—calm, lucid, aware—will our situation improve. I wish you good luck. Please be yourself, Please be that person.

I would like to suggest that in each home we have a small room for breathing. We have rooms for sleeping, eating, and cooking, why not have one room for breathing? Breathing is very important. I suggest that that room be decorated simply, and not be too bright. You may want to have a small bell, with a beautiful sound, a few cushions or chairs, and perhaps a vase of flowers to remind us of our true nature. Children can arrange flowers in mindfulness, smiling. If your household has five members, you can have five cushions or chairs, plus a few for guests. From time to time, you might like to invite a guest to come and sit and breathe with you for a few minutes.

I know of families where children go into a room like that after breakfast, sit down and breathe ten times, in-out-one, in-out-two, in-out-three, and so on, before they go to school. This is a beautiful practice. Beginning the day with being a Buddha is a very nice way to start the day. If we are a Buddha in the morning and we try to nourish the Buddha throughout the day, we may be able to come home at the end of a day with a smile—the Buddha is still there. It is really beautiful to begin the day by being a Buddha. Each time we feel ourselves about to leave our Buddha, we can sit and breathe until we return to our true self. Doing these kinds of things can change our civilization.

Days and Months

IT SEEMS LIKE only yesterday that I stopped by to see my dear friend, Nhat Chi Mai. Mai was a sister in the Dharma, my closest fellow traveler along the Buddha's path of understanding and love. Whenever she spoke, her voice was filled with affection and a unique blend of innocence and wisdom that my friends and I began to call "the special accent of Mai." "Where have you been? You're all covered with sweat," she said to me, with her eyebrows knit and her lips pursed, like a mother worrying about her only child.

"Do I look as if I've been working in the rice fields? I've just come from Tan Dinh Market collecting pledge money from our school's supporters." Mai laughed and served me a large glass of cool water— exactly what I needed that hot July day.

Her dress was as simple as a nun's robe, and it made her look especially beautiful. After a moment, I became serious and asked Mai what she thought about Thây's[1] appeal for peace. She sat silently, and then, stroking my hair, she said, "You know I love and respect Thây, especially his vision of social service, but his political activities worry me."

I understood. Thây's appeal for a cease-fire and the withdrawal of American troops was still very early. A "nationalist" wouldn't dare demand such a thing, and our government and newspapers condemned him. As the youngest in her family, protected by her parents, Mai had never even seen a bombed village, so how could she not worry

---

[1] Thây - Vietnamese for "teacher," a term commonly used for all Buddhist monks. In this account, "Thây" generally refers to Sister Chân Không's teacher, Thich Nhat Hanh.

when the radio, newspapers, and even the President himself accused Thây of being a communist?

Anxiously, on the verge of tears, I said, "Please consider this, dear sister. The Buddha taught us not to take life, so how can we sit by while our people kill one another? For 4,000 years, our country has defeated every single invader. Why do we need the help of foreign troops now? Mai, do you know that when Thây's 'Prayer for Peace' was printed in the *Buddhist Weekly,* I asked the Executive Council of the Buddhist Church to support eight of us in a fast until death as a prayer for peace? But the Council did not approve, and, without their backing, we knew that our act would be useless."

"Of course they wouldn't approve!" she interrupted. "Who would care for your aged mother?"

"I know that I would commit the sin of impiety towards my mother by killing myself, but if my death could help shorten the war and save lives, I would be willing to pay for the sin of impiety in another life."

Mai sat still for a long moment, then she took my hands, looked deeply into my eyes, and said, in a determined voice, "Dear younger sister, you are right. If there is ever another opportunity to fast for peace, count on me to join you." The sincerity of her words moved me so, and I wept.

Three months later Mai joined our work for peace at Van Hanh University. As the daughter of a well-off family, this kind of "underground" work was new to her, but with copies of Thây Nhat Hanh's book, *Lotus in a Sea of Fire,* hidden in her white Volkswagen, she delivered ten to this school, twenty to that, and through her efforts, Thây's book made its way into the hands of almost every teacher and student organization in Saigon.

One Saturday, during our weekly Day of Mindfulness, Mai invited me into her room, took my hand in hers and said, "Younger sister, I have an idea. Remember how the eight of you wanted to fast for peace? What if I and one other person joined you, and ten of us left a statement for peace and then disemboweled ourselves? Our act could reach many people, and it might move them to end this dreadful war! Fasting and even self-immolation no longer wake people up. We have to be imaginative!" I was shocked, but I promised Mai I would consider her proposal.

I stayed in my room for four days, weighing the pros and cons, and finally I told her that I thought we shouldn't do it. The eight of us had been single when we proposed the fast for peace. Now all the others were married, and some lived far away. I suspected there would be only Mai and me. "The peace movement is still quite weak," I said. "If we sacrifice ourselves, the only thing we can be sure of is that our brothers and sisters in the peace movement will be without us. And we promised Thây Nhat Hanh that we would help Thây Thanh Van manage the School of Youth for Social Service, at least until the first students complete their training." Mai knew that the financial crisis of the SYSS was critical after Thây Nhat Hanh's departure. If we two, the main fundraisers for the school, died, who would care for the students? I spoke with all my heart, and she agreed to abandon the idea, although she wanted to wait for the final word from Thây Nhat Hanh. She had sent him a letter but hadn't received a response yet. A week later, she cheerfully told me that Thây had written back forbidding the sacrifice.

Feeling a great sense of responsibility for the School of Youth for Social Service, Mai said to me, "We need to work as much as we can. You must make me work harder. You are so good in your work in the slums, the peace movement, and the school. I wish I could be more like you." I held her shoulder tenderly and said, "Dear elder sister Mai, each person is unique, and you are a beautiful flower. There is no need to be like anyone else, especially me!" At the beginning of the second year of the SYSS , we were having a severe financial crisis. When Nga and I collected more sacks of rice than Uyen or Mai, Mai reproached herself, but her disappointment caused her to be even more diligent in starting self-support projects for the school. Each week, she presented a new list of proposals.

Thây Nhat Hanh was far away, and no one had taught us Avalokiteshvara's great art of listening or the Buddha's art of Sangha building—living in harmony with those around you. So, instead of sitting with Mai, listening deeply, and kindly showing her the strong and weak points of each proposal, we became impatient and ignored her. Many people would have felt frustrated and accumulated internal wounds that might explode at some time, but Mai seemed able to look deeply into herself and heal and transform each wound with ease.

Every week, she would propose something new. In a soft voice, she said to me, "Phuong, if you are free Monday, please come with me to the rice market. We can buy large quantities of rice and then sell it in smaller amounts to raise money." The next week she would suggest, "Phuong, perhaps we can sell soap to the families that support the school." And the following week, she would have yet another plan, and the next week another. Her proposals were not particularly wise, but I did not want to hurt her, so I didn't say anything. Then one day, when too many silent disagreements had accumulated in my mind's "store consciousness," I answered in a very irritated way: "Just go ahead and do it, Mai! But don't force me to do everything with you. I have my own work."

As soon as the words left my mouth, I regretted them, but I could not take them back. At dinnertime, I walked up behind Mai, hugged her, and said, "Where would you like me to go Monday?" She smiled sweetly, and I knew she bore no grudge. The next Monday we went to the soap market together, and on Tuesday we went to the home of a sponsor to sell our soap. On Wednesday we picked up rice, and it was only on Thursday that I got around to my own work. Mai could have done those errands by herself, but she always insisted how much fun it would be to do things together.

To satisfy Mai, Uyen and I would have had to spend two or three days each week just accompanying her. Looking back, I wish we had done so. But at the time, we grumbled to each other, "We spent 1,000 *piasters* on rice, carried it across the city in traffic, and arrived at the home of a sponsor to sell it for a profit of fifteen piasters, while it cost us eight piasters for gas, and took the whole morning! I could earn 300 piasters an hour teaching math." Uyen and I had not yet learned the joy of just being together with a friend, the work, the rice sellers, and the sponsors. Uyen and I did not know how to practice peace with every step, but it seems that Mai did. With or without us, she embarked on many projects just to earn small amounts of money for the school. Then one day, she touched the heart of a wealthy man with her gentle way of being, and he gave the school 20,000 *dong* that we used to start many self-supporting projects. Little by little, we repaid the construction loans, and the sponsors' pledges were again used to buy food.

One evening after we had recited the *Tiep Hien* precepts, I suggested that we build a bungalow with six tiny meditation rooms for each Tiep Hien brother and sister to use for a half-day solitary retreat every week. I knew that would be a real treasure. Uyen and the other brothers and sisters were overjoyed by the idea, but Mai opposed it, saying that sharing a room with others was practicing the way also, that it would be too much of a luxury to have our own rooms. I did not want a fancy building, just a palm-leaf and bamboo hut, a place to be alone to calm our emotions after six days of strenuous work.

Mai sat silently and then reminded us that we did not have the money and that if we did, we should use it for the school, not to build a house for ourselves. I was afraid that if we did not build this bungalow, we might lose ourselves and be unable to serve anyone. Seeing my determination, Mai finally agreed. At times, I felt she did not understand my suffering. I suppose that was because she lived on a different level from most of us. She always seemed refreshed and in touch with her deepest self.

To raise the money, I began by asking my older sister, "Nam, if I get married, how much will you give me as a wedding gift?" My family had been concerned about me not getting married, so when Nam heard this, she answered right away, "Three thousand piasters!" "That's all?" I responded, "How about 5,000?" She said, "Okay, 5,000." I put out my hand and said, "For people who want a family, a wedding is important. But for someone who wants to be a resource for many people, having a special room to quiet her mind is equally important, don't you agree? How about giving it to me right now so we can build a bungalow for a solitary retreat?" Nam laughed and gave me 3,000 piasters.

Mai donated 5,000 piasters of her own money, and with a few other donations, we were able to build a small house. Uyen and I always had a simple arrangement of bamboo or wildflowers in our rooms, while the flowers in Mai's room were always arranged in the formal, traditional way. Every time I entered it, I was struck by the resplendent Buddha on gold paper hanging on her wall—the Buddha sat in a full lotus, surrounded by clouds, flowers, and a halo—and a set of eight pictures of Thây Quang Duc. Mai also had a hanging pot with a branch of golden plum flowers and one bright red, plastic rose. It was

exactly like entering an old-style nun's room, except that her bed always had many covers and a pink satin pillowcase—appropriate for
the favorite daughter of a well-to-do family!

One day Mai entered my room and exclaimed, "Your room is so
sad. There are no pictures at all here." When she looked more closely,
she noticed a tiny photo of a lake and a forest just above the floor, and
near my bed, at eye level, sketches of crying children.

Surprised, she asked, "Why are the pictures so close to the ground
where no one can see them?" I answered, "I did not arrange the room
for others. I placed the pictures low so I can see them when I lie down."
Mai shook her head and said, "How selfish!" When she accused me
of being selfish, I felt angry, but my irritation dissipated quickly when
I remembered how different her nature was from mine. We laughed,
and everything was fine.

One Saturday in April, when it was Mai's turn to read the Precepts
of the Order of Interbeing, her voice faltered as she said, "Do not kill.
Do not let others kill. Find whatever means possible to protect life and
build peace." From that moment on, she spoke so softly it was nearly
impossible to hear her. As we were putting the precept books back on
the shelves, Uyen asked, "What happened, Mai?" And I added, "You
seemed to lose your concentration during the recitation. Are you all
right?" Mai just smiled and returned to her room early that evening.

The following two Saturdays she did not come to our Days of
Mindfulness. Because the situation in Saigon was so dangerous—four
friends from the school had been murdered—I assumed that her parents had forbidden her from spending the night with us. But when
she didn't show up for a third Saturday, I thought that even if her
parents wanted her home at night, they would certainly let her recite
the precepts with us in the afternoon.

I wondered if something could be wrong, yet, at the same time, I
was upset with Mai for not taking our Days of Mindfulness more
seriously. At least she could have told us why she had missed the SYSS
staff meetings, the Days of Mindfulness, and her work at the university.

Then, on Sunday, May 14, 1967, she came to her last Morning of
Mindfulness. I was in my room, looking out the window onto a field
of green bamboo, and I didn't hear her car pull up. Uyen knocked

gently at my door and said, "Sister Mai is here, wearing a beautiful violet *ao dai* with gold embroidery!" I stood up and walked slowly from my room, intending to reproach her. But as I entered the hallway, I saw Mai surrounded by friends, all trying to tell her something, and then, like baby chicks with their mother, we all followed her into the dining room.

Mai's hair was arranged beautifully, and her new dress made her look as if she were about to attend a ceremony. Right away, she began slicing the banana cake she had baked especially for us. I smiled and said, teasingly, "First you abandon us for three weeks, and now you dress so beautifully and bring a delicious cake! Are you going to get married?" Others joined in, "Very possible! Mai looks so pretty today!" We all laughed, hut Mai just smiled silently.

I felt disappointed that, once again, our dream for peaceful social change was being pushed aside. So many young friends shared our aspiration, but then they married and had children, and always had excuses for not helping with the work. Now Mai was going too. At that moment, her voice pierced my thoughts, "Sister Chân Không, please come to Tu Nghiêm Pagoda early on Tuesday morning. It is Wesak, the Buddha's nativity, and something interesting will happen."

Mai was always kind to the old nuns at the pagoda, so I thought she was asking me to help decorate their temple for Wesak. "I respect your wish," I said, somewhat irritably, "but is it really necessary for me to be at the temple so early?" Nhat Chi Mai lookcd directly at me and said, "If you don't want to come, it's okay, hut please don't speak so strongly about it!" When she left, I felt ashamed, and I resolved to go to the pagoda early on Tuesday, just to please her.

On Tuesday morning, Ngoc ran frantically into my family's house and told me that Sister Mai had set herself on fire, right outside the Tu Nghiêm Pagoda! I couldn't believe my ears! I sat perfectly still for a long while, and then I said, "Sister Mai has sacrificed herself for peace." My mother, sitting next to me, burst into tears. "Your friend's act," she said, "will lead her parents to the grave!" She looked at me with each word, preparing herself for the day I might do the same.

Without a word, Ngoc and I went out, knowing that much needed to be done. I went straight to Mai's parents' home, and when I entered the house, they embraced me, sobbing. As we sat together, her mother actually passed out several times. Then I drove them to the pagoda, and they went inside. I don't know why, but I was unable to enter the pagoda and see Mai in death. Instead I ran to the Cau Muoi Market and told our vendor friends of Mai's sacrifice. As I was sharing the news with dear old Aunt Ba, I started to cry and she began to weep with me. Soon everyone in the market was in tears. Aunt Ba walked over to the taxi and pedicab drivers, spoke a few words to each, and immediately the drivers began to carry all the vendors from the market to the pagoda to see Mai for the last time.

The well-known writer, Bac Thieu Son, also came to the pagoda, joined by several other intellectuals. His face was drawn, and when he saw me, he could only manage to say, "Phuong!" and tears rolled down his cheeks. The printer who had refused to print our peace books was also there. He came up to me, sobbing, and said that in the future he would help us in any way we needed. Even government officials and military men came and offered to help our work for peace. It was only then that I realized that my words of advice to Mai against sacrificing ourselves—"We are too few. If we are gone, there will not be enough people to do the work"—were wrong. Her sacrifice had indeed moved the hearts of many people and caused the peace movement to swell like waves in a storm. Even friends who had become guerrillas in the jungle sent back news and asked, "How can we help realize Mai's wish for peace and reconciliation?"

Before she died, Nhat Chi Mai placed two statues in front of her, the Virgin Mary and Avalokiteshvara Bodhisattva. In her poems and letters, she asked Catholics and Buddhists to work together for peace so that people might realize the love of Jesus and the compassion of the Buddha.

I never saw Thây Tri Quang more moved. At one o'clock in the morning, he sent a message to Tu Nghiêm Pagoda to ask the nuns to provide a car for me to come to An Quang Pagoda. (He was afraid I would be arrested or kidnapped if I came by myself.) When I arrived at his pagoda, the gate was locked, and I had to climb over it. As I entered his room, he was trying to repair an old tape recorder, and he told me, "This machine hardly works, but I want to have a tape of someone reading the poems and letters of the young woman who sacrificed herself so I can come to know her better. Will you read them?

You are also a young woman from the South, so your voice must be close to hers."

The next day, at four o'clock in the morning, Thây Tri Quang disguised himself as a novice and had someone take him to Tu Nghiêm Pagoda. He had been under house arrest for some time, so he could not travel openly. In front of Mai's coffin, he chanted sutras for her. When he finished, he called me into a room of the pagoda and said, "You must find a way to print Mai's letters and distribute them widely. I will pay for the paper and the printing. Ask some of the Buddhist elders to lend you the money, and my younger sister will pay them back."

The following day, Thây Tri Quang called me again, "Mai's prayer was for all religions to work together for peace. I've heard that Father Nguyen Ngoc Lan is a progressive Catholic and close to us. Please ask him to write a preface to Mai's letters." I was very moved. In the past, Thây Tri Quang had been skeptical about working with Catholics. In fact, Father Lan had already offered to print Mai's letters and write a foreword to them. He even agreed to circulate them, a very dangerous thing to do. With each heartfelt act, I thought of Mai's smiling face, and I could hear her saying, "Isn't that wonderful?" Just as she had prayed, the elders of the Buddhist Church tried every day to find opportunities to work with the Catholics, and the Catholics also began to have more sympathy for the Buddhists. It all began with everyone's appreciation of Sister Mai.

During the three days her body lay in Tu Nghiêm Pagoda, I tried to keep busy. I went to meet students both inside and outside our movement. I went to all the markets. I visited many organizations and friends. When I saw Hiep and other friends sitting by her body, weeping and clutching the yellow cloth that covered her, I didn't have the courage to come near. I could only think that my body should be there too, or in a pagoda in Hue, Ben Tre, or Can Tho. Hadn't that been Mai's wish? But I was alive, able to stand, walk, eat, drink, and sleep.

Day after day, I met with friends to inform them of Mai's sacrifice for peace. And night after night, I stayed up translating her poems into English and French for newspapers and peace groups around the world. But it was not until Ngoc brought me Mai's final letters and poems that I understood how she had spent her last three weeks:

she had stayed with her parents in order to give them those last precious hours of her life. She was "sweet bananas, fragrant rice, and precious honey," a loving child for them, all the while preparing for her sacrifice.

Students came to the pagoda to prevent the police from taking Mai's body away. The police, afraid that the news of her sacrifice would travel to other provinces and inspire others to work for peace, tried to persuade her parents to bury her right away. Mai's father resisted, but his wife's grief was so great that finally, on the third day, he agreed to bring Mai's body to An Duong Dia in Phu Lam for cremation.

On the day after Mai's sacrifice, many newspapers carried blank spaces where the news of her act had been censored. Word of her death traveled only by friends, but even so, on the day of the cremation, a huge crowd came to the ceremony. When the funeral car reached Phu Lam Bridge, the crowd behind it stretched more than five kilometers, all the way back to the Tu Nghiêm Pagoda. Students and teachers, merchants and vendors, politicians and priests were all present. I was surprised to see so many wealthy men and women who, until then, had accused us of being under the control of the communists.

There was a fine, cool rain. The white dresses of young women students, the black shirts of poor workers, the monks' and nuns' robes, the simple rags of our street vendor friends from the markets, and the fine clothes of the well-to-do were all moistened by the gentle rain. My younger sister Thanh, with her gift for lightening even the saddest moments, whispered in my ear, "Sister, do you see Mai? She is sitting on the funeral car looking back at us, her face bright, saying, 'Oh, Phuong and Thanh, I feel very joyful. There really are a lot of people here, aren't there?'" I had been walking in the rain, immersed in my sadness, when I heard Thanh imitate Mai's special accent, and I had to smile. She was right. It was exactly what Mai would have said.

When you want something ordinary, you can just go out and buy it, but when you want something extraordinary, like love, understanding, and peace for a whole nation, you have to pay for it with something much more precious than money. My sister, Nhat Chi Mai, did not commit suicide. She loved life. She had a good education, and the conditions to live comfortably, even in the midst of the war. She sacrificed her life because, more than anything, she wanted the killing to stop. She tried to bring peace to Vietnam by paying for it with her life.

I remember Thây's poem, "Recommendation," that she read again and again just before she immolated herself:

Promise me,
promise me this day,
promise me now,
while the sun is overhead
exactly at the zenith,
promise me:

Even as they
strike you down
with a mountain of hate and violence;
even as they step on you and crush you
like a worm,
even as they dismember and disembowel you,
remember, brother,
remember:
man is not our enemy.

The only act worthy of you is compassion—
invincible, limitless, unconditional.
Hatred will never let you face
the beast in man.

One day, when you face this beast alone,
with your courage intact, your eyes kind,
untroubled,
(even as no one sees them),
out of your smile
will bloom a flower.
And those who love you
will behold you
across ten thousand worlds of birth and dying.

Alone again,
I will go on with bent head,
knowing that love has become eternal.
On the long, rough road,
the sun and the moon
will continue to shine.

After Nhat Chi Mai immolated herself for peace on May 16, 1967,
I became ever more determined to find ways to end the suffering of
Vietnam.

GARY SNYDER

Buddhism and the Possibilities
of a Planetary Culture

BUDDHISM HOLDS that the universe and all creatures in it are intrinsically in a state of complete wisdom, love, and compassion, acting in natural response and mutual interdependence. The personal realization of this from-the-beginning state cannot be had for and by one-"self,"—because it is not fully realized unless one has given the self up and away.

In the Buddhist view, that which obstructs the effortless manifestation of this is ignorance, which projects into fear and needless craving. Historically, Buddhist philosophers have failed to analyze out the degree to which ignorance and suffering are caused or encouraged by social factors, considering fear-and-desire to be given facts of the human condition. Consequently the major concern of Buddhist philosophy is epistemology and "psychology" with no attention paid to historical or sociological problems. Although Mahayana Buddhism has a grand vision of universal salvation, the actual achievement of Buddhism has been the development of practical systems of meditation toward the end of liberating a few dedicated individuals from psychological hang-ups and cultural conditionings. Institutional Buddhism has been conspicuously ready to accept or ignore the inequalities and tyrannies of whatever political system it found itself under. This can be death to Buddhism, because it is death to any meaningful function of compassion. Wisdom without compassion feels no pain.

No one today can afford to be innocent, or to indulge themselves in ignorance of the nature of contemporary governments, politics, and social orders. The national polities of the modern world are "states" which maintain their existence by deliberately fostered craving and fear: monstrous protection rackets. The "free world" has become economically dependent on a fantastic system of stimulation of greed which cannot be fulfilled, sexual desire which cannot be satiated, and hatred which has no outlet except against oneself, the persons one is supposed to love, or the revolutionary aspirations of pitiful, poverty-stricken marginal societies. The conditions of the Cold War have fumed most modern societies—both communist and capitalist—into vicious distorters of true human potential. They try to create populations of *preta*—hungry ghosts, with giant appetites and throats no bigger than needles. The soil, the forests, and all animal life are being consumed by these cancerous collectivities; the air and water of the planet is being fouled by them.

There is nothing in human nature or the requirements of human social organization which intrinsically requires that a society be contradictory, repressive, and productive of violent and frustrated personalities. Findings in anthropology and psychology make this more and more evident. One can prove it for oneself by taking a good look at Original Nature through meditation. Once a person has this much faith and insight, one will be led to a deep concern with the need for radical social change through a variety of nonviolent means.

The joyous and voluntary poverty of Buddhism becomes a positive force. The traditional harmlessness and avoidance of taking life in any form has nation-shaking implications. The practice of meditation, for which one needs only "the ground beneath one's feet," wipes out mountains of junk being pumped into the mind by the mass media and supermarket universities. The belief in a serene and generous fulfillment of natural loving desires destroys ideologies which blind, maim, and repress—and points the way to a kind of community which would amaze "moralists" and transform armies of men who are fighters because they cannot be lovers.

Avatamsaka (Kegon or *Hua-yen)* Buddhist philosophy sees the world as a vast, interrelated network in which all objects and creatures are necessary and illuminated. From one standpoint, governments, wars, or all that we consider "evil" are uncompromisingly contained in this totalistic realm. The hawk, the swoop, and the hare are one. From the "human" standpoint we cannot live in those terms unless all beings see with the same enlightened eye. The Bodhisattva lives by the sufferer's standard, and he or she must be effective in aiding those who suffer.

The mercy of the West has been social revolution; the mercy of the East has been individual insight into the basic self/void. We need both. They are both contained in the traditional three aspects of the Dharma path: wisdom *(prajña)*, meditation *(dhyana)*, and morality *(shila)*. Wisdom is intuitive knowledge of the mind of love and clarity that lies beneath one's ego-driven anxieties and aggressions. Meditation is going into the mind to see this for yourself—over and over again, until it becomes the mind you live in. Morality is bringing it back out in the way you live, through personal example and responsible action, ultimately toward the true community *(sangha)* of "all beings." This last aspect means, for me, supporting any cultural and economic revolution that moves clearly toward a truly free world. It means using such means as civil disobedience, outspoken criticism, protest, pacifism, voluntary poverty, and even gentle violence if it comes to a matter of restraining some impetuous crazy. It means affirming the widest possible spectrum of non-harmful individual behavior—defending the right of individuals to smoke hemp, eat peyote, be polygamous, polyandrous, or homosexual. Worlds of behavior and custom long banned by the Judaeo-Capitalist-Christian-Marxist West. It means respecting intelligence and learning, but not as greed or means to personal power. Working on one's own responsibility, but willing to work with a group. "Forming the new society within the shell of the old"—the I.W.W. slogan of 70 years ago.

The traditional, vernacular, primitive, and village cultures may appear to be doomed. We must defend and support them as we would the diversity of ecosystems; they are all manifestations of Mind. Some of the elder societies accomplished a condition of Sangha, with not a little of Buddha and Dharma as well. We touch base with the deep mind of peoples of all times and places in our meditation practice, and this is an amazing revolutionary aspect of the Buddhadharma. By a "planetary culture" I mean the kind of societies that would follow on a new understanding of that relatively recent institution, the National State, an understanding that might enable us to leave it behind. The State is greed made legal, with a monopoly on violence; a natural society is familial and cautionary. A natural society is one which "Follows the Way," imperfectly but authentically.

Such an understanding will close the circle and link us in many ways with the most creative aspects of our archaic past. If we are lucky, we may eventually arrive at a world of relatively mutually tolerant small societies attuned to their local natural region and united overall by a profound respect and love for the mind and nature of the universe.

I can imagine further virtues in a world sponsoring societies with matrilineal descent, free-form marriage, "natural credit" economics, far less population, and much more wilderness.

Genuine Compassion

I REALLY ADMIRE bees' sense of common responsibility. When you watch a beehive, you see that those small insects come from far away, take a few seconds' rest, go inside, and then hurriedly fly away. They are faithful to their responsibility. Although sometimes individual bees fight, basically there is a strong sense of unity and cooperation. We human beings are supposed to be much more advanced, but sometimes we lag behind even small insects.

We are social animals. If we were by nature solitary, there would be no towns or cities. Because of our nature, we have to live in a co-operative setting. People who have no sense of responsibility for the society or the common good are acting against human nature. For human survival, we need genuine cooperation, based on the sense of brotherhood and sisterhood.

Friends make us feel secure. Without friends, we feel a great loneliness. Sometimes, there is no proper person with whom we can communicate and share affection, so we prefer an animal, such as a dog or a cat. This shows that even those people who lose their trusted friends need someone to communicate and share affection with. I myself like my wristwatch, even though it never shows me any affection! In order to get mental satisfaction, as a human being, it is best to love another human being, and, if that is not possible, then some animal. If you show sincere affection, you will receive a response, and you will feel satisfaction. We all need friends.

There are different approaches to friendship. At times we may think that we need money and power to have friends, but that is not correct. When our fortune is intact, those kinds of friends may appear loyal, but when our fortune disappears, they will leave us. They are not true friends; they are friends of money or power. Alcohol is another unreliable friend. If you drink too much, you may collapse. Even your dreams will be unpleasant.

But there are other kinds of friends who, no matter what the situation, remain true. When our fortunes rise, even without friends, we can manage. But when they go down, we need true friends. In order to make genuine friends, we ourselves must create an environment that is pleasant. If we just have a lot of anger, not many people will be drawn close to us. Compassion or altruism draws friends. It is very simple.

All of the world's religions emphasize the importance of compassion, love, and forgiveness. Each may have a different interpretation, but, broadly speaking, everyone bases their understanding on the basis of brotherhood, sisterhood, and compassion. Those who believe in God usually see their love for their fellow human beings as an expression of their love for God. But if someone says, "I love God," and does not show sincere love towards his fellow human beings, I think that is not following God's teaching. Many religions emphasize forgiveness. Love and compassion are the basis of true forgiveness. Without them, it is difficult to develop forgiveness.

Love and compassion are basic human qualities. From a Buddhist point of view, love is an attitude of wanting to help other sentient beings enjoy happiness, and compassion is the wish for other sentient beings to be free from suffering. Compassion is not a selfish attitude, such as, "These are my friends, and therefore I want them to be free of suffering." Genuine compassion can be extended even towards one's enemies, because the very basis for generating compassion is seeing suffering in other living creatures, and that includes your enemies. When you see that your enemies are suffering, you are able to develop genuine compassion even towards those who have injured you.

Usual compassion and love give rise to a very close feeling, but it is essentially attachment. With usual love, as long as the other person appears to you as beautiful or good, love remains, but as soon as he or she appears to you as less beautiful or good, your love completely changes. Even though someone appears to you as a dear friend and you love him very much, the next morning the situation may completely change. Even though he is the same person, he feels more like an enemy. Instead of feeling compassion and love, you now feel hostility. With genuine love and compassion, another person's appearance or behavior has no effect on your attitude.

Real compassion comes from seeing the other's suffering. You feel a sense of responsibility, and you want to do something for him or her. There are three types of compassion. The first is a spontaneous wish for other sentient beings to be free of suffering. You find their suffering unbearable and you wish to relieve them of it. The second is not just a wish for their well-being, but a real sense of responsibility, a commitment to relieve their suffering and remove them from their undesirable circumstances. This type of compassion is reinforced by the realization that all sentient beings are impermanent, but because they grasp at the permanence of their identity, they experience confusion and suffering. A genuine sense of compassion generates a spontaneous sense of responsibility to work for the benefit of others, encouraging us to take this responsibility upon ourselves. The third type of compassion is reinforced by the wisdom that although all sentient beings have interdependent natures and no inherent existence, they still grasp at the existence of inherent nature. Compassion accompanied by such an insight is the highest level of compassion.

In order to cultivate and develop genuine compassion within yourself, you need to identify the nature of suffering and the state of suffering that sentient beings are in. Because you want sentient beings to be free from their suffering, first of all you have to identify what suffering is. When Buddha taught the Four Noble Truths, he spoke of three types of suffering: suffering that is obvious and acute, like physical pain; the suffering of change, such as pleasurable experiences that have the potential to turn into suffering; and pervasive suffering, which is the basic fact of conditioned existence. To cultivate compassion, first of all, you have to reflect on suffering and identify suffering as suffering. When reflecting in depth on the nature of suffering, it is always beneficial to search for an alternative—to see whether it is possible to ever get rid of suffering. If there is no way out, just reflecting on suffering will make you feel depressed, and that is not helpful. If there is no possibility of getting rid of the suffering, then it is better to not think about it at all.

After describing the origin of suffering, the Buddha spoke of the cessation of suffering and the path that leads to the cessation. When you realize that it *is* possible to eliminate the root that gives rise to suffering, that awareness will increase your determination to identify and reflect on suffering at all different levels, and that will inspire you to seek liberation.

After reflecting on the nature of suffering and feeling convinced that there is a path that leads to the cessation of suffering, then it is important to see that all sentient beings do not want suffering and do want happiness. Everyone has the right to be happy, to overcome suffering. When reflecting on ourselves, we find that we have a natural desire to be happy and to overcome suffering, and that this desire is just and valid. When we see that all living creatures have the natural right to be happy and overcome suffering and fulfill their wishes, we ourselves have a spontaneous feeling of self-worth.

The only difference between us and others is in number. We are just one individual among infinite others. No matter how important we are, we are just one sentient being, one single self, while others are infinite. But there is a close relationship of interdependence. Our suffering or happiness is very much related with others. That is also reality. Under these circumstances, if, in order to save one finger the other nine fingers are sacrificed, that is foolish. But if, in order to save nine fingers, one finger is sacrificed, it may be worth it. So you see the importance of others' rights and your own rights, and others' welfare and your own welfare. Because of numbers, the infinite numbers of others' rights and welfare naturally become most important. The welfare of others is important not only because of the sheer number, but also if you were to sacrifice the infinite others for your own happiness eventually you will lose. If you think more of others, taking care of others' rights and serving others, ultimately you will gain.

Not only when you are engaging in the meditative practices of the bodhisattva path is it harmful to sacrifice the welfare and happiness of infinite others for your own happiness, as it prevents you from making progress in the spiritual path, but if you were to sacrifice the benefit and welfare of infinite others for the sake of your own happiness and welfare in your daily life, you are the one who ultimately will lose and suffer the consequences.

If you want to be selfish, you should be selfish-with-wisdom, rather
than with foolishness. If you help others with sincere motivation and
sincere concern, that will bring you more fortune, more friends, more
smiles, and more success. If you forget about others' rights and neglect others' welfare, ultimately you will be very lonely.

Even our enemy is very useful to us because, in order to practice
compassion we need to practice tolerance, forgiveness, and patience,
the antidotes to anger. In order to learn tolerance, forgiveness, and
patience, we need someone to create some trouble. From this point
of view, there is no need to feel anger towards the enemy or the person who creates the problem for us. In fact, we should feel gratitude
for the opportunity he provides us. Regardless of whether he intended
to benefit us, whenever we find anything that is helpful, we can utilize the opportunity. Of course one might argue that the enemy has
no conscious intention to be of help, but on the contrary, has a strong
conscious intention to cause harm, and therefore, anger is justified.
This is true. We categorize someone as an enemy because he has the
intention to harm us. Even if a surgeon has to amputate our limb,
because surgeons do not generally have the intention to harm us, we
don't classify them as our enemy. Since our enemy has the intention
to be harmful to us, we classify and identify him as an enemy, and
therefore we have this opportunity to practice patience and tolerance
toward that person.

In order to practice compassion toward all living beings, it is important to be able to generate a genuine sense of patience and tolerance toward our enemies. In order to cultivate genuine patience toward
our enemy, there are certain types of mental trainings. For instance,
if you have been injured by gunfire, if you feel angry, you should analyze the situation and think, what is it that I am angry at? If I am angry
at the thing that injured me, I should be angry at the direct cause of
my injury, which is the bullet. If I should feel anger toward the ultimate cause of my injury, I should feel anger toward the anger within
the person who shot at me. But that is not the case. I don't feel angry
at the bullet or the other person's anger; I feel angry at the person, who
is just the medium. Under different circumstances, that person could
change into a good friend.

As long as that negative emotion is there, it acts like an enemy. But when a positive motivation develops, that person becomes our friend. The person himself can be changed under different circumstances, dominated by different factors of the mind. So, logically speaking, if we are to feel anger toward the thing that harmed us, it is the anger within that person that we should feel angry at. So, just as we see how destructive is the anger generated within us, how it destroys our peace of mind, mental balance, and so forth, so it is in the case of the anger generated within the enemy's mind. It affects his mind and his happiness.

Therefore, when someone dominated by anger harms you, instead of feeling angry toward him, you should feel a sense of compassion and pity because that person is suffering himself. When you reflect in this way, it will help reduce the force of your anger. When you train your mind in this way, gradually you will be able to extend your compassion toward all living creatures, including your enemy.

I myself, as a Buddhist monk who is supposedly a practitioner—although my practice is very lazy and not at all satisfying to myself—even a lazy practitioner with not enough time, step by step, little by little, can change. I can change my own mental attitude, and it brings me some real joy and inner strength. Brothers and sisters, please think along these lines. If you feel you can practice at a certain point, please try to carry it out as a kind of experiment. As time goes on, you may get some benefit. But if you feel it isn't working, don't worry. Don't be concerned at all.

Compassion, or altruistic motivation, is really wonderful. Sometimes I feel a sense of wonder that we human beings can develop such altruism. It is really a precious source of inner strength, happiness, and future success.

PART IV

THE GREENING OF THE SELF

Dharma Gaia

THE MORE TIME I spend sitting on my meditation cushion listening to what Peter Matthiessen calls the "ringing stillness of the universal mind," the more I feel the warm embrace of Gaia, our Mother Earth. It is an awareness of being cared for and nurtured, like being in a long slow dance with the Goddess. Buddhism has been called "the religion before religion," which means that anyone, of any faith, can practice. For Matthiessen, that phrase evokes the natural religion of our early childhood, when "heaven and a splendorous Earth were one." Only too soon is the child's clarity of vision obscured by a host of encrustations intrinsic to cultural conditioning—firm views, judgmentalism, and denial.

The Dharma—the teaching of Buddhism—is about putting an end to suffering by facing existing circumstances with equanimity and the resolve to do our best. Looking deeply at things as they are can be painful, and some call Buddhism pessimistic. But it has also been known as an ancient art and science of ecstasy. Thich Nhat Hanh tells us:

> Life is filled with suffering, but it is also filled with many wonders, like the blue sky, the sunshine, the eyes of a baby.... Whether or not we are happy depends on our awareness. When we have a toothache, we think that not having a toothache will make us very happy. But when we don't have a toothache, often we are still not happy. If we practice awareness, we suddenly become very rich, very happy. Practicing Buddhism is a clever way to enjoy life.

While the Earth is changing in response to human carelessness, and the problems that lie ahead are vast, perilous, and certain, the emerging ecocrisis is energizing a strong desire for a positive vision of the future. If Buddhism is to be relevant, must we not be able to imagine a real Buddha—to believe it possible that we can give rise to the quality and refinement of character exemplified by Gautama? And isn't it a realistic, achievable goal to develop ourselves into great flowers in the garden of humanity?

It is vital that we reduce pollution, plant trees, recycle, and so forth, and yet the most critical change that must take place is a transformation in our very relationship with the Earth. The Earth does not need to change in order to survive—she will survive with or without us. If *we* are to continue, it is our minds that need changing. The Buddha's insight that the Earth is also mind can serve us as we endeavor to define a new ecological ethic. The Dharma is a powerful companion for us on our journey from *ego*centricity to *eco*centricity— a true greening of our minds.

The fruit of Buddhism—mindful living—cultivates a view of human beings, nature, and their relationship that is fundamentally ecological. Awareness opens our perception to the interdependence and fragility of all life and our indebtedness to countless beings, living and dead, past and present, near and far. If we have any real identity at all in Buddhism, it is ecology itself—a massive, interdependent, self-causing dynamic energy-event against a backdrop of ceaseless change. From Indra's Net of the Hua-yen school, to the Japanese teaching of *esho-funi* (life and environment are one), to *interbeing* as taught by Thich Nhat Hanh, Buddhist philosophy and practice constitute what scholar Francis Cook calls a "cosmic ecology."

Having taken root in the West, Buddhism is following its classical migratory mode—forming a circle with the nature-based wisdom of indigenous cultures. The sophisticated ecological teaching that Native American life represents is grounded in an honorable partnership with a living Mother Earth, from which all life springs. The Lakota people have a prayer: *mitakuye oyasin,* which means "all my relations," that everything in our experience is part of us, and we are part of it. While Native American cosmology is generally centered around harmony, its history is fraught with war. Buddhism can help Native Americans find their path to peace while Native Americans can vivify the living Earth for Buddhists. Both traditions share the notion that nature is an active partner in all thought.

The great Mahayana teachings that swept through the East in the sixth century, including *The Avatamsaka Sutra,* the *Lotus Sutra,* and *The Vimalakirti Sutra,* speak as reverently of nature as they do of the Buddha. Locales are described in loving detail down to the colors of the leaves and the shapes of the trees and clouds. One chapter of *The Lotus Sutra,* entitled "The Parable of the Herbs," describes a mystical rain that fosters the growth of the Earth's trees and plants. This rain is our practice. All life on Earth, the sutra proclaims, plants, animals, trees, and the quality of life for all beings, is cultivated by correct practice. In another chapter of the same sutra, "Springing Up Out of the Earth," the planet gives rise to innumerable beings who will relieve the sufferings of the Earth.

The Buddhist tradition, in all of its historical and cultural manifestations, encourages greater identification with the natural world. At Todai-ji temple in Japan, visitors are reminded that the universe itself is a Buddha, that "the songs of the birds, the colors of the flowers, the currents of streams and the figures of clouds" are also his teachings. D. T. Suzuki said that the thought process of an enlightened mind is "like showers coming down from the sky, like waves rolling on the ocean, like the stars illuminating the nightly heavens, like green foliage shooting forth in the relaxing spring breeze—indeed [the Enlightened One] is the showers, the ocean, the stars, and the foliage."

In the West, our Cartesian, mechanical, anthropocentric world view, so culturally embedded as to be nearly invisible, seems to be giving way to an interrelated, intercausal universe similar to the world described in Native American wisdom, Buddhist philosophy, and modern physics. The Buddha observed a universe made up of phenomena and their mutual interactions. "This is like this," as Thich Nhat Hanh often paraphrases the Buddhist genesis, "because that is like that." *Paticca samuppada,* translated as dependent co-origination or the Great Wheel of Causation, is at the heart of Buddhist understanding. It suggests that all things—objects and beings—exist only *inter*dependently, not *in*dependently. This is the emptiness of *shunyata*—that nothing has a separate existence. In a Buddhist perception, everything is alive and influences everything else. All of nature is vibrating with life, even the air.

In fact, it was while observing the air that independent atmospheric scientist James Lovelock, then under contract from NASA, recognized dependent co-origination in the self-regulating, constantly changing atmosphere of the Earth. He hypothesized that the Earth is a homeostatic living organism that coordinates its vital systems to compensate for threatening environmental changes. At the suggestion of his friend, novelist William Golding, Lovelock called this theory the Gaia Hypothesis, after the Greek Goddess of the Earth. While unity is the essence of the Gaia principle, so is the fact that differences and variety in nature are not just to be tolerated, but encouraged. Our very survival depends on diversity.

Many ecologists recognize that our environmental problems are rooted in a spiritual crisis. We seem to be awash in a great sea of duality between our own aliveness and the life of the planet, between mind and body, and between the masculine and the feminine. Dr. Lovelock has predicted that an understanding of Gaia could conceivably become a scientifically verifiable religion. Such a faith might resemble a merging of Buddhism, deep ecology, and feminism and could be called "Dharma Gaia." Both component words have their origin in three-thousand-year-old cultures—and both are playing an increasingly significant role in the way the world is understood.

Dharma comes from the Sanskrit root *dhr*, which means "firmament," "that which is established firmly," "that which is confirmed," "that which is real." Dharma Gaia might therefore mean "the teaching of the living Earth." The place of the Buddha's enlightenment was Bodh Gaya in northeastern India. As meditation teacher and Green activist Christopher Titmuss has observed, both Gaia and Gaya share the same pronunciation—and a certain ancient intimacy with the Earth.

Buddhism offers a clearly defined system of ethics, a guide to ecological living, right here, right now. Meditation is its primary tool for raising ecological consciousness. In meditation, awareness of our environment deepens and our identity expands to include the multitude of circumstances and conditions that come together to form our existence. Curiosity and respect for the beauty and power of nature is enhanced, revealing an innate biospirituality. Re-sensitized to our feelings and immersed in awareness, we may find ways to avoid irreversible damage and ultimate self-destruction. With its emphasis on cooperation and interdependence, Buddhist practice can inspire the building of partnership societies with *need*-based, sustainable economies rather than *greed*-based, growth economies.

As the crisis of feeding the world's population grows, breeding of animals for human consumption becomes less acceptable—out of compassion for the suffering of animals and the awareness that it is a grossly inefficient use of water and grain. A new relationship with the animal kingdom is part of our changing perception of the Earth. Animals are part of us, and part of our practice.

The arms industry among the developed nations creates vast amounts of pollution, drains the planet's resources, and threatens the Earth's very survival as a life-sustaining body. But Buddhism helps us realize that it is futile to blame others as solely responsible. We are encouraged to take a closer look at the unwholesome tendencies in our own behavior. Are we recycling? Are we consuming conscientiously? Right livelihood becomes the fruit of our awakening and the salvation of our form of life.

Practice prepares us to glimpse the preciousness and immediacy of life so we can experience ourselves and nature as one—operationally. It brings a meditative attitude of complete attention and focus to all our activities. By practicing in community, or Sangha, with others who share a Green perception of the future, we are liberated from the myth of our separateness. Carl Sagan recently told an audience of scientists that "efforts to safeguard and cherish the environment need to be infused with a vision of the sacred." Inspired by Buddha, guided by Dharma, and supported by Sangha, we travel a path toward living in balance with ourselves, with all other forms of life, and with our true mother, the Earth.

There is an urgency to restore our deeper powers of perception. We are challenged to understand with our intellect, our heart, and with every molecule of our being, the seemingly ironic state in which we are both uniquely different from everything else *and* intrinsically interconnected with each other and the entire living cosmos. Every day is Earth Day. As Buddhists have chanted since ancient times, "May all beings be happy and free from suffering!"

CHATSUMARN KABILSINGH

Early Buddhist Views on Nature

BUDDHISM VIEWS HUMANITY as an integral part of nature, so that when nature is defiled, people ultimately suffer. Negative consequences arise when cultures alienate themselves from nature, when people feel separate from and become aggressive towards natural systems. When we abuse nature, we abuse ourselves. Buddhist ethics follow from this basic understanding. Only when we agree on this common ground can we save ourselves, let alone the world.

In order to explore the connection between Buddhism and nature, the World Wildlife Fund has sponsored a project called Buddhism and Nature Conservation. This project is particularly interested in finding teachings of the Buddha that relate to nature and its conservation. A team of researchers has combed the texts and discovered a surprisingly large store of beautiful and valuable teachings in Buddhism relating to nature and respect for wildlife and natural resources.

The *Jataka*, the richly narrated birth stories of Buddhism, are abundant with poetic appreciations of nature. Passage after passage celebrates forests, waters, and the Earth's wild creatures. Here we find a "Garden of Delight," where grass is ever green, all trees bear fruit good to eat, and streams are sweet and clean, "blue as beryl." Nearby is "a region overrun and beautified with all manner of trees and flowering shrubs and creepers, resounding with the cries of swans, ducks and geese...." Next is reported an area "yielding from its soil all manner of herbs, overspread with many a tangle of flowers," and listing a rich variety of wild animals: antelope, elephant, buffalo, deer, yak, lion, rhinoceros, tiger, panther, bear, hyena, otter, hare, and more.[1]

---

[1] *Jataka Stories*, edited by E. B. Cowell, VOL. IV-V (1957).

All Buddhist literature states that the Buddha was born in a grove of sal, lovely straight-backed trees with large leaves. According to legend, when the Buddha was born he took seven steps, and lotus flowers sprang up as he walked. As a youth, he is said to have meditated in the shade of the jambo, one of the 650 species of myrtle.

The Buddha's further study was in the company of a banyan, and his enlightenment was under the spreading branches of a tree recognized for its special place in human faith even in its scientific name, *Ficus religiosa*. Also known as the Bo, Bodhi, or peepul, this tree is sacred in both Buddhism and Hinduism.

The early Buddhist community lived in the forest under large trees, in caves, and in mountainous areas. Directly dependent on nature, they cultivated great respect for the beauty and diversity of their natural surroundings.

In the *Sutta Nipata*, one of the earliest texts, the Buddha says:

> Know ye the grasses and the trees.... Then know ye the worms, and the moths, and the different sorts of ants.... Know ye also the four-footed animals small and great, the serpents, the fish which range in the water, the birds that are borne along on wings and move through the air.... Know ye the marks that constitute species are theirs, and their species are manifold.[2]

There is a story of a monk who cut down the main branch of a tree: The spirit who resided in that tree came forward and complained to the Buddha that a monk had cut off his child's arm. From then on, monks were forbidden to cut down trees.[3]

The Buddha encouraged acting with compassion and respect for the trees, noting that they provide natural protection for the beings who dwell in the forest. On one occasion, the Buddha admonished some travelers who, after resting under a large banyan tree, proceeded to cut it down. Much like a friend, the tree had given them shade. To harm a friend is indeed an act of ingratitude.[4]

---

[2] *Sutta-Nipata*, translated by V. Fausboll (Delhi, India: Motilal Banarsidass, 1968).

[3] *Paccittiya, Bhutagama Vagga*, Thai Tripitaka, VOL. 2, p. 347.

[4] *Ibid.*, VOL. 27, p. 370.

The *Anguttara Nikaya* tells a similar story:

Long ago, Brahmin Dhamika, Rajah Koranya, had a steadfast king banyan tree and the shade of its widespread branches was cool and lovely. Its shelter broadened to twelve leagues. None guarded its fruit, and none hurt another for its fruit.

Now then came a man who ate his fill of fruit, broke a branch, and went his way. Thought the spirit dwelling in that tree: How amazing, how astonishing it is, that a man should be so evil as to break a branch off the tree after eating his fill. Suppose the tree were to bear no more fruit. And the tree bore no more fruit.[5]

What about the treatment of animals? Every healthy forest is home for wildlife, so when a monk accepts the forest as his home, he also respects the animals who live in the forest. Early Buddhists maintained this kind of friendly attitude toward their natural surroundings and opposed the destruction of forests or their wildlife.[6]

The first precept in Buddhism is "Do not kill." This precept is not merely a legalistic prohibition, but a realization of our affinity with all who share the gift of life. A compassionate heart provides a firm ground for this precept.

Those who make their living directly or indirectly from killing animals will experience the karmic consequences. The resultant pain is described in the texts as being "sharp as spears" and as terrifying as being "thrown head-down into a river of fire."[7] A person who tortures or kills animals will always harbor a deep sorrow within:

When, householder, the taker of life, by reason of his taking life, breeds dread and hatred in this world, or when he breeds dread and hatred in the next world, he experiences in the mind pain and grief; but he who abstains from taking life breeds no dread and hatred in this world and in the next world.... Thus that dread and hatred has ceased for him, who abstained from taking life.[8]

---

[5] *Anguttara Nikaya, Gradual Sayings,* VOL. 3, p. 262.

[6] *Payaka Jataka, op. cit.* VOL. 27:417, p. 107.

[7] *Ibid.,* Vol. 28:92, p. 35.

[8] *Gradual Sayings,* Vol. 4, p. 273.

The community of monks are forbidden by the *Vinaya*, the ancient rules of conduct, from eating ten different kinds of meat, mostly animals of the forest.[9] The Buddha taught his disciples to communicate to animals their wishes for peace and happiness. This was only possible when they did not eat the animals' flesh, and harbored no thoughts of harming them. When a monk died from a snakebite, the Buddha advised the community to generate compassion and dedicate the merit to the family of snakes.[10]

When we look at the Buddha's pronouncements on water conservation, it is astonishing to see that he actually set down rules forbidding his disciples to contaminate water resources. For example, monks were dissuaded from throwing their waste or leftover food into rivers and lakes, and they were urged to guard the lives of all living beings abiding there.[11] In the *Vinaya Pitaka* there are detailed descriptions of how to build toilets and water wells.[12] One of the eight good qualities of the ocean is "cleanliness," and another is that it "must be the abode of various kinds of fish." Those who destroy or contaminate water resources do so at great karmic peril.[13] This illustrates early awareness of the need to preserve natural resources.

The early Buddhist community lived comfortably within nature, and the Buddha included many examples and similes from nature in his teachings:

> Suppose there is a pool of water, turbid, stirred up and muddied. Just so a turbid mind. Suppose there is a pool of water, pure, tranquil and unstirred, where a man can see oysters and shells, pebbles and gravel, and schools of fish. Just so an untroubled mind.[14]

Buddhism holds a great respect for and gratitude toward nature. Nature is the mother that gives rise to all the joyful things in life.

---

[9] *Ibid.*, Vol. 4, p. 60–61.

[10] *Ibid.*, Vol. 7, p. 9.

[11] *Ibid.*, Vol. 25:300, p. 313.

[12] *Ibid.*, Vol. 7, p. 48.

[13] *Ibid.*, Vol. 26:104, p. 174.

[14] *Ibid.*, Vol. 1, p. 6–7.

Among the beautiful expressions in Buddhist literature showing mutual relation and interdependence of humankind and wildlife, there was early on a realization that survival of certain species was in danger, and that losing such creatures diminishes the Earth: "Come back, O Tigers! to the woods again, and let it not be leveled with the plain. For without you, the axe will lay it low. You, without it, forever homeless go."[15]

Another well-known and much loved teaching which exemplifies the central core of compassion in Buddhism is the *Metta Sutta:* "Thus, as a mother with her own life guards the life of her own child, let all embracing thoughts for all that lives be thine."[16]

His Holiness the Fourteenth Dalai Lama of Tibet who stands prominently among Buddhist leaders of the world who are farsighted, has repeatedly expressed his concern for environmental protection. "Our ancestors viewed the Earth as rich, bountiful and sustainable," said His Holiness. "We know this is the case, but only if we take care of it." In one of his recent speeches on the subject of ecology, he points out that the most important thing is to have a peaceful heart. Only when we understand the true nature lying within can we live harmoniously with the rest of the natural world.

In this respect, the Buddhist practice of cultivating awareness and calmness through meditation is vital. Buddhism is very much a religion of this world, this life, and the present moment. In the past it has often been misunderstood as otherworldly or life-denying. In fact, Buddhism can be meaningful only when it is relevant to our everyday lives and to our environment. The Buddhist tradition counsels us to treasure and conserve nature, of which human beings are an active part. Each of us must choose the extent to which we will bring to life the teachings of the Buddha. If we cannot hand over a better world to future generations, it is only fair that they have at least as green a world to live in as we do.

---

[15] *Khunddakapatha* (London: Pali Text Society, 1960).

[16] *Ibid.*

Watering the Seed of Mindfulness

IN LATE MARCH OF 1991, on the way to a retreat for environmentalists to be led by the eminent Vietnamese Zen master, poet, and peace
activist Thich Nhat Hanh, I took time for a walk up Malibu Creek,
in the Malibu Canyon State Park. Spring songbirds were numerous,
and a golden eagle sailed high overhead, crossing the Santa Catalina
Mountains of the Coast Range, and from a bridge over the creek I
saw a heavy brown-furred animal half-hidden behind rocks close to
the bank. From its striped ears, I knew it was a bobcat, stalking three
coot that had come ashore into the sedges. So intent was it upon its
prey that, moving out into the open, it looked back just once, the sun
catching the oval of light fur around the lynxish eyes. However, the
coot, sensing danger, swam away from shore, and as the bobcat made
its way downstream, striped bobbed tail twitching in frustration, the
slate gray birds with their ivory bills followed along, just off the bank,
peering and craning to see where the wildcat had got to.

The bobcat or bay lynx is not uncommon, but it is elusive, difficult to see; I have crossed paths with it perhaps eight times in fifty years
of wildlife observation, usually as it crossed a trail or a night road. This
was the first one I had ever watched for minutes at a time—ten minutes at the least—in open sunlight of mid-afternoon, scarcely fifty feet
away, a stirring event that seemed to me an auspicious sign for the
environmentalists' retreat that would begin that evening.

Originally the retreat was to take place at Ojai, but in recent weeks,
due to housing complications, it had been shifted to Camp Sholom,
a Jewish retreat in the Santa Catalinas, perhaps five miles inland from
the coast; the camp lies in a hollow in the dry chaparral hills, in a grove

of sycamore and live oak where two brooks come together. The hills were green and the brooks rushing from the heavy rains, which muddied the ground beneath the huge white tent and moved the whole retreat indoors.

My host was James Soshin Thornton, a student of Maezumi Roshi and the founding lawyer of the Los Angeles office of the Natural Resources Defense Council, which together with the Nathan Cummings Foundation, the Ojai Foundation, and the Community of Mindful Living, had sponsored the retreat. One of my own Zen students, Dennis Snyder, was also present, and so were several environmental acquaintances and friends-of-friends.

Zazen, which took place in the meeting hall on the first evening, after some welcoming remarks by Thich Nhat Hanh, Joan Halifax of Ojai, and James Thornton, was a new experience for most of the environmentalists among the 225 retreatants, some of whom were later obliged to move to chairs, but they persevered bravely and by the week's end, were sitting as assiduously as all the rest.

"When you take care of the environmentalist," said Thich Nhat Hanh, urging the use of a gentle smile to help us pay attention to each moment, "you take care of the environment." This remark might have been the theme of the whole retreat.

Thich Nhat Hanh, called "Thây" by his students, is a small, large-toothed man with a broad smile and kind, smiling eyes, so youthful in appearance that one scarcely believes he was nominated in 1968 (by Martin Luther King) for the Nobel Peace Prize.

In his first Dharma talk next morning (on breathing meditation: "When I breathe in, I am aware of my eyes…of the lovely morning…of my heart….") he stood in brown robes in the early sun that shimmered from the small hard shiny leaves of live oak and poured through the windowed wall behind him, filtered by a lovely wooden screen of six carved panels that Joan Halifax believes came originally from China. Like chinks of sun through the brown rosettes of the screen, Thây's white teeth glinted in that childlike wide-eyed smile.

"Sometimes we believe we would like to be someone else, but of course we cannot be someone else, we can only be ourselves, and even that is very difficult….To be ourselves, we must be in the present moment, and to be in the present moment we must follow our breath, be one with our breath, for otherwise we are overtaken by emotions and events...."

Thây's daily talks were pointed up by intermittent bell notes rung by his attendant Therese Fitzgerald (formerly of San Francisco Zen Center), and all meals, eaten in silence, were also punctuated by a bell, to remind retreatants to pay attention to this present moment.

Insight depends upon awareness of this moment, according to Thây's teaching, which leads inevitably to compassion and a natural state of being. His teaching returns again and again to the soft image of a flower, "showing its heart" as it opens to the sun. The mudra of gassho he likens to a closed lotus, the hands opening outward in gratitude and thanks for this extraordinary existence, in the way that a bean sprout opens, smiling, to the sun and wind. That half-smile on the lips will lead to an unforced well-being, contributing to a sincere joy in one's practice. "If your practice is not pleasurable," then some other practice might be more suitable, says Thây.

On the first evening, an informal panel—Thây's associate, the Vietnamese nun Sister Chân Không, James Thornton, and Randy Hayes of the Rainforest Action Network, also Joan Halifax and myself—took questions from the gathering of perhaps 225 persons that filled the meeting hall right to the walls. Sister Chân Không, a small dynamic person who administers one hundred social workers in Vietnam (all unknown to one another, since they may be harassed by the government), was articulate and eloquent; like Thich Nhat Hanh, she counseled returning to the breath as the foundation of this moment, of our very being. And the panel agreed that in time of distress, we must go into that distress, deeper and deeper, become one with it.

On other occasions, in a sweet voice, Sister Chân Không burst into song, manifesting the joy in this moment that Thây talks about. Discussing the anger she sometimes feels, seeing the waste of water and materials in our bathrooms and kitchens, she says she cures this by singing aloud, "When I go to the bathroom (kitchen, etc.), I feel happy, because I have learned to breathe deeply...." (After Thây's Dharma talk on the precepts, she remarked, "When you are truly mindful, you don't need the precepts.")

Each day began with two early periods of strong zazen, followed by recitation from the sutras or, on one occasion, a fine letter to Thây

from an environmental lawyer in the group who stressed the need for
the spiritual base for environmental work that has been sadly lacking
in most organizations. After silent breakfast in the dining hall, down
along the creek, Thây would talk to us again, in a Dharma talk that
one day ran close to two hours.

"We are only real when we are one with our breathing—our walking, our eating—and it is then that everything around us becomes
real…. Eating a bean, be conscious of the true nature of that bean,
the structure, all the non-bean elements that make up that bean, and
permit it to exist. If you look into a flower penetratingly, you will see
the sun, the minerals, the water that make up the flower, which contains all the non-flower elements in the world, just as a Buddhist contains all the non-Buddhist elements."

Thây's eyes sometimes remain sad even when he is smiling, and
more than once during the week he expressed distress over the actions
of President Bush in the Gulf War, which had almost deterred him
from making his annual visit to this country. He spoke to us of "sowing the seed of peace in our land," and attending to "the President Bush
within ourselves…" as we might attend to our greed, ignorance, and
anger.

"Take tender care of your anger, with mindfulness…don't suppress
it…it is you. You have been watering the seed of your anger rather
than the seed of your mindfulness; the anger comes from lack of understanding, and it comes very easily…. If mindfulness is there, you
are protected from anger and from fear."

And he spoke to us strongly against "sowing the seed of suffering"
in our speech and actions. Another day, he pointed out our compul-
sive behavior, our inability to stop: the more we eat (sleep, telephone,
watch television, drive in our car)—the more we fill the emptiness,
in short—the hungrier we become. We must fill every moment, we
cannot just be. "How can we stop the arms race when we cannot stop
ourselves?"

Following the Dharma talk came walking meditation in the hills,
then lunch, then afternoon meetings with various leaders, late afternoon zazen, supper, and more evening meetings, followed by a last
period of formal zazen. All of these events except zazen were inter-
spersed with semi-spiritual musical presentations by two guitarist-

singers, an evening of entertainment, and even a Passover supper, or seder. At times, Thây appeared vaguely mystified by these secular events, which were not, however, permitted to alter the warm and yet serious tone of the retreat.

Despite his gentle manner, Thich Nhat Hanh is a strict teacher with a strong adherence to the precepts. Talking informally one evening over green tea in his room, we discussed the fact that many if not most Zen teachers transgress the precepts in one way or another, and he said wryly, "They have the idea that this is all right for enlightened people."

He went on to describe his Rinzai training in Vietnam, where he became a monk in 1942 and founded the Tiep Hien Order in 1964; I had not realized that Rinzai Zen, which traveled eastward from China to Korea and Japan, then the United States, had also made its way south into Southeast Asia, where Theravadin Buddhism had held sway for centuries.

As the days passed and the rain ceased and concentration deepened, Thich Nhat Hanh's mild tones came and went like some wonderful soft voice from faraway in the mysterious stacks of a huge library. At times the whole brown-robed being seemed to shine, as if he and the sun-filled screen, the mountain light, were now all one. "We have to be a little bit mindful just to notice the moon, but we don't appreciate the intensity, the beauty of our life, until we are truly mindful in each moment."

World As Lover, World As Self

OUR PLANET IS in trouble. It is hard to go anywhere without being confronted by the wounding of our world, the tearing of the very fabric of life. I return this day from Germany, where I lived in the 1950s amidst the clear waters, rich green fields, and woodlands of Bavaria. Now there is an environmental plague there called *waldsterben*, "the dying of the trees," and the Black Forest is reckoned to be about 50% dead from industrial and automobile pollution.

South of the Black Forest rise the headwaters of the Rhine, which flows on down through Basel, across Europe, and into the North Sea. A 1986 fire at the Sandoz chemical plant in Basel washed 30,000 tons of mercury and dioxin-forming chemicals into that once great, life-bearing artery of Europe. Millions of fish floated belly-up, and the deaths of seals as far away as the North Sea have been traced to the accident. Along this majestic river, requiems were held. On its many bridges, people gathered, banging on pots, pans, and anything that could make a noise, and cried, *"Der Rhein ist tot!"* "The Rhine is dead!"

I went to Germany to lead a workshop, just south of the Black Forest, near the source of the Rhine. We came together to explore the inner resources that are needed to take action in today's world. The corner of Europe where we met, given the prevailing winds in April and May of 1986, received some of the heaviest radioactive fallout from the disaster at the nuclear power plant in Chernobyl. During the workshop, one participant brought out a loaf of bread and said, reverently, "This was made from grains harvested before Chernobyl! We can eat it without fear."

In the face of what is happening, how do we avoid feeling over-whelmed and just giving up, turning to the many diversions and de-mands of our consumer societies?

It is essential that we develop our inner resources. We have to learn to look at things as they are, painful and overwhelming as that may be, for no healing can begin until we are fully present to our world, until we learn to sustain the gaze.

These concerns, obviously, are not limited to Germany. Two weeks before going, I led a similar workshop in England at a neo-Gothic castle in the Lake District. We were fifteen minutes from Barrow, the great ship building town on the Irish Sea where the new British Tri-dent submarine, with its mammoth load of nuclear warheads, was being constructed. Half an hour up the coast, the dirtiest nuclear re-actor ever built, Sellafield, is turning the Irish Sea into the world's most radioactive body of water. Looking for the inner resources to deal with such a world, we felt very deeply the tragedies that are befalling it. As the poisoned winds of Chernobyl and the plutonium being dumped daily into the Irish Sea teach us, there are no boundaries to ecologi-cal disasters, no political borders to the perils that threaten us today.

Among the inner resources that we seek for sustaining our action and our sanity are what the Germans call *weltbild,* the way we view our world and our relationship to it. Let us reflect together on our basic posture vis-a-vis our world and how we may come to see it in ways that empower us to act.

By "our world," I mean the place we find ourselves, the scene upon which we play our lives. It is sending us signals of distress that have become so continual as to appear almost ordinary. We know about the loss of cropland and the spreading of hunger, the toxins in the air we breathe and the water we drink, and the die-off of fellow species; we know about our nuclear and so-called conventional weapons that are deployed and poised on hair-trigger alert and the conflicts that ignite in practically every corner of the world. These warning signals tell us that we live in a world that can end, at least as a home for conscious life. I do not say it will end, but it *can* end. This very possibility changes everything for us.

There have been small groups throughout history that have pro-claimed the end of the world, such as at the time of the first millen-

nium and again during the Black Plague in Europe. These expectations arose within the context of religious faith, of a belief in a just
but angry God ready to punish his wayward children. But now the
prospect is spelled out in sober scientific data, not religious belief, and
it is entirely devoid of transcendent meaning. I stress the unprec-
edented nature of our situation, because I want to inspire awe, respect,
and compassion for what we are experiencing. With isolated excep-
tions, every generation prior to ours has lived with the assumption that
other generations would follow. It has always been assumed, as an
integral part of human experience, that the work of our hands and
heads and hearts would live on through those who came after us,
walking on the same earth beneath the same sky. Plagues, wars, and
personal death have always taken place within that wider context, the
assurance of continuity. Now we have lost the certainty that we will
have a future. I believe that this loss, felt at some level of consciousness by everyone, regardless of political orientation, is the pivotal psychological reality of our time.

These signals of impending doom bring with them a sense of urgency to do something. But there are so many programs, strategies,
and causes that vie for our attention that we may feel overwhelmed.
So it is good to pause and ground ourselves, to look at our *weltbild*, at
the ways we see and relate to our world, and discover what ways can
best sustain us to do what must be done. With this in mind, I would
like to reflect on four particular ways that people on spiritual paths
look at the world. These are not specific to any particular religion; you
can find all of them in most spiritual traditions. These four are: world
as battlefield, world as trap, world as lover, world as self.

Many people view the *world as a battlefield*, where good and evil
are pitted against each other, and the forces of light battle the forces
of darkness. This ancient tradition goes back to the Zoroastrians and
the Manichaeans. It can be persuasive, especially when you feel threatened. Such a view is very good for arousing courage, summoning up
the blood, using the fiery energies of anger, aversion, and militancy.
It is very good, too, for giving a sense of certainty. Whatever the score
may be at the moment or whatever tactics you are using, there is the
sense that you are fighting God's battle and that ultimately you will

win. William Irwin Thompson has called this kind of certainty and the self-righteousness that goes with it, the "apartheid of good."

We see this in many areas of our world today, in Beirut and Belfast, in the Persian Gulf and South Asia, even in my beloved Sri Lanka, a home of the most tolerant of religions. And we see it in our own country. The Jerry Falwells of society evoke the righteousness of this divinely ordained battle, leading, as they see that it must, to Armageddon and the Second Coming of Christ. In this variety of Christian thought, nuclear war may be the catalyst for the millennial denouement, bringing just rewards to the elect, who will inherit the Earth—and the Bomb itself can appear as an instrument of God's will.

A more innocuous version of the battlefield image of the world is the one I learned from my grandparents. It is the world as a classroom, a kind of moral gymnasium where you are put through certain tests which would prove your mettle and teach you certain lessons, so you can graduate to other arenas and rewards. Whether a battlefield or classroom, the world is a proving ground, with little worth other than that. What counts are our immortal souls, which are being tested here. They count, and the world doesn't. For the sake of your soul, whether you are a Jerry Falwell or an Ayatollah Khomeini, you are ready to destroy.

If you feel our world has seen enough destruction already, this view may be unappealing. But it is strong among monotheistic religions, and it is contagious. Agnostics, too, can feel a tremendous do-or-die militancy and self-righteousness. Even adherents of more tolerant and non-theistic religions betray this kind of fundamentalism, a conviction that you are on the side of the good and, therefore, whatever you do is permitted, if not required. I don't expect many readers to leap to the defense of this view, especially as I am presenting it in so bald and biased a fashion. But it is important that we recognize its presence, its appeal, and its tenacity.

Let us turn to the second view: *the world as trap*. Here, the spiritual path is not to engage in struggle and vanquish a foe, but to disentangle ourselves and escape from this messy world. We try to extricate ourselves and ascend to a higher, supra-phenomenal plane. This stance is based on a hierarchical view of reality, where mind is seen as higher than matter and spirit is set over and above nature. This view encourages contempt for the material plane. Elements of it have entered all major religions of the last 3,000 years, regardless of their metaphysics.

Many of us on spiritual paths fall for this view. Wanting to affirm a transcendent reality distinct from a society that appears very materialistic, we place it on a supra-phenomenal level removed from confusion and suffering. The tranquility that spiritual practices can provide, we imagine, belongs to a haven that is aloof from our world and to which we can ascend and be safe and serene. This gets tricky, because we still have bodies and are dependent on them, however advanced we may be on the spiritual path. Trying to escape from something that we are dependent on breeds a love-hate relationship with it. This love-hate relationship with matter permeates our culture and inflames a twofold desire—to destroy and to possess. These two impulses, craving and aversion, inflame each other in a kind of vicious circle. In the terms of general systems theory, the desire to destroy and the desire to possess form a deviation-amplifying feedback loop. We can see this exemplified in our military arsenal. To back up our demands for the raw materials we want, we threaten their very existence. To sustain our technologies' capacity to destroy, we require increasing amounts of raw materials; and the vicious circle continues, exponentially.

Many on a spiritual path, seeking to transcend all impulses to acquire or to destroy, put great value on detachment. "Let us move beyond all desire or any actions that might inflame desire." And they are reluctant to engage in the hurly-burly work of social change. Some of my fellow Buddhists seem to understand detachment as becoming free from the world and indifferent to its fate. They forget that what the Buddha taught was detachment from ego, not detachment from the world. In fact, the Buddha was suspicious of those who tried to detach themselves from the realm of matter. In referring to some yogis who mortified the flesh in order to free the spirit, the Buddha likened their efforts to those of a dog tied by a rope to a stake in the ground. He said that the harder they tried to free themselves from the body, the more they would circle round and get closer to the stake, eventually wrapping themselves around it.

Of course, even when you see the world as a trap and posit a fundamental separation between liberation of self and transformation of society, you can still feel a compassionate impulse to help its suffering beings. In that case you tend to view the personal and the political in a sequential fashion. "I'll get enlightened first, and then I'll engage in social action." Those who are not engaged in spiritual pursuits put it differently: "I'll get my head straight first, I'll get psychoanalyzed, I'll overcome my inhibitions or neuroses or my hang-ups (whatever description you give to *samsara*) and *then* I'll wade into the fray." Presupposing that world and self are essentially separate, they imagine they can heal one before healing the other. This stance conveys the impression that human consciousness inhabits some haven, or locker-room, independent of the collective situation—and then trots onto the playing field when it is geared up and ready.

It is my experience that the world itself has a role to play in our liberation. Its very pressures, pains, and risks can wake us up—release us from the bonds of ego and guide us home to our vast, true nature. For some of us, our love for the world is so passionate that we cannot ask it to wait until we are enlightened.

So let us now discuss the third view: *world as lover.* Instead of a stage set for our moral battles or a prison to escape, the world is beheld as a most intimate and gratifying partner. In Hinduism, we find some of the richest expressions of our erotic relationship to the world. In early Vedic hymns, the first stirrings of life are equated with that primal pulse of *ergs*. In the beginning there was the sacred, self-existent one, Prajapati. Lonely, it created the world by splitting into that with which it could copulate. Pregnant with its own inner amplitude and tension, it gave birth to all phenomena, out of desire. Desire plays a creative, world-manifesting role here, and its charge in Hinduism pulses onward into Krishna worship, where devotional songs, or *bhajans*, draw on the erotic yearnings of body and soul. Krishna evokes them to bring to his devotees the bliss of union with the divine. As you sing your yearning for the sparkle of his eyes, the touch of his lips, the blue shade of his skin—like the thunderclouds that bring the refreshment and fertility of the monsoon—the whole world takes on his beauty and the sweetness of his flesh. You feel yourself embraced in the primal erotic play of life.

That erotic affirmation of the phenomenal world is not limited to Hinduism. Ancient Goddess religions, now being explored (at last!) carry it too, as do strains of Sufism and the Kabbalah, and Christianity has its tradition of bridal mysticism. It also occurs outside of religious metaphor. A poet friend of mine went through a period of such personal loss that she was catapulted into extreme loneliness. Falling apart into a nervous breakdown, she went to New York City and lived alone. She walked the streets for months until she found her wholeness again. A phrase of hers echoes in my mind: "I learned to move in the world as if it were my lover."

Another Westerner who sees the world as lover is Italian storyteller Italo Calvino. In his little book, *Cosmicomics,* he describes the evolution of life from the perspective of an individual who experienced it from the beginning, even before the Big Bang. The chapter I want to recount begins with a sentence from science. "Through the calculations begun by Edwin P. Hubble on the galaxies' velocity of recession, we can establish the moment when all the universe's matter was concentrated in a single point, before it began to expand in space."

"We were all there, where else could we have been?" says Calvino's narrator, Qfwfq, as he describes his experience. "We were all in that one point—and, man, was it crowded! Contrary to what you might think, it wasn't the sort of situation that encourages sociability...." Given the conditions, irritations were almost inevitable. See, in addition to all those people, "you have to add all the stuff we had to keep piled up in there: all the material that was to serve afterwards to form the universe...from the nebula of Andromeda to the Vosges Mountains to beryllium isotopes. And on top of that we were always bumping against the Z'zu family's household goods: camp beds, mattresses, baskets...."

So there were, naturally enough, complaints and gossip, but none ever attached to Mrs. Pavacini. (Since most names in the story have no vowels, I have given her a name we can pronounce.) "Mrs. Pavacini, her bosom, her thighs, her orange dressing gown," the sheer memory of her fills our narrator with a blissful, generous emotion.... The fact that she went to bed with her friend Mr. DeXuaeauX, was well-known. But in a point, if there's a bed, it takes up the whole point, so it isn't a question of *going* to bed but of *being* there, because anybody in the point is also in the bed. So consequently it was inevitable that she was in bed with each of us. If she'd been another person, there's no telling all the things that might have been said about her...

This state of affairs could have gone on indefinitely, but something extraordinary happened. An idea occurred to Mrs. Pavacini: "Oh boys, if only I had some room, how I'd like to make some pasta for you!" Here I quote in part from my favorite longest sentence in literature, which closes this particular chapter in Calvino's collection:

> And in that moment we all thought of the space that her round arms would occupy moving backward and forward over the great mound of flour and eggs...while her arms kneaded and kneaded, white and shiny with oil up to the elbows, and we thought of the space the flour would occupy and the wheat for the flour and the fields to raise the wheat and the mountains from which the water would flow to irrigate the fields...of the space it would take for the Sun to arrive with its rays, to ripen the wheat; of the space for the Sun to condense from the clouds of stellar gases and burn; of the quantities of stars and galaxies and galactic masses in flight through space which would be needed to hold suspended every galaxy, every nebula, every sun, every planet, and at the same time we thought of it, this space was inevitably being formed, at the same time that Mrs. Pavacini was uttering those words: "...ah, what pasta, boys!" The point that contained her and all of us was expanding in a halo of distance in light years and light centuries and billions of light millennia and we were being hurled to the four corners of the universe...and she dissolved into I don't know what kind of energy-light-heat, she, Mrs. Pavacini, she who in the midst of our closed, petty world had been capable of a generous impulse, "Boys, the pasta I could make for you" a true outburst of general love, initiating at the same time the concept of space and, properly speaking, space itself, and time, and universal gravitation, and the gravitating universe, making possible billions and billions of suns, and planets, and fields of wheat, and Mrs. Pavacinis scattered through the continents of the planets, kneading with floury, oil-shiny, generous arms and she lost at that very moment, and we, mourning her loss.

But is she lost? Or is she equally present, in every moment, her act of love embodied in every unfolding of this amazing world? Whether we see it as Krishna or as Mrs. Pavacini, that teasing, loving presence is in the monsoon clouds and the peacock's cry that heralds monsoon, and in the plate of good pasta. For when you see the world as lover, every being, every phenomenon, can become—if you have a clever, appreciative eye—an expression of that ongoing, erotic impulse. It takes form right now in each one of us and in everyone and everything we encounter—the bus driver, the clerk at the checkout counter, the leaping squirrel. As we seek to discover the lover in each life form, you can find yourself in the dance of *rasa-lila*, sweet play, where each of the milkmaids who yearned for Krishna finds him magically at her side, her very own partner in the dance. The one beloved has become many, and the world itself her lover.

Since, as Calvino reminds us, we were "all in one point" to begin with, we could as easily see the *world as self*. Just as lovers seek for union, we are apt, when we fall in love with our world, to fall into oneness with it as well. Hunger for this union springs from a deep knowing, to which mystics of all traditions give voice. Breaking open a seed to reveal its life-giving kernel, the sage in the *Upanishads* tells his student: "*Tat tvam asi*—That art thou." The tree that will grow from the seed, that art thou; the running water, that art thou, and the sun in the sky, and all that is, that art thou.

"There is a Secret One inside us," says Kabir, "the planets in all the galaxies pass through his hands like beads." Mystics of the Western traditions have tended to speak of merging self with God rather than with the world, but the import is often the same. When Hildegard of Bingen experienced unity with the divine, she gave it these words: "I am the breeze that nurtures all things green...I am the rain coming from the dew that causes the grasses to laugh with the joy of life."

In times like our own recent centuries, when the manifest world is considered less real and alive than ideas inside our heads, the mystic impulse reaches beyond it and seeks union with a transcendent deity. But once the bonds of limited ego snap, that blazing unity knows no limits. It embraces the most ordinary and physical of phenomena. The individual heart becomes one with its world, and expresses it in imageries of circle and net. The fifteenth century cardinal, Nicholas of Cusa, defined God as an infinite circle whose periphery is nowhere and whose center is everywhere. That center, that one self, is in you and me and the tree outside the door. Similarly, the Jeweled Net of

Indra, the vision of reality that arose with *Hua Yen* Buddhism, revealed a world where each being, each gem at each node of the net, is illumined by all the others and reflected in them. As part of this world, you contain the whole of it.

Today this perception arises in realms of science as well. The founder of general systems theory, biologist Ludwig von Bertalanffy, shows how all self-organizing systems are created and sustained by the dynamics at play in the larger systems of our universe. The part contains the whole, he says, and acknowledges his debt to Nicholas of Cusa. Systems thinker Gregory Bateson describes cognitive open systems, our minds, in terms of a flow-through of information, where no separate self can be delimited. Mind itself is immanent in nature, he says, extending far beyond the tiny spans illumined by our conscious purposes.

The way we define and delimit the self is arbitrary. We can place it between our ears and have it looking out from our eyes, or we can widen it to include the air we breathe, or, at other moments, we can cast its boundaries farther to include the oxygen-giving trees and plankton, our external lungs, and beyond them the web of life in which they are sustained.

I used to think that I ended with my skin, that everything within the skin was me and everything outside the skin was not. But now you've read these words, and the concepts they represent are reaching your cortex, so "the process" that is me now extends as far as you. And where, for that matter, did this process begin? I certainly can trace it to my teachers, some of whom I never met, and to my husband and children, who give me courage and support to do the work I do, and to the plant and animal beings who sustain my body. What I am, as systems theorists have helped me see, is a "Flow-through." I am a flow-through of matter, energy, and information, which is transformed in turn by my own experiences and intentions. Systems theory seeks to define the principles by which this transformation occurs, but not the stuff itself that flows through, for that, in the last analysis, would be a metaphysical endeavor. Systems thinkers Kenneth and Elise Boulding suggest that we could simply call it *agape*— the Greek and early Christian word for "love."

Systems thinking is basic to the swiftly developing science of ecology, and its import for our relationship to the world is expressed most clearly in the movement of thought called "deep ecology." This term was coined in the mid-1970s by Norwegian philosopher and mountain-climber, Arne Naess, to contrast with the environmentalism that still sets the self apart from its world. Environmental efforts that focus on cleaning up the Hudson River or San Francisco Bay for the sake of our own species are inadequate. These tend to be short-term, technological fixes, band-aid approaches to ecological problems, because they do not address the sources of these problems, which is our stance in relation to our world. What is destroying our world is the persistent notion that we are independent of it, aloof from other species, and immune to what we do to them. Our survival, Naess says, requires shifting into more encompassing ideas of who we are.

To experience the world as an extended self and its story as our own extended story involves no surrender or eclipse of our individuality. The liver, leg, and lung that are "mine" are highly distinct from each other, thank goodness, and each has a distinctive role to play. The larger selfness we discover today is not an undifferentiated unity. Our recognition of this may be the third part of an unfolding of consciousness that began a long time ago, like the third movement of a symphony.

In the first movement, our infancy as a species, we felt no separation from the natural world around us. Trees, rocks, and plants surrounded us with a living presence as intimate and pulsing as our own bodies. In that primal intimacy, which anthropologists call "participation mystique," we were as one with our world as a child in the mother's womb.

Then self-consciousness arose and gave us distance on our world. We needed that distance in order to make decisions and strategies, in order to measure, judge and to monitor our judgments. With the emergence of free-will, the fall out of the Garden of Eden, the second movement began—the lonely and heroic journey of the ego. Nowadays, yearning to reclaim a sense of wholeness, some of us tend to disparage that movement of separation from nature, but it brought great gains for which we can be grateful. The distanced and observing eye brought us tools of science, and a priceless view of the vast, orderly intricacy of our world. The recognition of our individuality brought us trial by jury and the Bill of Rights.

Now, harvesting these gains, we are ready to return. The third movement begins. Having gained distance and sophistication of perception, we can turn and recognize who we have been all along. Now it can dawn on us: we are our world knowing itself. We can relinquish our separateness. We can come home again—and participate in our world in a richer, more responsible and poignantly beautiful way than before, in our infancy.

Because of the journey we undertook to distance ourselves from our world, it is no longer undifferentiated from us. It can appear to us now both as self and as lover. Relating to our world with the full measure of our being, we partake of the qualities of both. I think of a poem, "The Old Mendicant," by Thich Nhat Hanh. In it he evokes the long, wondrous evolutionary journey we all have made together, from which we are as inseparable as from our own selves. At the same time, it is a love song. Hear these lines, as if addressed to you.

Being rock, being gas, being mist, being Mind,
being the mesons traveling among galaxies
at the speed of light,
you have come here, my beloved....
You have manifested yourself
as trees, grass, butterflies, single-celled beings,
and as chrysanthemums.
But the eyes with which you looked at me this morning
tell me you have never died.

We have all gone that long journey, and now, richer for it, we come home to our mutual belonging. We return to experience, as we never could before, that we are both the self of our world and its cherished lover. We are not doomed to destroy it by the cravings of the separate ego and the technologies it fashioned. We can wake up to who we really are, and allow the waters of the Rhine to flow clean once more, and the trees to grow green along its banks.

The Sun My Heart

WHEN I FIRST left Vietnam, I had a dream in which I was a young boy, smiling and at ease, in my own land, surrounded by my own people, in a time of peace. There was a beautiful hillside, lush with trees and flowers, and on it was a little house. But each time I approached the hillside, obstacles prevented me from climbing it, and then I woke up.

The dream recurred many times. I continued to do my work and to practice mindfulness, trying to be in touch with the beautiful trees, people, flowers, and sunshine that surrounded me in Europe and North America. I looked deeply at these things, and I played under the trees with the children exactly as I had in Vietnam. After a year, the dream stopped. Seeds of acceptance and joy had been planted in me, and I began to look at Europe, America, and other countries in Asia as also my home. I realized that my home is the Earth. Whenever I felt homesick for Vietnam, I went outside into a backyard or a park, and found a place to practice breathing, walking, and smiling among the trees.

But some cities had very few trees, even then. I can imagine someday soon a city with no trees in it at all. Imagine a city that has only one tree left. People there are mentally disturbed, because they are so alienated from nature. Then one doctor in the city sees why people are getting sick, and he offers each person who comes to him this prescription: "You are sick because you are cut off from Mother Nature. Every morning, take a bus, go to the tree in the center of the city, and hug it for fifteen minutes. Look at the beautiful green tree and smell its fragrant bark."

After three months of practicing this, the patient will feel much better. But because many people suffer from the same malady and the doctor always gives the same prescription, after a short time, the line of people waiting their turn to embrace the tree gets to be very long, more than a mile, and people begin to get impatient. Fifteen minutes is now too long for each person to hug the tree, so the city council legislates a five-minute maximum. Then they have to shorten it to one minute, and then only a few seconds. Finally, there is no remedy at all for the sickness.

If we are not mindful, we might be in that situation soon. We have to remember that our body is not limited to what lies within the boundary of our skin. Our body is much more immense. We know that if our heart stops beating, the flow of our life will stop, but we do not take the time to notice the many things outside of our bodies that are equally essential for our survival. If the ozone layer around our Earth were to disappear for even an instant, we would die. If the sun were to stop shining, the flow of our life would stop. The sun is our second heart, our heart outside of our body. It gives all life on Earth the warmth necessary for existence. Plants live thanks to the sun. Their leaves absorb the sun's energy, along with carbon dioxide from the air, to produce food for the tree, the flower, the plankton. And thanks to plants, we and other animals can live. All of us—people, animals, plants, and minerals—"consume" the sun, directly and indirectly. We cannot begin to describe all the effects of the sun, that great heart outside of our body.

When we look at green vegetables, we should know that it is the sun that is green and not just the vegetables. The green color in the leaves of the vegetables is due to the presence of the sun. Without the sun, no living being could survive. Without sun, water, air, and soil, there would be no vegetables. The vegetables are the coming-together of many conditions near and far.

There is no phenomenon in the universe that does not intimately concern us, from a pebble resting at the bottom of the ocean, to the movement of a galaxy millions of light years away. Walt Whitman said, "I believe a blade of grass is no less than the journey-work of the stars...." These words are not philosophy. They come from the depths of his soul. He also said, "I am large, I contain multitudes."

This might be called a meditation on "interbeing endlessly inter-
woven." All phenomena are interdependent. When we think of a speck
of dust, a flower, or a human being, our thinking cannot break loose
from the idea of unity, of one, of calculation. We see a line drawn
between one and many, one and not one. But if we truly realize the
interdependent nature of the dust, the flower, and the human being,
we see that unity cannot exist without diversity. Unity and diversity
interpenetrate each other freely. Unity is diversity, and diversity is
unity. This is the principle of interbeing.

If you are a mountain climber or someone who enjoys the countryside or the forest, you know that forests are our lungs outside of
our bodies. Yet we have been acting in a way that has allowed millions of square miles of land to be deforested, and we have also destroyed the air, the rivers, and parts of the ozone layer. We are
imprisoned in our small selves, thinking only of some comfortable
conditions for this small self, while we destroy our large self. If we want
to change the situation, we must begin by being our true selves. To
be our true selves means we have to be the forest, the river, and the
ozone layer. If we visualize ourselves as the forest, we will experience
the hopes and fears of the trees. If we don't do this, the forests will
die, and we will lose our chance for peace. When we understand that
we inter-are with the trees, we will know that it is up to us to make
an effort to keep the trees alive. In the last twenty years, our automo-
biles and factories have created acid rain that has destroyed so many
trees. Because we inter-are with the trees, we know that if they do not
live, we too will disappear very soon.

We humans think we are smart, but an orchid, for example, knows
how to produce noble, symmetrical flowers, and a snail knows how
to make a beautiful, well-proportioned shell. Compared with their
knowledge, ours is not worth much at all. We should bow deeply
before the orchid and the snail and join our palms reverently before
the monarch butterfly and the magnolia tree. The feeling of respect
for all species will help us recognize the noblest nature in ourselves.

An oak tree is an oak tree. That is all an oak tree needs to do. If an
oak tree is less than an oak tree, we will all be in trouble. In our former
lives, we were rocks, clouds, and trees. We have also been an oak tree.
This is not just Buddhist; it is scientific. We humans are a young spe-

cies. We were plants, we were trees, and now we have become humans. We have to remember our past existences and be humble. We can learn a lot from an oak tree.

All life is impermanent. We are all children of the Earth, and, at some time, she will take us back to herself again. We are continually arising from Mother Earth, being nurtured by her, and then returning to her. Like us, plants are born, live for a period of time, and then return to the Earth. When they decompose, they fertilize our gardens. Living vegetables and decomposing vegetables are part of the same reality. Without one, the other cannot be. After six months, compost becomes fresh vegetables again. Plants and the Earth rely on each other. Whether the Earth is fresh, beautiful, and green, or arid and parched depends on the plants.

It also depends on us. Our way of walking on the Earth has a great influence on animals and plants. We have killed so many animals and plants and destroyed their environments. Many are now extinct. In turn, our environment is now harming us. We are like sleepwalkers, not knowing what we are doing or where we are heading. Whether we can wake up or not depends on whether we can walk mindfully on our Mother Earth. The future of all life, including our own, depends on our mindful steps.

Birds' songs express joy, beauty, and purity, and evoke in us vitality and love. So many beings in the universe love us unconditionally. The trees, the water, and the air don't ask anything of us; they just love us. Even though we need this kind of love, we continue to destroy them. By destroying the animals, the air, and the trees, we are destroying ourselves. We must learn to practice unconditional love for all beings so that the animals, the air, the trees, and the minerals can continue to be themselves.

Our ecology should be a deep ecology—not only deep, but universal. There is pollution in our consciousness. Television, films, and newspapers are forms of pollution for us and our children. They sow seeds of violence and anxiety in us and pollute our consciousness, just as we destroy our environment by farming with chemicals, clear-cutting the trees, and polluting the water. We need to protect the ecology of the Earth and the ecology of the mind, or this kind of violence and recklessness will spill over into even more areas of life.

Our Earth, our green beautiful Earth is in danger, and all of us know it. Yet we act as if our daily lives have nothing to do with the situation of the world. If the Earth were your body, you would be able to feel many areas where she is suffering. Many people are aware of the world's suffering, and their hearts are filled with compassion. They know what needs to be done, and they engage in political, social, and environmental work to try to change things. But after a period of intense involvement, they become discouraged, because they lack the strength needed to sustain a life of action. Real strength is not in power, money, or weapons, but in deep, inner peace. If we change our daily lives—the way we think, speak, and act—we change the world. The best way to take care of the environment is to take care of the environmentalist.

Many Buddhist teachings help us understand our interconnectedness with our Mother, the Earth. One of the deepest is *The Diamond Sutra,* which is written in the form of a dialogue between the Buddha and his senior disciple, Subhuti. It begins with this question by Subhuti: "If sons and daughters of good families want to give rise to the highest, most fulfilled, awakened mind, what should they rely on and what should they do to master their thinking?" This is the same as asking, "If I want to use my whole being to protect life, what methods and principles should I use?"

The Buddha answers, "We have to do our best to help every living being cross the ocean of suffering. But after all beings have arrived at the shore of liberation, no being at all has been carried to the other shore. If you are still caught up in the idea of a self, a person, a living being, or a life span, you are not an authentic bodhisattva." Self, person, living being, and life span are four notions that prevent us from seeing reality.

Life is one. We do not need to slice it into pieces and call this or that piece a "self." What we call a self is made only of non-self elements. When we look at a flower, for example, we may think that it is different from "non-flower" things. But when we look more deeply, we see that everything in the cosmos is in that flower. Without all of the non-flower elements—sunshine, clouds, earth, minerals, heat, rivers, and consciousness—a flower cannot be. That is why the Buddha teaches that the self does not exist. We have to discard all distinctions between self and non-self. How can anyone work to protect the environment without this insight?

The second notion that prevents us from seeing reality is the notion of a person, a human being. We usually discriminate between humans and non-humans, thinking that we are more important than other species. But since we humans are made of non-human elements, to protect ourselves we have to protect all of the non-human elements. There is no other way. If you think, "God created man in His own image and He created other things for man to use," you are already making the discrimination that man is more important than other things. When we see that humans have no self, we see that to take care of the environment (the non-human elements) is to take care of humanity. The best way to take good care of men and women so that they can be truly healthy and happy is to take care of the environment.

I know ecologists who are not happy in their families. They work hard to improve the environment, partly to escape family life. If someone is not happy within himself, how can he help the environment? That is why the Buddha teaches that to protect the non-human elements is to protect humans, and to protect humans is to protect non-human elements.

The third notion we have to break through is the notion of a living being. We think that we living beings are different from inanimate objects, but according to the principle of interbeing, living beings are comprised of non-living-being elements. When we look into ourselves, we see minerals and all other non-living-being elements. Why discriminate against what we call inanimate? To protect living beings, we must protect the stones, the soil, and the oceans. Before the atomic bomb was dropped on Hiroshima, there were many beautiful stone benches in the parks. As the Japanese were rebuilding their city, they discovered that these stones were dead, so they carried them away and buried them. Then they brought in live stones. Do not think these things are not alive. Atoms are always moving. Electrons move at nearly the speed of light. According to the teaching of Buddhism, these atoms and stones are consciousness itself. That is why discrimination by living beings against non-living beings should be discarded.

The last notion is that of a life span. We think that we have been alive since a certain point in time and that prior to that moment, our life did not exist. This distinction between life and non-life is not correct. Life is made of death, and death is made of life. We have to accept death; it makes life possible. The cells in our body are dying every day, but we never think to organize funerals for them. The death of one cell allows for the birth of another. Life and death are two aspects of the same reality. We must learn to die peacefully so that others may live. This deep meditation brings forth non-fear, non-anger, and non-despair, the strengths we need for our work. With non-fear, even when we see that a problem is huge, we will not burn out. We will know how to make small, steady steps. If those who work to protect the environment contemplate these four notions, they will know how to be and how to act.

In another Buddhist text, *The Avatamsaka (Adorning the Buddha with Flowers) Sutra,* the Buddha further elaborates his insights concerning our "interpenetration" with our environment. Please meditate with me on the "Ten Penetrations":

The first is, "All worlds penetrate a single pore. A single pore penetrates all worlds." Look deeply at a flower. It may be tiny, but the sun, the clouds, and everything else in the cosmos penetrates it. Nuclear physicists say very much the same thing: one electron is made by all electrons; one electron is in all electrons.

The second penetration is, "All living beings penetrate one body. One body penetrates all living beings." When you kill a living being, you kill yourself and everyone else as well.

The third is, "Infinite time penetrates one second. One second penetrates infinite time." A *ksana* is the shortest period of time, actually much shorter than a second.

The fourth penetration is, "All Buddhist teachings penetrate one teaching. One teaching penetrates all Buddhist teachings." As a young monk, I had the opportunity to learn that Buddhism is made of non-Buddhist elements. So, whenever I study Christianity or Judaism, I find the Buddhist elements in them, and vice versa. I always respect non-Buddhist teachings. All Buddhist teachings penetrate one teaching, and one teaching penetrates all Buddhist teachings. We are free.

The fifth penetration is, "Innumerable spheres enter one sphere. One sphere enters innumerable spheres." A sphere is a geographical space. Innumerable spheres penetrate into one particular area, and one particular area enters into innumerable spheres. It means that when you destroy one area, you destroy every area. When you save one area, you save all areas. A student asked me, "Thây, there are so many urgent problems, what should I do?" I said, "Take one thing and do it very deeply and carefully, and you will be doing everything at the same time."

The sixth penetration is, "All sense organs penetrate one organ. One organ penetrates all sense organs"—eye, ear, nose, tongue, body, and mind. To take care of one means to take care of many. To take care of your eyes means to take care of the eyes of innumerable living beings.

The seventh penetration is, "All sense organs penetrate non-sense organs. Non-sense organs penetrate all sense organs." Not only do non-sense organs penetrate sense organs, they also penetrate non-sense organs. There is no discrimination. Sense organs are made of non-sense-organ elements. That is why they penetrate non-sense organs. This helps us remember the teaching of *The Diamond Sutra.*

The eighth penetration is, "One perception penetrates all perceptions. All perceptions penetrate one perception." If your perception is not accurate, it will influence all other perceptions in yourself and others. Suppose a bus driver has an incorrect perception. We know what may happen. One perception penetrates all perceptions.

The ninth penetration is, "Every sound penetrates one sound. One sound penetrates every sound." This is a very deep teaching. If we understand one sound or one word, we can understand all.

The tenth penetration is, "All times penetrate one time. One time penetrates all times—past, present, and future. In one second, you can find the past, present, and future." In the past, you can see the present and the future. In the present, you can find the past and future. In the future, you can find the past and present. They "inter-contain" each other. Space contains time, time contains space. In the teaching of interpenetration, one determines the other, the other determines this one. When we realize our nature of interbeing, we will stop blaming and killing, because we know that we inter-are.

Interpenetration is an important teaching, but it still suggests that things outside of one another penetrate into each other. Interbeing is a step forward. We are already inside, so we don't have to enter. In contemporary nuclear physics, people talk about implicit order and explicit order. In the explicit order, things exist outside of each other—the table outside of the flower, the sunshine outside of the cypress tree. In the implicit order, we see that they are inside each other—the sunshine inside the cypress tree. Interbeing is the implicit order. To practice mindfulness and to look deeply into the nature of things is to discover the true nature of interbeing. There we find peace and develop the strength to be in touch with everything. With this understanding, we can easily sustain the work of loving and caring for the Earth and for each other for a long time.

JOANNA MACY

The Greening of the Self

SOMETHING IMPORTANT is happening in our world that you are not going to read about in the newspapers. I consider it the most fascinating and hopeful development of our time, and it is one of the reasons I am so glad to be alive today. It has to do with what is occurring to the notion of the *self.*

The self is the metaphoric construct of identity and agency, the hypothetical piece of turf on which we construct our strategies for survival, the notion around which we focus our instincts for self-preservation, our needs for self-approval, and the boundaries of our self-interest. Something is happening to the self!

The conventional notion of the self with which we have been raised and to which we have been conditioned by mainstream culture is being undermined. What Alan Watts called "the skin-encapsulated ego" and Gregory Bateson referred to as "the epistemological error of Occidental civilization" is being unhinged, peeled off. It is being replaced by wider constructs of identity and self-interest—by what you might call the ecological self or the eco-self, co-extensive with other beings and the life of our planet. It is what I will call "the greening of the self."

At a recent lecture on a college campus, I gave the students examples of activities which are currently being undertaken in defense of life on Earth—actions in which people risk their comfort and even their lives to protect other species. In the Chipko, or tree-hugging, movement in north India, for example, villagers fight the deforestation of their remaining woodlands. On the open seas, Greenpeace activists are intervening to protect marine mammals from slaughter.

After that talk, I received a letter from a student I'll call Michael. He wrote:

> I think of the tree-huggers hugging my trunk, blocking the chain-saws with their bodies. I feel their fingers digging into my bark to stop the steel and let me breathe. I hear the bodhisattvas in their rubber boats as they put themselves between the harpoons and me, so I can escape to the depths of the sea. I give thanks for your life and mine, and for life itself. I give thanks for realizing that I too have the powers of the tree-huggers and the bodhisattvas.

What is striking about Michael's words is the shift in identification. Michael is able to extend his sense of self to encompass the self of the tree and of the whale. Tree and whale are no longer removed, separate, disposable objects pertaining to a world "out there"; they are intrinsic to his own vitality. Through the power of his caring, his experience of self is expanded far beyond that skin-encapsulated ego. I quote Michael's words not because they are unusual, but to the contrary, because they express a desire and a capacity that is being released from the prison-cell of old constructs of self. This desire and capacity are arising in more and more people today as, out of deep concern for what is happening to our world, they begin to speak and act on its behalf.

Among those who are shedding these old constructs of self, like old skin or a confining shell, is John Seed, director of the Rainforest Information Center in Australia. One day we were walking through the rainforest in New South Wales, where he has his office, and I asked him, "You talk about the struggle against the lumbering interests and politicians to save the remaining rainforest in Australia. How do you deal with the despair?"

He replied, "I try to remember that it's not me, John Seed, trying to protect the rainforest. Rather I'm part of the rainforest protecting myself. I am that part of the rainforest recently emerged into human thinking." This is what I mean by the greening of the self. It involves a combining of the mystical with the practical and the pragmatic, transcending separateness, alienation, and fragmentation. It is a shift that Seed himself calls "a spiritual change," generating a sense of profound interconnectedness with all life.

This is hardly new to our species. In the past poets and mystics have been speaking and writing about these ideas, but not people on the barricades agitating for social change. Now the sense of an encompassing self, that deep identity with the wider reaches of life, is a motivation for action. It is a source of courage that helps us stand up to the powers that are still, through force of inertia, working for the destruction of our world. I am convinced that this expanded sense of self is the *only* basis for adequate and effective action.

When you look at what is happening to our world—and it is hard to look at what's happening to our water, our air, our trees, our fellow species—it becomes clear that unless you have some roots in a spiritual practice that holds life sacred and encourages joyful communion with all your fellow beings, facing the enormous challenges ahead becomes nearly impossible.

Robert Bellah's book *Habits of the Heart* is not a place where you are going to read about the greening of the self. But it is where you will read *why* there has to be a greening of the *self*, because it describes the cramp that our society has gotten itself into with its rampant, indeed pathological, individualism. Bellah points out that the individualism that sprang from the Romantic movement of the eighteenth and nineteenth centuries (the seeds of which were planted even earlier than that) is accelerating and causing great suffering, alienation and fragmentation in our century. Bellah calls for a moral ecology which he defines as a moral connectedness or interdependence. He says, "We have to treat others as part of who we are, rather than as a 'them' with whom we are in constant competition."

To Robert Bellah, I respond, "It is happening." It is happening in the arising of the ecological self. And it is happening because of three converging developments. First, the conventional small self, or ego-self is being impinged upon by the psychological and spiritual effects we are suffering from facing the dangers of mass annihilation. The second thing working to dismantle the ego-self is a way of seeing that has arisen out of science itself. It is called the systems view, cybernetics, or new paradigm science. From this perspective, life is seen as dynamically composed of self-organizing systems, patterns that are sustained in and by their relationships. The third force is the resurgence in our time of non-dualistic spiritualities. Here I am speaking from my experience with Buddhism, but it is also happening in other faith-systems and religions, such as "creation spirituality" in Christianity. These developments are impinging on the self in ways that are undermining it, or helping it to break out of its boundaries and old definitions. Instead of ego-self, we witness the emergence of an eco-self!

The move to a wider ecological sense of self is in large part a function of the dangers that are threatening to overwhelm us. Given nuclear proliferation and the progressive destruction of our biosphere, polls show that people today are aware that the world, as they know it, may come to an end. I am convinced that this loss of certainty that there will be a future is the pivotal psychological reality of our time. The fact that it is not talked about very much makes it all the more pivotal, because nothing is more preoccupying or energy-draining than that which we repress.

Why do I claim that this erodes the old sense of self? Because once we stop denying the crises of our time and let ourselves experience the depth of our own responses to the pain of our world—whether it is the burning of the Amazon rainforest, the famines of Africa, or the homeless in our own cities—the grief or anger or fear we experience cannot be reduced to concerns for our own individual skin. It can never be the same.

When we mourn over the destruction of our biosphere, it is categorically distinct from mourning over our own death. We suffer with our world—that is the literal meaning of compassion. It isn't some private craziness. Yet, when I was weeping over the napalming of villages in Vietnam twenty years ago, I was told that I was suffering from a hangover of Puritan guilt. When I expressed myself against President Reagan, they said I had unresolved problems regarding my own father. How often have you had your concerns for political and ecological realities subjected to reductionistic pop-therapy? How often have you heard, "What are you running away from in your life that you are letting yourself get so concerned about those homeless people? Perhaps you have some unresolved issues? Maybe you're sexually unfulfilled?" It can go on and on. But increasingly it is being recognized that a compassionate response is neither craziness nor a dodge. It is the opposite; it is a signal of our own evolution, a measure of our humanity. We are capable of suffering with our world, and that is the true meaning of compassion. It enables us to recognize our profound interconnectedness with all beings. Don't ever apologize for crying for the trees burning in the Amazon or over the waters polluted from mines in the Rockies. Don't apologize for the sorrow, grief, and rage you feel. It is a measure of your humanity and your maturity. It is a measure of your open heart, and as your heart breaks open there will be room for the world to heal. That is what is happening as we see people honestly confronting the sorrows of our time. And it is an adaptive response.

The crisis that threatens our planet, whether seen from its military, ecological, or social aspect, derives from a dysfunctional and pathological notion of the self. It derives from a mistake about our place in the order of things. It is a delusion that the self is so separate and fragile that we must delineate and defend its boundaries, that it is so small and so needy that we must endlessly acquire and endlessly consume, and that it is so aloof that as individuals, corporations, nation-states, or species, we can be immune to what we do to other beings.

This view of human nature is not new, of course. Many have felt the imperative to extend self-interest to embrace the whole. What is notable in our situation is that this extension of identity can come not through an effort to be noble or good or altruistic, but simply to be present and own our pain. And that is why this shift in the sense of self is credible to people. As the poet Theodore Roethke said, "I believe my pain."

This "despair and empowerment" work derives from two other forces I mentioned earlier: systems theory, or cybernetics, and nondualistic spirituality, particularly Buddhism. I will now turn to what we could call the cybernetics of the self.

The findings of twentieth-century science undermine the notion of a separate self distinct from the world it observes and acts upon. Einstein showed that the self's perceptions are shaped by its changing position in relation to other phenomena. And Heisenberg, in his uncertainty principle, demonstrated that the very act of observation changes what is observed.

Contemporary science, and systems science in particular, goes farther in challenging old assumptions about a distinct, separate, continuous self, by showing that there is no logical or scientific basis for construing one part of the experienced world as "me" and the rest as "other." That is so because as open, self-organizing systems, our very breathing, acting and thinking arise in interaction with our shared world through the currents of matter, energy, and information that move through us and sustain us. In the web of relationships that sustain these activities there is no clear line demarcating a separate, continuous self.

As postmodern systems theorists say, "There is no categorical 'I' set over against a categorical 'you' or 'it.'" One of the clearer expositions of this is found in the teachings and writings of Gregory Bateson, whom I earlier quoted as saying that the abstraction of a separate "I" is the epistemological fallacy of Western civilization. He says that the process that decides and acts cannot be neatly identified with the isolated subjectivity of the individual or located within the confines of the skin. He contends that "the total self-corrective unit that processes information is a system whose boundaries do not at all coincide with the boundaries either of the body or what is popularly called 'self' or 'consciousness.'" He goes on to say, "The self is ordinarily understood as only a small part of a much larger trial-and-error system which does the thinking, acting, and deciding." Bateson offers two helpful examples. One is the woodcutter, about to fell a tree. His hands grip the handle of the axe, there is the head of the axe, the trunk of the tree. Whump, he makes a cut, and then whump, another cut. What is the feedback circuit, where is the information that is guiding that cutting down of the tree? It is a whole circle; you can begin at any point. It moves from the eye of the woodcutter, to the hand, to the axe, and back to the cut in the tree. That is the self-correcting unit, that is what is doing the chopping down of the tree.

In another illustration, a blind person with a cane is walking along the sidewalk. Tap, tap, whoops, there's a fire hydrant, there's a curb. What is doing the walking? Where is the self then of the blind person? What is doing the perceiving and deciding? That self-corrective feedback circuit is the arm, the hand, the cane, the curb, the ear. At that moment that is the self that is walking. Bateson's point is that the self is a false reification of an improperly delimited part of a much larger field of interlocking processes. And he goes on to maintain that:

this false reification of the self is basic to the planetary ecological crisis in which we find ourselves. We have imagined that we are a unit of survival and we have to see to our own survival, and we imagine that the unit of survival is the separate individual or a separate species, whereas in reality through the history of evolution, it is the individual plus the environment, the species plus the environment, for they are essentially symbiotic.

The self is a metaphor. We can decide to limit it to our skin, our person, our family, our organization, or our species. We can select its boundaries in objective reality. As the systems theorists see it, our consciousness illuminates a small arc in the wider currents and loops of knowing that interconnect us. It is just as plausible to conceive of mind as coexistent with these larger circuits, the entire "pattern that connects," as Bateson said.

Do not think that to broaden the construct of self this way involves an eclipse of one's distinctiveness. Do not think that you will lose your identity like a drop in the ocean merging into the oneness of Brahman. From the systems perspective this interaction, creating larger wholes and patterns, allows for and even requires diversity. You become more yourself. Integration and differentiation go hand in hand.

The third factor that is aiding in the dismantling of the ego-self and the creation of the eco-self is the resurgence of non-dualistic spiritualities. Buddhism is distinctive in the clarity and sophistication with which it deals with the constructs and the dynamics of self. In much the same way as systems theory does, Buddhism undermines categorical distinctions between self and other and belies the concept of a continuous, self-existent entity. It then goes farther than systems theory in showing the pathogenic character of any reifications of the self. It goes farther still in offering methods for transcending these difficulties and healing this suffering. What the Buddha woke up to under the Bodhi tree was the *paticca samuppada*, the co-arising of phenomena, in which you cannot isolate a separate, continuous self.

We think, "What do we do with the self, this clamorous 'I,' always wanting attention, always wanting its goodies? Do we crucify it, sacrifice it, mortify it, punish it, or do we make it noble?" Upon awaking we realize, "Oh, it just isn't there." It's a convention, just a convenient convention. When you take it too seriously, when you suppose that it is something enduring which you have to defend and promote, it becomes the foundation of delusion, the motive behind our attachments and our aversions.

For a beautiful illustration of a deviation-amplifying feedback loop, consider *Yama* holding the wheel of life. There are the domains, the various realms of beings, and at the center of that wheel of suffering are three figures: the snake, the rooster and the pig—delusion, greed and aversion—and they just chase each other around and around. The linchpin is the notion of our self, the notion that we have to protect that self or punish it or do *something* with it.

Oh, the sweetness of being able to realize: I am my experience. I am this breathing. I am this moment, and it is changing, continually arising in the fountain of life. We do not need to be doomed to the perpetual rat-race. The vicious circle can be broken by the wisdom, *prajña*, that arises when we see that "self" is just an idea; by the practice of meditation, *dhyana*; and by the practice of morality, *shila*, where attention to our experience and to our actions reveals that they do not need to be in bondage to a separate self.

Far from the nihilism and escapism that is often imputed to the Buddhist path, this liberation, this awakening puts one *into* the world with a livelier, more caring sense of social engagement. The sense of interconnectedness that can then arise, is imaged—one of the most beautiful images coming out of the Mahayana—as the jeweled net of Indra. It is a vision of reality structured very much like the holographic view of the universe, so that each being is at each node of the net, each jewel reflects all the others, reflecting back and catching the reflection, just as systems theory sees that the part contains the whole.

The awakening to our true self is the awakening to that entirety, breaking out of the prison-self of separate ego. The one who perceives this is the bodhisattva—and we are all bodhisattvas because we are all capable of experiencing that—it is our true nature. We are profoundly interconnected and therefore we are all able to recognize and act upon our deep, intricate, and intimate inter-existence with each other and all beings. That true nature of ours is already present in our pain for the world.

When we turn our eyes away from that homeless figure, are we indifferent or is the pain of seeing him or her too great? Do not be easily duped about the apparent indifference of those around you.

What looks like apathy is really the fear of suffering. But the bodhisattva knows that to experience the pain of all beings is necessary to experience their joy. It says in *The Lotus Sutra* that the bodhisattva hears the music of the spheres, and understands the language of the birds, while hearing the cries in the deepest levels of hell.

One of the things I like best about the green self, the ecological self that is arising in our time, is that it is making moral exhortation irrelevant. Sermonizing is both boring and ineffective. This is pointed out by Arne Naess, the Norwegian philosopher who coined the phrase "deep ecology." This great systems view of the world helps us recognize our embeddedness in nature, overcomes our alienation from the rest of creation, and changes the way we can experience our self through an ever-widening process of identification.

Naess calls this self-realization, a progression "where the self to be realized extends further and further beyond the separate ego and includes more and more of the phenomenal world." And he says,

> In this process, notions such as altruism and moral duty are left behind. It is tacitly based on the Latin term "ego" which has as its opposite the "alter." Altruism implies that the ego sacrifices its interests in favor of the other, the alter. The motivation is primarily that of duty. It is said we *ought* to love others as strongly as we love our self. There are, however, very limited numbers among humanity capable of loving from mere duty or from moral exhortation.
>
> Unfortunately, the extensive moralizing within the ecological movement has given the public the false impression that they are being asked to make a sacrifice—to show more responsibility, more concern, and a nicer moral standard. But all of that would flow naturally and easily if the self were widened and deepened so that the protection of nature was felt and perceived as protection of our very selves.

Please note this important point: virtue is *not* required for the greening of the self or the emergence of the ecological self. The shift in identification at this point in our history is required precisely *be-*

cause moral exhortation doesn't work, and because sermons seldom hinder us from following our self-interest as we conceive it.

The obvious choice, then, is to extend our notions of self-interest. For example, it would not occur to me to plead with you, "Oh, don't saw off your leg. That would be an act of violence." It wouldn't occur to me because your leg is part of your body. Well, so are the trees in the Amazon rain basin. They are our external lungs. And we are beginning to realize that the world is our body.

This ecological self, like any notion of selfhood, is a metaphoric construct and a dynamic one. It involves choice; choices can be made to identify at different moments, with different dimensions or aspects of our systemically interrelated existence—be they hunted whales or homeless humans or the planet itself. In doing this the extended self brings into play wider resources—courage, endurance, ingenuity—like a nerve cell in a neural net opening to the charge of the other neurons.

There is the sense of being acted through and sustained by those very beings on whose behalf one acts. This is very close to the religious concept of grace. In systems language we can talk about it as a synergy. But with this extension, this greening of the self, we can find a sense of buoyancy and resilience that comes from letting flow through us strengths and resources that come to us with continuous surprise and sense of blessing.

We know that we are not limited by the accident of our birth or the timing of it, and we recognize the truth that we have always been around. We can reinhabit time and own our story as a species. We were present back there in the fireball and the rains that streamed down on this still molten planet, and in the primordial seas. We remember that in our mother's womb, where we wear vestigial gills and tail and fins for hands. We remember that. That information is in us and there is a deep, deep kinship in us, beneath the outer layers of our neocortex or what we learned in school. There is a deep wisdom, a bondedness with our creation, and an ingenuity far beyond what we think we have. And when we expand our notions of what we are to include in this story, we will have a wonderful time and we will survive.

Ecocentric Sangha

IN HIS BOOK, *A Sand County Almanac*, ecologist Aldo Leopold re-
counts expeditions he and his friends made into the wilderness of the
American Southwest in the early part of this century. He tells about
his relentless campaign to kill all the wolves. One day, spotting a wolf
down ridge from the hunting party, he shot first and then moved to
where the body of the wolf was lying.

> We reached the old wolf in time to watch a fierce green fire dying in
> her eyes. I realized then, and have known ever since, that there was
> something new to me in those eyes—something known only to her
> and to the mountain. I was young then, and full of trigger-itch; I
> thought that fewer wolves meant more deer, that no wolves would
> mean hunter's paradise. But after seeing the green fire die, I sensed
> that neither the wolf nor the mountain agreed with such a view.[1]

Leopold entitled this section of his book "Thinking Like a Mountain," a phrase that has become a slogan for the deep ecology movement.[2] Buddhists trained to cultivate mindfulness can appreciate the
possibilities for true understanding embodied in that slogan.

During the past few centuries almost every ecosystem and primal
culture on the Earth has been disrupted, and in many cases totally
despoiled, by aggressive human beings. This multitude of ruins is

---

[1] Aldo Leopold, *A Sand County Almanac* (New York: Oxford University Press, 1949), p.
130.

[2] John Seed, *Thinking Like a Mountain: Towards a Council of All Beings* (Philadelphia:
New Society Publishers, 1988).

embedded in our consciousness—the massive deforestation, the human caused increase in the rate of species extinction, and the replacement of complex and diverse plant and animal communities with monocultures of cereal grain or tree plantations.

Some beings must die in order that human beings may live. However, when whole forests of ancient growth are clear-cut, and when whales and other marine mammals are threatened with extinction to satisfy narrow human needs, it is clear that nature is being wantonly exploited.

Buddhist teachings emphasize the middle way. Right livelihood, self-realization, nonviolence, doing no harm...principles that are affirmed in our practice. Practice gives rise to mindfulness and true attention to the place wherein we dwell. Practicing within our bioregion, the interpenetration of all beings becomes more evident.

Dharma comes forth in Gaia, and the Earth manifests in the Buddha way. The power and beauty of nature turning through the seasons links each being inexorably into the song of interbeing. The richness and fullness of life is found here and now in the ways of Earth.

Earth is forthcoming, and we are forthcoming as part of the Earth. We are empowered in the present moment by touching the whole of our interbeing. Great compassion leads to great love. This love is powerful and helps human beings connect deeply with all other beings.

Some people say, "I love the Earth. I want to help all living beings." But such statements are abstractions. We can conceptualize the Earth as a system of interactions, as Gaia. But can we explore a true understanding of the whole Earth? Can we expand our self-identity sufficiently to feel true solidarity with the entire Earth?

Perhaps a few extraordinary people can develop such an identification, but I suspect most of us have much difficulty understanding the entire Earth. We can relate only with a few beings in our lifetime. We have long-term intimate relationships with a few people—our spouse, the other members of our family, our parents, perhaps a few close friends maintained over many years, and a house pet. We understand the universal through the specific.

Buddhism wears a unique face whenever and wherever it manifests. Frequently, Buddhism enters a culture and presents the image of that

culture most denied by its participants. Buddhism in Japan revolution-
ized the cultural meaning of death. In the West, Buddhism presents
a new face to the environmental crisis—which is, on a deeper level, a
crisis of character and cultural integrity.

I suggest that in North America, as well as in Europe and Australia, Buddhists will develop an ecocentric Sangha, an international
community that practices the Way together. An ecocentric Sangha is
not human-centered, but centered in the biosphere. Participants will
be dedicated to self-realization for all beings, not just human beings.
The Sangha is a witness for the bioregion, engendering new growth
and affirming the rights of other species.

In an ecocentric Sangha we are members, not stewards or master
elites, in the land community. Each bioregion is graced with sacred
places. Each bioregion exists beyond artificial boundaries of counties,
states, or nations. Mountains are mountains and rivers are rivers.
Mountains and rivers are becoming realized beings.

There is a Sangha in every bioregion, perhaps marked by a specific mountain, forest, section of coastline, or watershed. The
ecocentric Sangha encourages service to the place wherein all beings
dwell. Members serve in order to maintain a continuous harmony
within the place. Out of this wider responsibility comes great expan-
sion of self into the greater Self of the bioregion.

I dwell in a bioregion noted for its redwood trees. Redwood trees
are only one species among many in the forest, but they are very big
and sometimes very old. Many people, including some ecologists (who
should recognize that the trees are not the forest), call my homeland
the Redwood Forest. Instead of calling ourselves the Redwood Zendo
or even the Zendo in the Redwoods, it might be more appropriate to
call ourselves People of the Redwoods or better still, People in Service to the Redwood Forest. When our self is very broad, deep, and
tall, serving the forest is the same as serving ourselves.

Only a small area of this Earth can be our homeland during this
lifetime. Dwelling mindfully in a bioregion, caring for it, becoming
intimate with its seasons, its moods, and becoming friends with its co-
dwellers—the plants and animals—requires clear intent and regular
practice. In our ecocentric Sangha, we appreciate and hasten our self-

realization through the Self-realization of all beings. Practicing in our bioregion, our life affirms all other life.

"All beings are Buddha," said the Enlightened One. Though all animals are Buddhas too, I frequently notice people acting as if this applies only to their personal domesticated pets, particularly dogs and cats. We often project our own fear and ignorance of other species onto so-called wild animals who happen to come into our space.

In my bioregion, for example, some people express fear of black bears. Occasionally, during the early winter months, a few bears will come out of the forest and amble through yards, search through dumpsters for tasty morsels, and perhaps growl at the family cat. Some people shoot any bears found on or near their property. Others call the police, who will usually shoot the bear as well.

Yet in the eighteenth century, when Spanish adventurers first arrived in what is now called California, they discovered native Americans fishing almost side by side with bears. The bears respected the space of the humans, and the humans respected the space of the bears. All shared in the feast of fish returning from the sea to spawn in the freshwater rivers. Respect for the space essential to other life forms is a precept for our Sangha.

The bioregion of an ecocentric Sangha might include a vast wilderness area where humans beings come to visit, but only a few at a time, and more in the fashion of a pilgrimage than an intrusion. Sangha members practice allowing all other creatures, especially wild creatures, all the space they need to be fruitful and happy. Buddhism teaches us that there are no real enemies in the world, except our own delusion born of ignorance, fear, and greed.

Before the last wild condor was captured and relocated in protective custody to the San Diego zoo, a well-known environmental leader in California, David Brower, wrote the following words:

> A condor is 5 percent feathers, flesh, blood, and bone. All the rest is place. Condors are soaring manifestations of the place that built them and coded their genes. That place requires space to nest in, to teach fledglings, to roost in unmolested, to bathe and drink in, to find other condors in and not too many biologists, and to fly over wild and free. If it is to be worthy at all, our sense of ethics about other living things requires our being able to grant that their place transcends our urge

to satisfy our curiosity, to probe, to draw blood, to insult, to incarcerate. We can respect the dignity of a creature that has done our species no wrong—except, perhaps, to prefer us at a distance.[3]

People in an ecocentric Sangha work with the rich bounty given to them without striving for great wealth at the expense of the life forms of the bioregion. A truly rich and full life can be expected from serving "all our relatives," as Native Americans say. Great diversity characterizes the ecocentric Sanghas. Some serve the ancient forests and glaciers of southeastern Alaska, while others serve a desert.

Some will serve in nuclear waste repositories or toxic waste dumps. The level of discipline held by people in such a Sangha would make most monasteries look like models of anarchy. Their practice will be guided in part by scientific knowledge of these toxic wastes, the rates of decay, and the extent of harm that can come to beings when exposed to these toxic substances.

Knowledge of appropriate ways of handling and monitoring these toxic substances will be very highly valued. People of the Toxic Waste Dump will probably experience higher rates of cancer than most other people. Perhaps they will choose to not have children, and recruit other Sangha members to join them in nuclear practice.

The Dharma teaches us that all is impermanent. All is changing. Change, in the form of evolution, has no direction, no finality. However, evolutionary change tends to develop greater diversity. Protection of biodiversity is another precept of an ecocentric Sangha.

Buddhist wisdom, including the awareness that everything is related to everything else and that the mind is a vast ocean of ignorance, is echoed in the modern science of ecology. Barry Commoner, author of *The Closing Circle*, summarized one of the laws of ecology in this way: Nature is more complex than we know and possibly more complex than we *can* know.[4]

Another law of ecology can be stated as follows: Nature knows best. Massive human intervention in ecosystems tends to be detrimental to those systems. Humans frequently oversimplify the complex, diverse

---

[3] "The Condor and a Sense of Place," in *The Condor Question* (San Francisco: Friends of the Earth, 1981), p. 275.

[4] Barry Commoner, *The Closing Circle* (New York: Knopf, 1971).

systems of nature due to limitations in their understanding of self-realization and their commitment to commercially exploit all possible
by-products. The suicidal practice of clear-cutting in ancient-growth
forests is still subsidized in most timber-producing nations, in spite
of the fact that human beings cannot create a rainforest or put the
chain of life back together once the whole ecosystem has unraveled.

Dwelling in harmony means dwelling as if life in the broadest
sense, not just human life, really matters. It means liberating our minds
from the shallow and anthropocentric attitudes drilled into us by a
consumer culture that rewards the desire to manipulate others for
selfish purposes; violence as a way to solve problems; egocentric individualism; and an intense fear of nature.

Dwelling in place means cultivating mindfulness of the multitude
of blessings that flow freely to us each day. Freed from the desire for
greater worldly wealth or political power and liberated from the belief in unrestrained growth, we can settle effortlessly into the delightful
flow of energy we call nature. Joyful moments and rewarding experiences multiply when socially perpetuated illusions and false needs, so
artfully promoted in our culture, are allowed to drop away.

In a bioregion, Sangha members are not stewards of the land, nor
are they managers of a plantation. Indeed, the term *plantation* implies
a master-slave relationship. In the Klamath-Siskiyou bioregion, where
I dwell, the U.S. Forest Service practices clear-cutting. Loggers cut
every tree in a certain parcel of land, remove the commercially valuable trees, and burn the rest. New trees are planted in this clear-cut
area, and it is thereafter called a plantation. Plantations are not sustainable forests. Sustainable forests are expressions of the soil, air, and
water—rich, diverse communities coevolving. Sustainable forests are
necessary for sustainable human communities.[5]

Mindful practice in an ecocentric Sangha includes the recognition
that genetically engineered organisms have been introduced into the
free environment and some living beings may have been biologically
altered or genetically engineered by human beings. Should they be
killed to prevent them from reproducing or joining with another

5 Chris Maser, *The Redesigned Forest* (San Diego: R. and E. Miles, 1988).

organism? How will we treat genetically engineered beings if we follow the principle of harmlessness?

We can be compassionate with genetically altered organisms just as we are compassionate with exotic species introduced to our bioregion by European settlers. To demonstrate compassion, however, does not mean deliberately propagating exotic or genetically engineered organisms. Many people will oppose further experimentation by the genetic engineering industry, and while the pace of genetic engineering may be slowed, it is unlikely that Sanghas will be spared from dealing with this issue.

Buddhist teachings include numerous references to a deep sense of oneness with all beings. In addition to zazen and other meditative practices, an increasing number of individuals are exploring socially engaged Buddhism. An ecocentric Sangha is both socially engaged and practicing what Thich Nhat Hanh calls *interbeing*. One of the precepts of the Order of Interbeing states:

> Do not live with a vocation that is harmful to humans and nature. Do not invest in companies that deprive others of their chance to live. Select a vocation which helps realize your ideal of compassion.[6]

In an ecocentric Sangha there is compassionate discussion of dilemmas and paradoxes that members living in complicated societies must face, including issues around ethical investments, political activism, and social relationships.

Walking meditation is a way that the ecocentric Sangha practices directly with the bioregion. A Sangha in the foothills of the California Sierras holds a "mountains and rivers sesshin." Walking meditation in the mountains might include contemplation of Dogen's "Mountains and Rivers Sutra."

Some Sanghas may be located in large cities. Nonhuman life forms can also be included in the urban Sanghas. Discussion among the members of the Sangha will concern many questions: What is the essential nature of the place where this city has been built? Where are the rivers or streams? (Under the streets, turned into sewers?) What

---

[6] Thich Nhat Hanh, *Interbeing: Fourteen Guidelines for Engaged Buddhism* (Berkeley: Parallax Press, 1993), pp. 39–41.

native species are no longer found within this city? Have land owners introduced exotic plants in this city and, if so, what impact have they had on the habitat of native species? How can human beings and wildlife live harmoniously in the city? Where does the city obtain its water supply? Have dams been built that impede fish from returning to their spawning grounds? Does the city government encourage recycling?

The people of an urban ecocentric Sangha practice diligently, just as do members of an ecocentric Sangha in the countryside or in a wilderness. Cities, however, are home to many alienated intellectuals who live in delusion and serve the circles of power by manipulating language and images to enhance the appearance of human competence and success. Skillful practice in large cities and in regions where technology is idolized and runs rampant, such as major industrial centers, military bases, or factories where nuclear bombs or hazardous chemical compounds are created, may require a willingness to take on the suffering created by these human inventions.

The ideals of right practice and right livelihood take on new meaning in the context of ecocentric Sanghas. Perhaps the greatest challenge for members of an ecocentric Sangha is to let go of feeling that they are in control. Industrial civilization is out of control at the present time. Ways to help bring it under control include smashing the illusion that we can burn fossil fuels, or create new species of animals with biotechnology, or control the growth of trees on plantations through the use of chemical herbicides and fertilizers without threatening the very continuation of life on Earth.

The quality and richness of life manifests from a deep understanding of ourselves in relation to a place. In our technocratic culture there is widespread belief that we can satisfy any desire, anywhere. By participating in an ecocentric Sangha, we become more honest with ourselves and identify more profoundly with the other sentient beings in our midst. The journey home is joyful and simple. Settling down into our rightful place as human beings in harmony with our bioregions, we find rich companionship with life.

PART V

COMMUNITY

RICHARD BAKER

Building Sangha

THE BUDDHIST SANGHA is one of the oldest continuing institutions in the world. It represents the potential or capacity of a society to live together—if a few people can find a way to live together, then many people can find a way to live together. It is this effort and example, rather than the scale of its success, that offer a society a model and an opportunity to deepen its expression. A community can give us the space and support needed to express ourselves individually and with others in the simplest, most adequate way.

The physical care and expression of our situation and life are very important in Zen practice. The bonding aspect of a Buddhist community is that we meditate together and share a daily practice, which produces a common life. Meditation is both a mode for personal change and the provider of a deep sense of openness and space that reduce many of the problems that naturally occur in community.

The actual physical space is an important part of what makes people able to live together and develop the bonds of community. The bells, drums, and sounding boards of a Buddhist community articulate and relate space and events. The visual space should be varied, related, and if possible visually interlocking. The space of physical passage should be designed according to what will be done there—people walking slowly and quietly, for example. Stone walkways can bring you the long way around a building so that you change your pace and enter the building with familiarity. Passage within and between buildings can be designed according to how often people will meet each other and the significance of the activities and buildings joined by the passage.

Work is an essential part of the practice in a Zen community. It is the way we spend time together and take care of the needs of our environmental and social existence. The work we do together is too valuable to sacrifice to machines or the saving of time.

Our society, if it is to survive, needs every kind of community. In the West, the identity and good of the individual has been given such singular priority that every association is seen as serving the individual. Few people understand or act through the responsibility of association and mutuality. Community represents that compassionate good will and realistic regard for others and ourselves that establishes and maintains a humane social order. It is the natural expression and necessary basis of real freedom.

Community As a Resource

ONE TIME THE BUDDHA visited a small community of three monks in a bamboo forest near Kosambi. Anuruddha, Nandiya, and Kimbila were extremely happy to see the Buddha—Nandiya took the Buddha's bowl, Kimbila took his outer robe, and they cleared a place for him to sit next to a yellow bamboo thicket. With their palms joined, the three monks bowed to the Buddha, and the Buddha invited them to sit down. "How is your practice going?" he asked. "Are you content here? Do you encounter difficulties while begging for alms or sharing the teachings?"

Anuruddha answered, "Lord, we are most content here. It is calm and peaceful. We receive ample food offerings, we are able to share the Dharma, and we are making progress in our practice."

The Buddha then asked, "Do you live in harmony?"

Anuruddha replied, "Lord, we do live in harmony, like milk and honey. Living with Nandiya and Kimbila is a great blessing. I treasure their friendship. Before saying or doing anything, I always reflect on whether my words or actions will be helpful for my brothers. If I feel any doubt, I refrain from speaking or acting. Lord, we are three, but we are also one."

The Buddha nodded in assent and looked at the other two monks. Kimbila said, "Anuruddha speaks the truth. We live in harmony and care deeply for each other." Nandiya added, "We share all things—our food, our insight, and our experience."

The Buddha praised them, "Excellent! I am most pleased to hear how you live. A community is truly a community when there is harmony. You demonstrate real awakening."

The Buddha stayed with the monks for a month, and he observed the way they went begging each morning after meditation. Whoever returned first prepared a place for the other two, gathered water for washing, and set out an empty bowl, into which he would place some food in case one of his brothers did not receive enough offerings. After all three monks finished eating, they placed their leftover food on the ground or in the stream, careful not to harm any of the creatures who lived there. Then they washed their bowls together. When one of them noticed something that needed tending, he did it at once, and all of them worked together on tasks that required more than one person. And they sat together regularly to share their insights and experiences.

Before leaving the Bamboo Forest, the Buddha told the three monks, "The nature of a community is harmony, and harmony can be realized by following the Six Concords: sharing space, sharing the essentials of daily life, observing the same precepts, using only words that contribute to harmony, sharing insights and understanding, and respecting each other's viewpoints. A community that follows these principles will live happily and in peace. Monks, please continue to practice this way." The monks were overjoyed to spend a month with the Buddha and to receive such encouragement from him.

When we were in our mother's womb, we felt secure—protected from heat, cold, and hunger. But the moment we were born and came into contact with the world's suffering, we began to cry. Since then, we have yearned to return to the security of our mother's womb. We long for permanence, but everything is changing. We desire an absolute, but even what we call our "self" is impermanent. We seek a place where we can feel safe and secure, a place we can rely on for a long time.

When we touch the ground, we feel the stability of the earth and feel confident. When we observe the steadiness of the sunshine, the air, and the trees, we know that we can count on the sun to rise each day and the air and the trees to be there tomorrow. When we build a house, we build it on ground that is solid. Before putting our trust in others, we need to choose friends who are stable, on whom we can rely. "Taking refuge" is not based on blind faith or wishful thinking. It is gauged by our real experience.

We all need something good, beautiful, and true to take refuge in. To take refuge in mindfulness, our capacity of being aware of what is going on in the present moment, is safe and not at all abstract. When we drink a glass of water and know we are drinking a glass of water, that is mindfulness. When we sit, walk, stand, or breathe and know that we are sitting, walking, standing, or breathing, we touch the seed of mindfulness in us, and, after a few days, our mindfulness will grow stronger. Mindfulness is the light that shows us the way. It is the living Buddha inside of us. Mindfulness gives rise to insight, awakening, and love. We all have the seed of mindfulness within us and, through the practice of conscious breathing, we can learn to touch it.

Taking refuge in our capacity to wake up is a daily practice. If we wait for difficulties to arise before we begin to practice, it will be too late. When the bad news arrives, we will not know how to cope. If we cultivate our own strengths and abilities by taking refuge in our breathing and our mindfulness every day, several times a day, we will be solid and will know what to do and what not to do to help the situation.

When we cut our skin, our body has the capacity to heal itself. We only need to wash the wound, and our body will do the rest. The same is true of our consciousness. When we feel anger, distress, or despair, if we breathe consciously and recognize the feeling, our consciousness will know what to do to heal these wounds. To practice mindful living is to take refuge in our body, and also in our mind.

> I take refuge in the Buddha,
> the one who shows me the way in this life.
> I take refuge in the Dharma,
> the way of understanding and love.
> I take refuge in the Sangha,
> the community that lives in harmony and awareness.

Taking refuge in the Three Jewels is a very deep practice. It means, first of all, to take refuge in ourselves. Taking refuge in the Buddha in myself, I vow to realize the Great Way in order to give rise to the highest mind. Taking refuge in the Dharma in myself, I vow to attain understanding and wisdom as immense as the ocean. Taking refuge in the Sangha in myself, I vow to build a community without obstacles.

If, for example, you are a single parent and think that you need to be married in order to have stability, please reconsider. You may have more stability right now than with another person. Taking refuge in yourself protects the stability you already have. Taking refuge in what is solid helps you become more solid and develop yourself into a ground of refuge for your child and your friends. Please make yourself into someone we can rely on. We need you—the children need you, the trees and the birds also need you. Please practice going back to yourself, living each moment of your life fully, in mindfulness. Walking, breathing, sitting, eating, and drinking tea in mindfulness are all ways of taking refuge.

Taking refuge in a Sangha means putting your trust in a community of solid members who practice mindfulness together. It is difficult if not impossible to practice mindfulness without a Sangha. Teachers and teachings are important for the practice, but a community of friends is the most essential ingredient. We need a Sangha to support our practice.

When we practice breathing, smiling, and living mindfully with our family, our family becomes our Sangha. If there is a bell at home, the bell is also part of the Sangha, because the bell helps us to practice. Our meditation cushion is a part of our Sangha, too. Many elements help us practice.

We can begin our Sangha-building by inviting one friend to come over for tea meditation, sitting meditation, walking meditation, precept recitation, or Dharma discussion. These are all efforts to establish a Sangha at home. Later, when others wish to join, we can form a small group and meet weekly or monthly. Someday in the future we may even wish to set up a country retreat center. But the practice is not to seclude ourselves for many years in order to attain enlightenment. Real transformation, real enlightenment, is possible only when we stay in touch.

Every Sangha has its problems. It is natural. If you suffer because you do not have confidence in your Sangha and feel on the verge of leaving, I hope you will make the effort to continue. You do not need a perfect Sangha. An imperfect one is good enough. We do our best to transform the Sangha by transforming ourselves into a positive element of the Sangha, accepting the Sangha, and building on it. The principle is to organize the Sangha in a way that is enjoyable for everyone.

Siddhartha, the Buddha-to-be, invited the children of Uruvela village, the water of the Neranjara River, the Bodhi tree, the kusha grass, and many birds and flowers into his Sangha. We have more possibilities available in each moment than we may realize. I know of people in prisons and reeducation camps in Vietnam who practice walking meditation in their cells. We should not miss the opportunity to set up a Sangha. The Sangha is a jewel.

Ditthadhamma sukhavihari means "dwelling happily in the present moment." We don't rush to the future, because we know that everything is here in the present moment. We know that we have arrived. Walking meditation can help a lot. We walk and touch our deepest happiness. In Plum Village, we always walk mindfully, and we are a bell of mindfulness for others. I practice for you, and you practice for me. Other people are very important.

We do not have to practice intensively. If we allow ourselves to be in a good Sangha, transformation will come naturally. Just being in a Sangha where people are happy, living deeply the moments of their days, is enough. Transformation will happen without effort. The most important thing a Dharma teacher can offer his or her students is the art of Sangha-building. Knowing the sutras is not enough. The main concern is building a happy Sangha—taking care of each person, looking into his pain, her difficulties, his aspirations, her fear, his hopes in order to make everyone comfortable and happy. This takes time and energy.

When the Buddha was eighty years old, King Prasenajit, who was also eighty, told him, "My Lord, when I look at your Sangha, I feel confidence in the Lord." When the king observed the Buddha's community of monks and nuns and saw the peace and joy emanating from them, he felt great confidence in the Buddha. When we see a Sangha whose practice reveals peace, calm, and happiness, confidence is born in us right away. Through the Sangha, you see the teacher. A teacher without a Sangha is not effective enough. The value of a doctor, a psychotherapist, or a Dharma teacher can be seen in the Sangha around her. Looking at the Sangha, we can see her capacity for helping people.

It is a joy to be in the midst of a Sangha where people are practicing well together. Each person's way of walking, eating, and smiling can be a source of inspiration. If we just put someone who needs to be helped in the midst of such a Sangha, even if that person does not practice, he will be transformed. The only thing he has to do is allow himself to be there. As a teacher, I am always nourished by my Sangha. Any achievement in the Sangha supports me and gives me strength. It is so important to build a Sangha that is happy, where communication is open.

If you don't have a good Sangha yet, please spend your time and energy building one. If you are a psychotherapist, a doctor, a social worker, a peace worker, or an environmentalist, you need a Sangha. Without a Sangha, you will burn out very soon. A psychotherapist can choose among his clients who have overcome their difficulties, who recognize him as a friend or a brother in order to form a group. We need brothers and sisters in the practice in order to continue. In Vietnam we say, "When a tiger leaves his mountain and goes to the lowlands, he will be caught by humans and killed." When a practitioner leaves her Sangha, at some time she will abandon her practice. She will not be able to continue practicing very long without a Sangha. Sangha-building is a crucial element of the practice.

If there is no Sangha in your area, try to identify elements for a future Sangha—your children, your partner, a path in the woods, the blue sky, some beautiful trees—and use your creative talents to develop a Sangha for your own support and practice. We need you to water the seeds of peace, joy, and loving kindness in yourself and others so that all of us will blossom.

Every time I see someone without roots, I see him or her as a hungry ghost. In Buddhist mythology, a hungry ghost is a wandering soul whose throat is too narrow for food or drink to pass through. Hungry ghosts need love, but they do not have the capacity to receive it. They understand in principle that there is beauty in life, but they are not capable of touching it. Something is preventing them from touching the refreshing and healing elements of life. They want to forget life, and they turn to all kinds of intoxicants to help them forget. If we tell them not to, they will not listen. They have heard enough. What they need is something to take refuge in, something that proves to them that life is meaningful. To help a hungry ghost, first of all we have to listen deeply to him or her, to provide an atmosphere of family, and to help him or her experience something beautiful and true to believe in.

Our society produces millions of hungry ghosts, people of all ages. I have seen children just ten years old who have no roots at all, who have never experienced happiness at home and have nothing to believe in or belong to. This is the main sickness of our time. With nothing to believe in, how can a person survive? How can he find the energy to smile or touch the linden tree or the beautiful sky? He is lost, living with no sense of responsibility. Alcohol, drugs, and promiscuity are destroying his body and soul, but he has nowhere to turn. The availability of drugs is a secondary cause of the problem. The primary cause is the lack of meaning in people's lives. Those who abuse drugs or alcohol are unhappy; they do not accept themselves, their families, their society, or their traditions. They have renounced them all.

We cannot be by ourselves alone, we can only "inter-be" with everyone else, including our ancestors and future generations. Our "self" is made only of non-self elements. Our sorrow and suffering, our joy and peace have their roots in society, nature, and those with whom we live. When we practice mindful living and deep looking, we see the truth of interbeing.

I hope communities of practice will organize themselves in warm, friendly ways, as families. We need to create environments in which people can succeed easily in the practice. If each person is an island, not communicating with others, transformation and healing cannot be obtained. To practice meditation, we must be rooted. Buddhism helps us get rooted again in our society, culture, and family. The Buddha never suggested that we abandon our own roots in order to embrace something else.

Interpersonal relationships are the key to the practice. With the support of even one person, you develop stability, and later you can reach out to others. In Asian Buddhist communities, we address one another as Dharma brother, Dharma sister, Dharma uncle, or Dharma aunt, and we call our teacher Dharma father or Dharma mother. A practice center needs to possess that kind of familial brotherhood and sisterhood for us to be nourished. Aware that we are seeking love, Sangha members will treat us in a way that helps us get rooted. In a spiritual family, we have a second chance to get rooted.

In the past, we lived in extended families. Our houses were surrounded by trees and hammocks, and people had time to relax together. The nuclear family is a recent invention. Besides mother and father, there are just one or two children. When the parents have a problem, the atmosphere at home is heavy and there is nowhere to escape, not even enough air to breathe. Even if the child goes into the bathroom to hide, the heaviness pervades the bathroom. The children of today are growing up with many seeds of suffering. Unless we intervene, they will transmit those seeds to their children.

At Plum Village, children are at the center of attention. Each adult is responsible for helping the children feel happy and secure. We know that if the children are happy, the adults will be happy, too. I hope that communities of practice will take this kind of shape in the West, with the warmth and flavor of an extended family. I have seen some practice centers where children are regarded as obstacles to the practice. We have to form communities where children are viewed as the children of everyone. If a child is hitting another child, his parents are not the only ones responsible. Everyone in the community has to work together to find ways to help the children. One adult might try holding the child tightly, not as a policeman, but as an uncle or aunt. Of course, the parents should prevent their child from hitting others, but if they cannot discipline their child, they have to let an uncle or an aunt do it. In the practice center, there should be a garden where the children can play, and there should be people skillful in helping children. If we can do that, everyone—parents and non-parents—will enjoy the practice. If we form practice communities as extended families, the elderly will not have to live apart from the rest of society. Grandparents love to hold children in their arms and tell them fairy tales. If we can do that, everyone will be very happy.

Nowadays, when things become difficult, couples think of divorce. In traditional cultures, the whole community worked together to help the couple find ways to live in harmony and understanding together. Some people today divorce three, four, or five times. This is an issue that Buddhist practice has to address. How can we create a community that supports couples? How can we support single parents? How can we bring the practice community into the family and the family into the practice community?

If you are a single parent raising your child alone, you have to be both a mother and a father. You have to let go of the idea that you will not be complete unless that "someone" or "something" is with you. You yourself are enough. You can transform yourself into a cozy, stable hermitage, filled with light, air, and order, and you will begin to feel great peace and joy.

A father's love is somewhat different from a mother's. A father says, "If you act like this, you will receive my love. If you don't, you will not get my love." It's a kind of deal. A mother's love is unconditional. As the child of your mother, you are loved by her. There is no other reason. To a mother, her child is an extension of herself, and she uses her body and mind to protect that very soft, vulnerable part of herself. This is beautiful, but it can create problems in the future. Mother has to learn that her son or daughter is a separate person.

It is not easy for a single mother to also be a father, but with a good Sangha helping by being uncles and aunts, you can do your best to play both roles. One day the Abbot of Kim Son Monastery in California said to me, "Thây, you are our mother." Something in me has the manner of being a mother. When I am with children, I can play the role of a mother as well as a father.

Single parenting is widespread in the West. If you succeed in bringing your child up happily, then you can share the fruit of your practice with many people. Single parenting is a Dharma door. Parenting is a Dharma door. We need retreats and seminars to discuss the best ways to raise our children. We do not accept the ancient ways of parenting, but we have not fully developed modern ways of doing so. We need to draw on our practice and our experience to bring new dimensions to family life. Combining the nuclear family with the practice community may be a successful model. We bring our children to the practice center, and all of us benefit. When the children are happy, the adults will be happy also, and everyone will enjoy the practice.

Many people were abused or beaten by their parents, and many more were severely criticized or rejected by them. These people have so many seeds of unhappiness in their consciousness that they do not even want to hear their father's or mother's name. When I meet someone like this, I usually suggest that he or she practice the meditation on the five-year-old child. It is a kind of mindfulness massage.

"Breathing in, I see myself as a five-year-old child. Breathing out, I smile to the five-year-old child in me." During the meditation, you try to see yourself as a five-year-old child. If you look deeply at that child, you see that you are vulnerable and can be easily hurt. A stern look or a shout can cause internal formations in your store consciousness. When your parents fight, your five-year-old receives many seeds of suffering. I have heard young people say, "The most precious gift my parents can give is their own happiness." Because he himself was unhappy, your father made you suffer a lot. Now you visualize yourself as a five-year-old child. Smiling at that child in yourself, you experience real compassion. "I was so young and tender, and I received so much pain."

The next day, I would advise you to practice, "Breathing in, I see my father as a five-year-old child. Breathing out, I smile to that child with compassion." We are not accustomed to thinking of our father as a child. We picture him as having always been an adult—stern and with great authority. We do not take the time to see our father as a tender, young boy who was easily wounded by others. To help you visualize your father as a young boy, you can peruse the family album and study images of your father when he was young. When you are able to see him as fragile and vulnerable, you may realize that he must have been the victim of someone also, perhaps his father. If he received too many seeds of suffering from his father, it is natural that he will not know how to treat his own son properly. He made you suffer, and the circle of samsara continues. Unless you practice mindfulness, you will probably behave exactly the same way towards your children. But if you see your father as himself a victim, compassion will be born in your heart and you will smile. By bringing mindfulness and insight into your pain, your anger toward him will begin to dissolve, and one day, you will be able to say, "Dad, I understand you. You suffered very much during your childhood."

One fourteen-year-old boy who practices at Plum Village told me this story. He said that every time he fell down and hurt himself, his father would shout at him. The boy vowed that when he grew up, he would not act that way. But one time his little sister was playing with other children and she fell off a swing and scraped her knee, and the boy became very angry. His sister's knee was bleeding and he wanted to shout at her, "How can you be so stupid! Why did you do that?" But he caught himself. Because he had been practicing breathing and mindfulness, he was able to recognize his anger and not act on it.

While the adults were taking care of his sister, washing her wound and putting a bandage on it, he walked away slowly and meditated on his anger. Suddenly he saw that he was exactly the same as his father. He told me, "I realized that if I did not do something about the anger in me, I would transmit it to my children." He saw that the seeds of his father's anger must have been transmitted by his grandparents. This was a remarkable insight for a fourteen-year-old boy. Because he had been practicing, he could see clearly like that.

It is important that we realize that we are the continuation of our ancestors through our parents. By making peace with our parents *in us,* we have a chance to make real peace with our real parents.

For those who are alienated from their families, their culture, or their society, it is sometimes difficult to practice. Even if they meditate intensively for many years, it is hard for them to be transformed as long as they remain isolated. We have to establish links with others. Buddhist practice should help us return home and accept the best things in our culture. Reconnecting with our roots, we can learn deep looking and compassionate understanding. Practice is not an individual matter. We practice with our parents, our ancestors, our children, and their children.

There are gems in our own tradition that have come down to us, and we cannot ignore them. Even the food we eat has our ancestors in it. How can we believe that we can cut ourselves off from our culture? We must honor our tradition. It is in us. Meditation shows us the way to do so. Whether we are Christian, Jewish, Muslim, Buddhist, or something else, we have to study the ways of our ancestors and find the best elements of the tradition. We have to allow the ancestors in us to be liberated. The moment we can offer them joy, peace, and freedom, we offer joy, peace, and freedom to ourselves, our children, and their children at the same time. Doing so, we remove all limits and discrimination and create a world in which all traditions are honored.

Some of us do not like to talk or think about our roots, because we have suffered so much. We want something new, but our ancestors in us are urging us to come back and connect with them—their joy and their pain. The moment we accept this, transformation will take place right away, and our pain will begin to dissolve. We realize that we are a continuation of our ancestors and that we are the ancestors of all future generations. It is crucial for us to "return home" and make peace with ourselves and our society.

There is no need to be afraid of going home. It is at home that we touch the most beautiful things. Home is in the present moment, which is the only moment we can touch life. If we do not go back to the present moment, how can we touch the beautiful sunset or the eyes of our dear child? Without going home, how can we touch our heart, our lungs, our liver, or our eyes to give them a chance to be healthy? At home, we can touch the refreshing, beautiful, and healing elements of life.

When we touch the present moment deeply, we also touch the past, and all the damage that was done in the past can be repaired. The way to take care of the future is also to take good care of the present moment.

One Frenchwoman I know left home at the age of seventeen to live in England, because she was so angry at her mother. Thirty years later, after reading a book on Buddhism, she felt the desire to reconcile with her mother, and her mother felt the same. But every time the two of them met, there was a kind of explosion. Their seeds of suffering had been cultivated over many years, and there was a lot of habit energy. The willingness to make peace is not enough. We also need to practice.

I invited her to come to Plum Village to practice sitting, walking, breathing, eating, and drinking tea in mindfulness, and through that daily practice, she was able to touch the seeds of her anger. After practicing for several weeks, she wrote a letter of reconciliation to her mother. Without her mother present, it was easier to write such a letter. When her mother read it, she tasted the fruit of her daughter's flower watering, and peace was finally possible.

If you love someone, the greatest gift you can give is your presence. The most meaningful declaration we can offer is, "Darling, I am here for you." Without your attention, the person you love may die slowly. When she is suffering, you have to make yourself available right away: "Darling, I know that you are suffering. I am here for you." This is the practice of mindfulness. If you yourself suffer, you have to go to the person you love and tell him, "Darling, I am suffering. Please help." If you cannot say that, something is wrong in your relationship. Pride does not have a place in true love. Pride should not prevent you from going to him and saying that you suffer and need his help. We need each other.

One day in Plum Village, I saw a young woman walking who looked like a hungry ghost. The flowers were blooming everywhere, but she could not touch them. She seemed to be dying of loneliness. She had come to Plum Village to be with others, but when she was there, she was not able to be with anyone. I thought she must come from a broken family, from a society that does not appreciate her, and from a tradition not capable of nourishing her. I have met many people without roots. They want to leave their parents, their society, and their nation behind and find something that is good, beautiful, and true to believe in. People like that come to meditation centers, but without roots, they cannot absorb the teaching. They do not trust easily, so the first thing we have to do is earn their trust.

In Asian countries, we have an ancestors' altar in each home and offer flowers, fruits, and drink to them. We feel that our ancestors are with us. But, at the same time, we are aware that many hungry ghosts have nowhere to go. So once a year we set up a special table and offer them food and drink. Hungry ghosts are hungry for love, understanding, and something to believe in. They have not received love, and no one understands them. It is difficult for them to receive food, water, or love. Our society produces thousands of hungry ghosts every day. We have to look deeply to understand them.

We need two families—blood and spiritual—to be stable and happy. If our parents are happy together, they will transmit the love, trust, and the values of our ancestors to us. When we are on good terms with our parents, we are connected with our blood ancestors through them. But when we are not, we can become rootless, like a hungry ghost.

Transmission has three components—the one who transmits, the object transmitted, and the receiver. Our body and our consciousness have been transmitted to us by our parents, and we are the receiver. When we look deeply, we can see that the three components are one. In Buddhism, we call this the "emptiness of transmission." Our parents did not transmit anything less than themselves—their seeds of suffering, happiness, and talent, which they received, at least in part, from their ancestors. We are very much a continuation of our parents and our ancestors. To be angry at our parents is to be angry at ourselves. To reconcile with our parents is to make peace with ourselves.

An American young man who came to Plum Village told me that he was extremely angry at his father even after his father had passed away. So the young man put a photo of his father on his desk, and practiced looking into the eyes of his father. Doing this, he was able to see his father's suffering and he realized that his father had been incapable of transmitting seeds of love and trust, because he had not touched these seeds in himself. When the young man became aware of that, he was able to forgive his father. He also realized that if he did not practice mindfulness, the seeds of love and trust in him would remain buried. He made peace with his parents, and through this act, reconnected with all of his blood ancestors.

In our spiritual family, we have ancestors, too, those who represent the tradition. But if they were not happy, if they were not lucky enough to receive the jewels of the tradition, they will not be able to transmit them to us. If we do not respect our pastor, our rabbi, our priest, we may decide to leave the tradition. Disconnected from our spiritual ancestors, we suffer, and our children suffer, too. We have to look deeply to see what is wrong. When those who represent our tradition do not embody the best values of the tradition, there must be causes, and when we see the causes, insight and acceptance arise.

Then we are able to return home, reconnect with our spiritual mentors, and help them.

Through the practice of mindfulness, we can discover the jewels of our spiritual traditions. In Christianity, for example, Holy Communion is an act of mindfulness—eating our bread deeply in order to touch the entire cosmos. In Judaism, mindfulness is there when you set the table or light the Sabbath candles. Everything is done in the presence of God. The equivalents of the Three Jewels can be found in Christianity, Judaism, Islam, and other great traditions. After practicing mindfulness, you will be able to return to your spiritual home and discover the jewels of your own tradition. I hope you will do so, for your nourishment and the nourishment of your children. Without roots, we cannot be happy and our children cannot be happy. Returning home and touching the wondrous jewels of our blood and spiritual traditions, we become whole.

We need to establish retreat centers where we can go from time to time to renew ourselves. The features of the landscape, the buildings, even the sound of the bell can be designed to remind us to return to awareness. The residential community there does not need to be large. Ten or fifteen people who emanate freshness and peace, the fruits of living in awareness, are enough. When we are there, they care for us, console us, support us, and help us heal our wounds. Even when we cannot actually go there, just thinking of the center makes us smile and feel more at peace.

The residents can organize larger retreats occasionally to teach the art of enjoying life and taking care of each other. Mindful living is an art, and a retreat center can be a place where joy and happiness are authentic. The community can also offer Days of Mindfulness for people to come and live happily together for one day, and they can organize study courses on mindfulness, conscious breathing, Buddhist psychology, and transformation. We must work together with everyone in peace and harmony. Using each person's talents and ideas, we can organize retreats and Days of Mindfulness that children and adults love and want to practice more.

Most of the retreats can be for preventive practice, developing the habit of practicing mindfulness before things get too bad. But some retreats should be for those who are undergoing extreme suffering, although even then two-thirds of the retreatants should be healthy and stable for the practice to succeed. The depth and substance of the practice are the most important. The forms can be adapted.

At the retreat center, we can enjoy doing everything in mindfulness, and our friends will see the value of the practice through us—not through what we say, but through our being. We can also enjoy the practice at home, at work, or at school. For the practice to succeed, we have to find ways to incorporate it into our daily lives. Going to a retreat center from time to time can help a lot. Forming a Sangha at home is crucial.

Two thousand, five hundred years ago, the Buddha Shakyamuni predicted that the next Buddha will be named Maitreya, the "Buddha of Love." I think the Buddha of Love may be born as a community and not just as an individual. Communities of mindful living are crucial for our survival and the survival of our planet. A good Sangha can help us resist the speed, violence, and unwholesome ways of our time. Mindfulness protects us and keeps us going in the direction of harmony and awareness. We need the support of friends in the practice. You are my Sangha. Let us take good care of each other.

The Six Principles of Harmony

AFTER SEEING HOW Anuruddha, Kimbila, and Nandiya lived in harmony together, the Buddha arrived at the Six Concords, principles for being happy together.

The first is "the body as a principle of harmony." In a community, we try to learn how to be both individuals and community members at the same time. In the West we stress individualism. At Plum Village we are trying to learn ways to diminish our individualism while, at the same time, learning how to practice in a way that is creative and full of our own initiative.

We share common space in a community, but we have to take into account that we are many different bodies. Everyone is a member of the family, but each person is responsible for looking after his own health. We don't want to become a burden on the community, so we try our best to stay healthy. If someone is a little sick, everyone feels a little sick at the same time. When someone catches a cold, the whole community worries and gives advice.

We also learn to breathe together. Everyone's breath is a little different. If we are sensitive to another person, we can breathe with him or her. Sometimes, rather than talking with someone, we just breathe together. Those who work with the dying know how to harmonize their breath with the person who is dying. This can be a wonderful practice.

The Buddha's second principle, "the sharing principle," is about sharing material things with the community. The Buddha observed that when the monks returned from their almsrounds, they would always set aside some food for the monk who was last to return.

In the larger community of the Buddha, there was a monk who shared everything he had, even a glass of water. The other monks were impressed by this and told the Buddha, who replied, "He was not always this way. In a past life, he was a king who never shared anything. One day, he desired some special porridge with rice, curds, honey, and sesame seeds, and he thought, If I make this porridge in my castle, others will want some, so I'd better take the ingredients to the forest and cook the porridge there.

"Some gods saw what he was doing and disguised themselves as beggars in order to ask him for some of his porridge. At that time, people ate off of leaves, so the gods went to a special tree with huge leaves, and picked one large leaf each. Along the road, the gods smelled the porridge and went to the king. 'We were just walking by,' they began, but the king interrupted: 'Why are you walking past here?'

"They replied, 'We are going to Vaishali,' and the king interrupted again: 'This is the wrong way to Vaishali. Go back in the other direction immediately!'

"Then one of the beggars said, 'We're extremely hungry. We haven't eaten for a long time. Can you give us a serving of your porridge?'

"The king said, 'Okay, but you cannot use those big leaves. Go and pick some smaller leaves first.'

"When they returned with smaller leaves, the king gave them each a tiny portion of porridge, and then he served himself the rest. Immediately one of the gods turned himself into a dog and urinated right in the king's porridge. The gods ate their small portions happily and told the king, 'If you don't share, things are not worth having.' From that time on," the Buddha said, "the king learned to share. In fact, he became the most generous person in the kingdom."

The third principle of harmony is practicing the same precepts. At Plum Village, we ask that everyone who joins the community keep the Five Precepts.

When we work in the plum orchard or the garden, for example, we are very aware of the First Precept—not to kill. We try not to use products that will result in killing or come from killing. To do this, we need to take more time. But if we know how to live simply, we will have the time. The slugs are really a problem, so every day we pick them up and transport them in a tin can to someplace where they won't eat the vegetables. The Five Wonderful Precepts are necessary for the wholesomeness of the community.

The fourth principle of harmony has speech as its basis. Much of our speech is habitual—it comes from things we have said before or have heard others say. When we were children, our parents repeated certain things over and over, and their habits have become a part of our own way of speaking. We need to develop new harmonious patterns of speech. Anuruddha and the other two monks told the Buddha that before they said anything they would ask themselves, "If I say this, will it make my two brothers happy?" That has to do with breaking our negative patterns of speech. If we stop and follow our breathing, there is a kind of renewal, and a new kind of speaking comes out. Before speaking, we ask ourselves, "Will it make the other person happy? Will it help the other members of the community?"

The fifth principle, harmony of views, may be the most important. We have to learn to tone down our individualism. We have strong views and deep feelings. When we hear someone speak, we usually react, "That is what I think, so it must be right," or "That is not what I think, so it must be wrong." In a community, when someone offers an idea, we need to listen deeply and take what has been said seriously. If someone else disagrees, we try to find ways that take both points of view into account.

Sharing views includes sharing our experience in the practice. It is important not just to share positive things that are happening to us, but our mistakes as well, asking others for help when needed. If we have a good experience, we shouldn't think, I'm more advanced than the others. Maybe they're not quite up to hearing this yet. We share it with them in the best way we can.

Even though it is true that the essence of what is happening to us can never be described in words, words are our vehicle. When the Buddha sat under the Bodhi tree and reached enlightenment, for seven weeks he did not know what to say. He felt he had nothing to communicate. It was only when he came into contact with the five ascetics and felt their suffering deeply that the words came to him to describe what he had experienced, and he was able to formulate the Four Noble Truths, the Twelve Links of Interdependent Origination, and the Middle Way. The Middle Way was an obvious teaching to present to those practicing extreme asceticism. It did not arise from the Buddha having a certain view. It came from seeing how the wrong view of the ascetics was leading them to suffer. In a Dharma discussion, when we present our ideas on the practice, it is partly to learn ways to talk about our experience that are helpful to ourselves and others.

The sixth principle of harmony has the mind as its basis. We use our mind, our thinking, to help others in the community. It is as if we keep a file on everyone else. We see what brings them joy and what causes them to suffer. If someone has some physical suffering, we keep that in our minds. If they tell us a story about their past, that becomes part of our file. Gradually we learn more and more about each person, and we are able to see how we can practice meditation to love them more. That is how we keep the harmony by means of the mind. Just as Ananda always kept the welfare of the Buddha in his mind, we always keep in mind the welfare of all the other members of our community.

Precious Jewel

EVERY NEW YEAR'S DAY in some countries in Asia, monks and nuns write their last wills and testament. They light incense, sit quietly, following their breathing and looking deeply at birth and death, and think, soon it will be the New Year. What kind of will should I write?

What can we inherit? What can we pass on? What kind of treasure are we? Over time we receive many things, enjoy them, share them with others, and pass them on. We especially want to pass on what is most precious, so we look after those things most carefully. Whatever we receive, whatever we are—our robes, bowl, lamps, body, mind, feelings, emotions, understanding, love, and support—are all part and parcel of the precious jewel we want to pass on.

We want this heritage to go to its rightful heirs. Normally our family members are considered to be the rightful heirs, but what is it that makes an heir rightful? To me, one who is lacking in whatever is to be given is what makes him or her a rightful heir. There is a famous story about a shepherd in France who planted trees. He had lost his wife and son, and so he spent his time gathering the healthiest acorns in the forest and planting them in barren, deserted areas where nothing would grow and no one lived. Carrying a stick with a metal point, he made little holes in the ground and planted an acorn in each one. As years passed, trees sprang up and soon the barren land was transformed into a green, fertile oasis that became a national park.

For the universe to be whole, no one should lack what is essential. If food is lacking, we give food. If shelter is lacking, we give shelter. If love is lacking, we give love.

It is easy to love someone lovable. He is lovable because he already has love. He is love. But those who do not have love are the ones who need it. They ought to be the rightful heirs of our love. Someone who has love and is happy is like a beautiful landscape that we enjoy entering. Someone who has no love, who is sad or angry, is like a barren landscape where nothing will grow and no one wants to enter. However, that barren land is like that because we are like this, because we turn away from it. Let us not turn away from it, but approach it, and plant acorns there so that it will transform itself into a fresh and fragrant oasis that offers peace and joy to all.

A tiny little acorn has the totality of the tree in it. The same is true of us. We inherited from our parents their whole being—including their parents, teachers, friends, and environment, everyone and everything that made them, as well as everyone and everything that made our parents' teachers, friends, and parents, and their parents, teachers, friends, and so on—and that jewel is in us in its totality. We are the receiver of the heritage of the whole universe, and we are also the one who passes it on, day and night, without stopping. When we transform something negative in us into something more wholesome, we do it for everyone, and we make everyone else's transformation easier.

Once we know who our heirs are, we naturally become mindful and take good care of our heritage, our universal jewel. Our parents, grandparents, ancestors, teachers, friends, and everything that was, is, and will be are in their totality in us, and we are in our totality in everything that ever was, is, and will be. Seeing this, we understand what can be inherited and what we are passing on. Happy continuation.

Acceptance

I WAS BORN with a congenital heart disease that has limited my physical activity and more than once has brought me to the brink of death. Mental aspects of this handicap have, on the whole, been hardest to handle. The gap between my wish to be active and the limits set by my heart condition has been difficult at times, but the feeling that my disability made me worthless has been the real problem. I don't know how early in life this feeling started to grow, or why, but I think it has been with me for a long time. It probably was nourished by other people's fear and denial about disease and handicaps, and their aversion to suffering. In my teens, this feeling grew into a wish to hide my heart completely and to restrain my breath carefully, never to sound out-of-breath. I fought hard to pretend that all was well. Carrying my "dark secret," it has taken me many years of meditation to open up.

I believe this is a universal experience. The pressures from society's expectations and hopes—other people's as well as our own—shape us into patterns that do not fit. Our healthy emotional tissue gets scarred by all the cosmetic surgery that is performed on our mind.

After meeting Thây, it became clear to me that practicing acceptance is essential for healing. Acceptance is not fatalistic passivity where we believe that we just have to endure. Acceptance is to acknowledge a situation for what it is and to calm down inside of it. If we then find we can bring about change, very good! If not, then we must acknowledge and accept that. In both cases, a clear, open heart and mind are useful.

Recently I woke up with my heart beating extremely fast and out of rhythm. Though unpleasant physically, I noticed that I didn't feel the strong sense of failure that this illness has triggered in me in the past. I was able to stay calm and reasonably happy, dwelling in the present moment. This felt very satisfying and has given me further trust in mindfulness practice. It also showed that acceptance is very close to patience. Physical or mental pain often brings a burning sense of restlessness. When we can stay aware and not be carried away by it, we can be present and not make things worse by futile attempts to escape that only bring tension and conflict.

Even more useful than accepting difficult situations is accepting our own reactions to them. When our feelings and thoughts are not calm and patient, but rather angry, jealous, or petty, they are often difficult to accept. Our self-image is threatened. It is helpful to remember that thoughts and feelings arise naturally. The question is how we react to them.

The Buddha mentions three ways of reacting that create difficulties. One is escaping from an unpleasant situation into sensual pleasures or fantasy through entertainment, food, sex, or shopping. We lose important opportunities to learn how to cope with difficulties and easily become victims of the many toxins in modern culture. The second way is to cling to experiences. As everything changes, this attitude also removes us from the way things are. The third is to try to block off large parts of ourselves. With concentration, we can become aware of these habits, and they will no longer dominate us. Practicing acceptance, we can allow more of our imperfections to be visible. We can learn more about ourselves and walk more lightly through life. This also makes us more tolerant of others. We won't need to project our dark sides onto others, and we become more open-minded.

Accepting and seeing ever more subtle feelings, thoughts, and impulses can be quite a challenge. I sense how I'd like to be perfect and tend not to allow myself much leeway. I can see that both the thirst for situations to go away and the wish to be someone special bring strain and unpleasantness. Slowly, as I accept myself, I let go more and more. We can remember that our internal knots—desire, aversion, ignorance, pride, indecision—are universal. There is no need to blame ourselves for them.

If our intentions are good and honest and we are willing to use difficulties as a way to learn, *The Sutra of Assembled Treasures* has this encouraging comment: "Just as the excrement and garbage disposed by the people living in big cities will yield benefit when placed in vineyards and sugarcane fields, so the residual afflictions of a bodhisattva will yield benefits because they are conducive to all-knowing understanding." Another exercise is to celebrate imperfection instead of seeing it as something undesirable. We acknowledge that life will never be perfect and we can actually enjoy this fact!

On their first visit to Plum Village, many people have difficulties with the simple living conditions, constantly changing schedule, and lack of orderly silence. Both this situation and our reactions to it can be very valuable, as they challenge our habits and expectations. I have a hunch that this is one of the reasons why Plum Village allows people to get in touch with deep aspects of themselves so remarkably quickly. (Of course, love, beauty, and a happy atmosphere help.)

The practice of acceptance helps us attain the stillness described in *The Miracle of Mindfulness:* "Once your feelings and thoughts no longer disturb you, at that time mind begins to dwell in mind. Your mind will take hold of mind in a direct and wondrous way, which no longer differentiates between subject and object." We can be alive and cheerful, moving from one moment to the next, shedding our sorrows as we go.

Smiling

IN PLUM VILLAGE, our mindfulness practice is the practice of joy and happiness. Everything we do here is to cultivate joy and happiness, and the foundation of our joy and happiness is the capacity of smiling. We practice smiling in every look, in every step, and in every breath. Practicing mindfulness without a smile makes us feel heavy, tired and bored, and very soon we abandon our practice. Sometimes people feel overwhelmed because of their unjoyful practice. It is not always easy to smile. But if we continuously practice smiling, it becomes a habit. The more we smile, the happier we are. Every morning when I wake up, I go back to my breathing and recite this gatha:

Waking up this morning, I smile.
Twenty-four brand new hours are before me.
I vow to live fully in each moment
and to look at all beings with eyes of compassion.

Just reciting this gatha while breathing consciously, a smile comes easily to my lips. Sometimes I forget to smile but when I open the window, the birds singing remind me.

During sitting meditation, I establish myself firmly in my conscious breathing and I smile. Joy and happiness are always there but we have to recognize them, and a smile makes it easy. Living as a young monk with a beautiful Sangha and feeling calm in the practice of sitting is very pleasant. Joy and happiness spring up naturally through my smiling. My smile brings joy and happiness into the atmosphere of my Sangha and I can feel it.

In the morning, we greet each other with an early smile, and we also welcome our guests with a big smile. Before leaving us, an American friend said, "Thank you for your support in the practice, especially your smile. It has made a great change in me."

We usually eat our meals in silence. From time to time we look up at our Sangha and smile. I usually smile in the formal meal because my younger sister Chân Tuê Nghiêm sits right in front of me. I like to eat in silence because I can touch the food deeply. Just eating rice, feelings of joy and happiness arise in me. I see my brothers and sisters in Vietnam through the rice. Feeling like this makes the food more precious and tasty.

In guided meditation, we practice smiling to our bodies, our feelings, our pain, and our anger because a smile has the power to heal and to calm our feelings, our pain, and our anger, and to nourish our joy and happiness. A smile is a flower and it can blossom on the lips of everyone.

PART VI

FOR A FUTURE TO BE POSSIBLE

THICH NHAT HANH

Diet for a Mindful Society

TO REALIZE PEACE in our daily lives, we need some guidelines. Two thousand five hundred years ago, the Buddha offered five wonderful precepts to Anathapindika and his friends as a practice to help them live a peaceful and wholesome life. Since that time in many Asian countries, these guidelines have served as the ethical basis of a happy life. I would like to present them to you in a way that makes their applicability clear for our situation today. Violence, racial injustice, alcoholism, sexual abuse, environmental exploitation, and so many other problems compel us to find ways to stop the suffering that is rampant in ourselves and in society. I hope you will reflect on these five precepts and try to practice them, either in this form or in the way they are presented in your own tradition.

The First Precept
Aware of the suffering caused by the destruction of life, I vow to cultivate compassion and learn ways to protect the lives of people, animals, plants, and minerals. I am determined not to kill, not to let others kill, and not to condone any act of killing in the world, in my thinking and in my way of life.

The foundation of all precepts is mindfulness. With mindfulness, we see that lives everywhere are being destroyed, and we vow to cultivate compassion as a source of energy for the protection of people, animals, plants, and our entire planet. Just feeling compassion is not enough. We also have to develop understanding so we know what kind of action to take. We must make the effort to stop all wars.

The mind is the basis of our actions. To kill with the mind is more dangerous than to kill with the body. When you believe that you have the only way and that everyone who does not follow your way is your enemy, millions may be killed. So it is not just by killing with our hands that we break the first precept. If, in our thinking and our way of life, we allow killing to go on, this is also an offense. We must look deeply. When we buy something or consume something, we may be participating in an act of killing. This precept reflects our determination not to kill, either directly or indirectly, and also to prevent others from killing. Vowing to practice this precept, we commit ourselves to protecting our planet and becoming bodhisattvas energized to practice love and compassion.

The Second Precept
Aware of the suffering caused by exploitation, social injustice, stealing, and oppression, I vow to cultivate loving kindness and learn the ways of working for the well-being of people, animals, plants, and minerals. I vow to practice generosity by sharing my time, energy, and material resources with those who are in real need. I am determined not to steal and not to possess anything that should belong to others. I will respect the property of others, but I will prevent others from profiting from human suffering or the suffering of other species on Earth.

Stealing comes in many forms. Oppression is one form of stealing, and it causes much suffering both here and in the Third World. Countries are torn by poverty and oppression. We want to help hungry children help themselves, for example, but we are caught in a way of life that keeps us so busy that we do not have time. We do not need a lot of money to help them. Sometimes they only need one pill or one bowl of food, but because we cannot free ourselves from our own small problems and our lifestyles, we don't do anything.

This precept is also about awareness of suffering and cultivating loving kindness. We may have the capacity of being generous, but we must also develop specific ways to express our generosity. Time is more than money. Time is for bringing joy and happiness to other people and thus to ourselves. There are three kinds of gifts—the gift of material resources, the gift of helping people rely on themselves, and the gift of non-fear. Helping people not be destroyed by fear is the greatest gift of all. This precept teaches us the very deep practice of sharing time, energy, and material resources with those who are in real need and truly reflects the bodhisattva ideal of compassion.

The Third Precept

Aware of the suffering caused by sexual misconduct, I vow to culti-vate responsibility and learn ways to protect the safety and integrity of individuals, couples, families, and society. I am determined not to engage in sexual relations without love and a long-term commitment. To preserve the happiness of myself and others, I am determined to respect my commitments and the commitments of others. I will do everything in my power to protect children from sexual abuse and to prevent couples and families from being broken by sexual misconduct.

We practice this precept to help ourselves and others avoid being wounded, and to restore peace and stability in ourselves, our families, and society. A sexual relationship is an act of communion that should be performed in mindfulness, with love, care, and respect. "Love" is a beautiful word, and we have to restore its meaning. When we say, "I love hamburgers," we spoil the word. We have to make the effort to heal words by using them properly and carefully. True love includes a sense of responsibility and accepting the other person as he or she is, with all strengths and weaknesses. If you like only the best things in a person, that is not love. You have to accept his or her weaknesses and bring your patience, understanding, and energy to help the per-son transform. This kind of love is safe.

We use the phrase "love sickness" to describe the kind of love that makes us sick. It is a kind of attachment, or addiction. Like a drug, it makes us feel wonderful, but once we are addicted, we cannot have peace. We cannot study, work, or sleep. We think only about the other person. This kind of love is possessive, even totalitarian. We want to own the object of our love, and we don't want anyone to prevent us from possessing him or her totally. It creates a kind of prison for our beloved one. He or she is deprived of the right to be himself or her-self.

The feeling of loneliness is universal in our society, and it can push us into a relationship. We believe naively that having a sexual relationship will make us feel less lonely. But when there is no real communication between you and the other person, a sexual relationship will only widen the gap and cause both of you to suffer.

The phrase "long-term commitment" is not strong enough to express the depth of our love, but we need to say something so people will understand. To love our child deeply, we have to make a long-term commitment and help him or her through the journey of life as long as we are alive. When we have a good friend, we also make a long-term commitment. How much more so the person with whom we want to share our body and soul. It is important to make such a commitment in the context of a community—family or friends—to witness and support you. The feeling between the two of you may not be enough to sustain your happiness in times of adversity. Even if you do not accept the institution of marriage, it is still important to express your commitment in the presence of friends who love and support you. It will give you peace, stability, and a greater chance for real happiness.

This precept also applies to society. There are many ways our families and society are destroyed by sexual misconduct. Many people suffer every day because they were molested as children. When you practice this precept, you vow to protect children and also those who sexually abuse children. The ones who cause suffering must also become the objects of your love and protection. They are the product of an unstable society, and they need our help. Our society needs bodhisattvas who practice in this field to prevent suffering and the breaking up of relationships, families, and individual lives.

The Fourth Precept
Aware of the suffering caused by unmindful speech and the inability to listen to others, I vow to cultivate loving speech and deep listening in order to bring joy and happiness to others and relieve others of their suffering. Knowing that words can create happiness or suffering, I vow to learn to speak truthfully, with words that inspire self- confidence, joy, and hope. I am determined not to spread news that I do not know

to be certain and not to criticize or condemn things of which I am not sure. I will refrain from uttering words that can cause division or discord, or that can cause the family or the community to break. I will make all efforts to reconcile and resolve all conflicts, however small.

Loving speech is an act of generosity. When we are motivated by loving kindness, we can bring happiness to many others through our kind words. When we have a lot of pain, it is difficult to speak lovingly, so it is important to look deeply into the nature of our anger, despair, and suffering in order to be free of it. If we use words that inspire self-confidence and trust, especially with our children, they will flower.

In my tradition, whenever we want to inspire ourselves to practice the art of deep listening, we recite this verse:

> We invoke your name, Avalokiteshvara. We aspire to learn your way of listening in order to help relieve the suffering in the world. You know how to listen in order to understand. We invoke your name in order to practice listening with all our attention and openheartedness. We will sit and listen without any prejudice. We will sit and listen without judging or reacting. We will sit and listen in order to understand. We will sit and listen so attentively that we will be able to hear what the other person is saying and also what is being left unsaid. We know that just by listening deeply, we already alleviate a great deal of pain and suffering in the other person.

Deep listening is the basis for reconciliation. To reconcile means to bring peace and happiness to members of our family, society, and other nations. To promote the work of reconciliation, we have to refrain from aligning ourselves with one party or another so that we understand both. This work takes courage; we may be suppressed or even killed by those we wish to help. After listening to both sides, we can tell each side of the suffering of the other. This alone will bring about greater understanding. People are sorely needed to do this in many places in the world, including South Africa, Eastern Europe, the Middle East, and Southeast Asia. Our society needs bodhisattvas who can bridge the huge gaps between religions, races, and peoples.

The Fifth Precept
Aware of the suffering caused by unmindful consumption, I vow to
cultivate good health, both physical and mental, for myself, my family, and my society by practicing mindful eating, drinking, and consuming. I vow to ingest only items that preserve peace, well-being, and
joy in my body, in my consciousness, and in the collective body and
consciousness of my family and society. I am determined not to use
alcohol or any other intoxicant or to ingest foods or other items that
contain toxins, such as certain TV programs, magazines, books, films,
and conversations. I am aware that to damage my body or my consciousness with these poisons is to betray my ancestors, my parents,
my society, and future generations. I will work to transform violence,
fear, anger, and confusion in myself and in society by practicing a diet
for myself and for society. I understand that a proper diet is crucial
for self-transformation and for the transformation of society.

In the West, people have the impression that their body belongs
to them, that they can do anything they want to their body. They feel
they have the right to live their lives however they please. And the law
supports them. This is individualism. But according to the teaching
of interbeing, your body is not yours alone. Your body belongs to your
ancestors, your parents, and future generations, and it also belongs to
society and all other living beings. All of them have come together to
bring about the presence of this body. Keeping your body healthy is
an expression of gratitude to the whole cosmos—the trees, the clouds,
everything. You practice this precept for everyone. If you are healthy,
physically and mentally, all of us will benefit. We are what we consume and metabolize. We have to eat, drink, and consume, but
unless we do it mindfully, we may destroy our bodies and our consciousness, expressing a lack of gratitude to our ancestors, parents, and
future generations. Mindful consuming is the main subject of this
precept.

It is important for each family to have at least one meal together
every day. This meal should be an occasion to practice mindfulness,
and to be aware of how fortunate we are to be together. After we sit
down, we look at each person and, breathing in and out, smile to him

or her for a few seconds. This practice can produce a miracle. It can make you real, and it can make the others at the table real also.

Then we practice meditation on the food. One person looks at one dish on the table and describes its content and history. Children and adults can learn from this and have a deeper look into the nature of the food. This may take only a few minutes, but it will help everyone enjoy the food much more. For example, someone says aloud, "This bread, made from wheat, Earth, sun, and rain, comes to us after much hard work. The wheat was grown organically by a farmer in Texas, and a considerable amount of fuel was used to transport the flour to a conscientious bakery in our home town. May we live in a way that is worthy of this food, and appreciate the positive and negative elements that are present in each bite."

Eating in silence, even for a few minutes, is a very important practice. It takes away all the distractions that can keep us from really touching the food. Our mindfulness may be fragile and it may be too difficult to carry on a conversation and really honor the food at the same time. So for the first five or ten minutes, it is wonderful to eat in silence. In my monastic tradition, we practice the Five Contemplations before eating. The second Contemplation is, "We vow to be worthy of this food." I think the best way to make ourselves worthy of this food is to eat it mindfully. The whole cosmos has come together to make this food available, and someone has spent an hour or more preparing the food. It would be a pity if we didn't eat it in mindfulness.

After the period of quiet, we can practice mindful talking, the kind of talking that can increase the happiness in the family. We should never talk of things that can separate us; we should never reproach someone during the meal. That would spoil everything. Parents should refrain from discussing the mistakes their children have made, and young people should also only say things that will help bring about more happiness and nourish the mindfulness in the family, such as "Daddy, isn't this soup fantastic?" Speaking this way waters the seeds of happiness in the whole family. Life is an art. We should all be artists in order to live a happy life. We will have time later to discuss our business projects or what happened in school. During dinnertime we feel grateful that we are together, we have food to eat, and we really enjoy the food and the presence of each other.

It is important that we maintain a healthy diet. There are so many wonderful things to eat and drink; we have to refrain from consuming the things that harm us. Alcohol causes a lot of suffering. So many people have grown up receiving some form of abuse from an alcoholic parent. The fruit and grain that produce alcoholic beverages use farmland that could be producing food for those who are hungry. And so many traffic accidents involve someone who is intoxicated. When we understand that we are practicing not only for ourselves, we will stop drinking alcohol. To stop drinking is a statement to our children and our society that this is a substance not worthy of our support. Even if we don't drink alcohol, we may get killed by a drunken driver. In persuading one person to refrain from drinking, we make the world a safer place. Drinking wine is an element running deep in Western civilization, as is evident in the Eucharist and the Sabbath meal. I have spoken with priests and rabbis to see whether it might be possible to substitute grape juice or some other beverage for the wine, and they think it is possible.

Sometimes we don't need to consume as much as we do. Consuming itself can become a kind of addiction, because we feel so lonely. Loneliness is one of the afflictions of modern life. When we are lonely, we ingest food in our body and into our consciousness that can bring toxins into us. Just as we make every effort to maintain a proper diet for our body, we must also maintain a proper diet for our consciousness, refraining from ingesting toxic intellectual and spiritual food. When we watch TV, read magazines or books, or pick up the telephone, we only make our condition worse if our consuming is not mindful. During one hour watching a film filled with violence, we water the seeds of violence, hatred, and fear in us. We do that, and we let our children do that. We need to have family meetings to discuss an intelligent policy for television watching. We may have to label our TV sets the same way we label our cigarette packs: "Warning: Watching TV can be hazardous to your health." Children see so many violent images on television. We need an intelligent policy concerning the use of television.

Of course there are many healthy and beautiful programs, and we should arrange our time so that the family will benefit from these. We don't have to destroy our TV sets. We only have to use them with mindfulness. We can ask television stations to broadcast healthier programs and encourage the boycott of those who refuse. We can even support the manufacture of TV sets that only receive signals from stations that produce healthy, educational programs. We need to be protected because the toxins are overwhelming, and they are destroying our society, our families, and us.

The idea of a diet is the essence of this precept. Our collective consciousness has so much violence, fear, craving, and hatred in it, and it manifests in wars and bombs. Bombs are a product of the fear in our collective consciousness. Just to remove the bombs is not enough. Even if we were able to transport all the bombs to the moon, we would not be safe, because the roots of the war and the bombs are still in our collective consciousness. We will not abolish war with angry demonstrations. We have to transform the toxins in our own consciousness and in our collective consciousness. We have to practice a diet for ourselves, our families, and our society, and we have to work with artists, writers, filmmakers, lawyers, psychotherapists, and others if we want to stop the kind of consuming that is poisoning our collective consciousness.

The problem is very big. It is not just a question of enjoying one glass of wine. If you stop drinking alcohol altogether or stop watching unwholesome films and tv programs, you do it for the whole society. When you see that we are in great danger, refraining from the first glass of wine is a manifestation of your enlightenment. You are setting an example for your children, your friends, and all of us. On French television, they say, *"Une verre, ça va, deux verres, bonjour les dégâts."* "One glass is all right, but two glasses are destructive." They don't say that if there were no first glass, there could not be a second.

Please join me in writing down three things. First, what kind of toxins do you already have in your body, and what kind of toxins do you already have in your psyche, your consciousness? What makes you suffer now? If you need to practice sitting or walking meditation in order to look deeply enough, please do so. When you have done this, please sit quietly for a few moments, and then look into the bodies and souls of your children, your spouse, or others who are close to you, since all of you are practicing together. Recognizing these toxins and

listing them on a sheet of paper is meditation—looking deeply in order to call things by their true names.

Second, please ask yourself, "What kind of poisons am I putting
into my body and my consciousness every day?" What am I ingesting
every day that is toxic to my body and my consciousness? What is my
family ingesting? What are my city and my nation ingesting concerning violence, hatred, and fear? The beating of Rodney King is a manifestation of how much hatred, fear, and violence are in our society.
What kinds of poisons do we ingest every day in our families, our cities, and our nation? This is a collective meditation.

Third, write down a prescription that arises from your insight. For
example, "I vow that from today I will not ingest more of this, this,
and this. I vow only to use this, this, and this to nourish my body and
my consciousness." This is the foundation of practice— the practice
of loving kindness to yourself. You cannot love someone else unless
you love and take care of yourself. Practicing in this way is to practice
peace, love, and insight. When you look deeply, you have insight, and
your insight brings about compassion.

Before you begin to eat, breathe in and out and look at the table
to see what is good for your body and what is not. This is to practice
the precept of protecting your body. When you want to watch TV or
go to the movies, first look deeply in order to determine what should
be viewed and what should not be viewed by you and your children.
Think about the books and magazines you read, and decide what
should be read and what should not be read by you and your children.
Practicing together as a community, we don't need to take refuge in
entertaining ourselves with any more poisons. Based on our own insight, we can decide what to ingest and what not to ingest into our
bodies and our souls.

Please discuss with your family and friends a diet for your body, a
diet for your consciousness, and also a diet for the collective consciousness of our society. This is a meditation practice, and it is true peace
work. Peace begins with each of us taking care of our bodies and our
minds every day.

I hope you will practice according to the letter and spirit of these
five precepts, reciting them regularly, and discussing them with
friends. If you prefer to use the equivalent from your own tradition,

that is wonderful. At Plum Village, we recite these precepts every week. One person reads each precept slowly and then breathes three times before saying, "This is the (first) of the five precepts. Have you made an effort to study and to practice it during the last week?" We do not answer yes or no. We just breathe three times and let the question enter us. That is good enough. "Yes" would not be entirely correct, but "No" would not be correct either. No one can practice these precepts perfectly. If you are a vegetarian, for example, the food you eat still contains living beings. But we have to do something, and practicing the precepts is a direction we can follow to produce the dramatic changes that are needed in ourselves and in society.

Precepts and Responsible Practice

As WESTERN BUDDHISTS we acknowledge our monastic heritage but tend to consider ourselves beyond that archaic, restrictive, and exclusive way of religious practice. Most of us are not ordained monks or nuns. Our Buddhist centers are not monasteries in any traditional sense. Yet it is our common purpose to carry forward the work of the Buddha Shakyamuni and his Asian successors in our own time and place and cultures. Are we doing it? Is our lay practice a natural outgrowth of the old in new circumstances? Or is there a risk that we might be fabricating something out of contemporary materials that have merely a Buddhist veneer?

We are not the first to struggle with such questions. After Buddhism was introduced to China, the next step was the establishment of monasteries and merit fields of lay devotees—but with a Chinese flavor. The ancient way of life without labor was set aside. "A day without work is a day without eating," Pai-chang, the founder of the Ch'an Buddhist monastic system declared. However, it was maintenance work for the most part. Dana was and is still the foundation of the East Asian Buddhist institution. The role of laypeople has largely been to support monks or priests and their temples. In Japan, temple membership is made up of *danka* ("dana families").

Layicization has proceeded. To take Japan as an example again, the Kamakura reformation in the thirteenth century shifted responsibility for realizing the Dharma to laypeople to some degree. There has been a general deterioration of the religion during this process, but still one can find ordinary people reciting the Buddha's name or doing zazen, consulting with priests about their practice, or taking part in retreats with monks. In new schools of Buddhism, such as the Rissho Koseikai, the leaders are not even ordained and function like Protestant ministers.

In our Western Mahayana centers, monks of both sexes are ordained, though the old rules of celibacy which eroded during earlier reformations are generally not observed. Benedictine rules of work have been applied and some of the centers seek self-sufficiency through business enterprise. Laypeople are in the majority and practice together with ordained monks. Theravada and Vajrayana centers have appeared in the West as well—Theravada with scarcely any deference to the monastic tradition and Vajrayana without much ordination.

It is surely time, high time, for us as Western Buddhists to take stock. To begin with the Buddha's intention: it is clear that he intended the Sangha to be more than a fellowship of people who shared common religious aspirations. As a treasure of the Way, the Sangha for him was the natural grouping that offered the only means for people to find liberation from their anguish. Moreover, the precepts, derived from formulations from the misty past in India and Persia, were for him the comportment of all followers of the Way.

With all the changes in Buddhism, its followers have remained true to this view of the Sangha as the order of Dharma and the precepts as the Sangha mode of life. Still, as a living organism, the Sangha too is evolving. Joanna Macy has shown how Theravada monks in Sri Lanka take their turns with the spade in the Sarvodaya Shramadana, the broadly based village self-sufficiency movement of that country. Lay Western Buddhists expect as a matter of course to take responsibility for their own religious practice.

Thich Nhat Hanh, the "Thây" or "Master" of Vietnamese Buddhism in the West, has given much thought to the Sangha treasure. His Tiep Hien Order includes monks and nuns in Europe and across the world. His peripatetic retreats provide them and lay followers with the kind of Sangha renewal the ancient sages found in their monsoon retreats. As with the original Sangha of the Buddha, the first teaching is the Vinaya, the moral way. His students learn decency with each other, and as decent people set about saving the many beings.

As a foundation for this practice, Thây takes up the *pañca-śila*, the five fundamental precepts of the ancient Way. He frames each of these precepts positively while maintaining their trenchant, negative vigor. His wording is true to the Buddha's profound intention, and, at the same time, it is relevant for modern students who are ready to take full responsibility for their practice. "I vow not to kill" thus becomes: "Aware of the suffering caused by the destruction of life, I vow to cultivate compassion and learn ways to protect the lives of people, animals, plants, and minerals. I am determined not to kill, not to let others kill, and not to condone any act of killing in the world, in my thinking, and in my way of life."

Making this vow our own, we make this way of life our own, modestly assenting, "With all my weaknesses and faults, I accept my role as bodhisattva." The way of the bodhisattva is the practice of "not killing," but what is "not killing" but nurturing life in fact with each smile and encouraging word? And what are the other "nots" in the precepts—"not stealing," "not speaking falsely," and so on—but the intimate practice of compassion and protecting people, animals, plants, and minerals! Thây's beautiful words enlarge the scope of the precepts—and this is the goal of most Western teachers, I believe. If in centuries past, the precepts were pro forma pledges or metaphysical formulations, that time has passed. In most of our centers, the precepts are examined in classes or in orientation programs that are required for the Refuge Ceremony. With such study and with the ceremonies themselves comes a clear understanding that we are human whatever our state of realization might be. There is no perfection except the perfection in our hearts which we seek to fulfill as best we can in our families, among our friends and colleagues, and in the world. As teachers and students alike, we take the precepts to heart and apply them in our daily lives as conscientiously as possible—or we are only make-believe Buddhists who can cause widespread harm, as we have seen to our sorrow.

According to *The Avatamsaka Sutra*, when the youth Sudhana entered the magnificent pagoda of Maitreya at the end of his long pilgrimage, he found that it contained an infinite number of pagodas, each of them beautifully adorned. If he entered one of those inner pagodas, he would find that it too contained an infinite number of pagodas. Thus Sudhana realized—made real for himself—the Net of Indra, in which each point is a jewel that perfectly reflects all other jewels. Each being, each element of each being, perfectly includes all others. He came into his own with full awareness, as his own flesh-and-blood treasure of interbeing at last.

Like all folk stories, the sojourn of Sudhana is itself a pagoda to be entered and made real for oneself, as heroine as well as hero, as adult and even elderly, as well as youthful. It is a personalization that is not just a goal that culminates a religious pilgrimage, but it forms the dimension of each step of the way.

This "dimension of each step" is illumined by the precepts of the Buddha. What is "not killing" but the practice of the ultimate intimacy we celebrate in Sudhana, making that intimacy more and more real in fact with each nurturing smile and encouraging word. And what are the other "nots" in the precepts—"not stealing," "not misusing sex," and so on—but Ms. and Mr. Sudhana in this time and place showing their perennial jewels!

And what of the conspiracy of ruin that mocks the metaphors and could bring the kalpa of Kuan-yin and Maria and Murasaki and Bach to the flames of total devastation? Somehow we must find expedient means to make real the jeweled network within and alongside consumer exploitation and national interest. This is a step beyond the monastery walls, uncharted by the old teachers. But it is a step, a path, that the unholy alliance of greed, state ego, racism, androcentrism, and technology has made imperative. Not an easy path, certainly. I am grateful to Thich Nhat Hanh for his light and his staff that guide us.

MAXINE HONG KINGSTON

Precepts for the Twenty-First Century

TO WRITE OUT the precepts again, we contend with them, and keep them; we build our humanity, and keep our humanity alive. After the Buddha gave the Five Precepts to the world, there have been many editions and translations, trying for language that would enlighten minds in changing times and places. Thich Nhat Hanh has written a strong version; it will inspire us and our difficult end-of-the-Twentieth-Century world. His thinking has gone through fire—war in and outside of Vietnam, the destruction and building of communities, the conditions of life in the East and in the West. These then are the precepts of Buddhism as they have evolved through the most exacting tests.

We people who have studied with Thich Nhat Hanh in person and/or through his writing should consider ourselves also authors of this book. Our teacher, Thây, learned from us as we struggled with how to live the precepts. Some of us debated their wording like lawyers (especially arguing over the Third Precept, its once-wording, "No sex without marriage"); some rebelled at the very idea of rules. In mindful understanding of our complex, modern, American lives, interacting—"interbeing"—with us, Thây has enworded and reworded the precepts until they are in their present rigorous form. (In the discussion of the Third Precept, he helps us distinguish between "marriage" and "commitment," the latter having more permanence.) Each precept has two parts: "I vow to ..." and "I am determined not to ...." Going beyond what thou shalt not do, we assert positive actions. The doers and authors of these precepts—war veterans and peace veterans, men and women, children, citizens of many countries, heterosexuals and homosexuals—are bringing into being through words and deeds a compassionate world community.

Thây has named the precepts "wonderful"—the Five Wonderful Precepts. Wonderful because they have lived for more than 2,500 years, through holocausts and devastations. Wonderful because they are a practicable, useful map and working plan for our lives in the real world. They teach us to effect that world with methods that are reasonable, logical, ethical—no impossible magic here. Wonderful because they can protect us, and show us how to live a joyous life, an interesting, adventurous, deep, large life, and how to be with one another, and with animals, plants, and all the Earth and universe. Wonderful because when we practice the precepts, we existentially become humane, we embody loving kindness.

During the 1991 firestorm through the Oakland-Berkeley hills, I stood in the middle of my street, while the houses on either side burned. I was bereft of my house, neighborhood, the book I was writing, and my father, who had died three weeks previously. Suddenly, I felt the emptiness fill with ideas, spirit, history, all that I have thought and lived. Standing in the midst of burning ruins, I was glad that I knew the precepts. Though I kept their tenets imperfectly, even in aspiration I created some invisible good that could not be destroyed. There is an actuality that surrounds and permeates words and things, and exists in their absence. The Five Wonderful Precepts give clear and simple directions to finding that life. In devastation, I have blueprints for making home anew.

PATRICIA MARX ELLSBERG

The Five Precepts
and Social Change

AFTER ATTENDING two retreats with Thich Nhat Hanh, I had the feeling of being "in love" with Thây and Sister Chân Không and with a whole community and way of life. And when I vowed to follow the precepts, I felt as if I were making a commitment as serious and profound as taking marriage vows.

I have no doubt of the powerful and far-reaching effect the precepts can have on my life if I take them to heart. And yet, during the retreats I found a question persistently recurring as to the relevance of my own personal practice of the precepts to social change. In the face of massive violence and injustice in the world, what difference does it make if I follow the precepts, or even if all the thousands of people Thây has touched with his teachings live by them more fully? How would this bring about the radical social transformations that are necessary?

I found myself uncomfortable with what I perceived to be an underlying premise of the retreat: that if enough individuals change, society will change. In my understanding, society is not simply an aggregate of individuals. It is also shaped by social structures and concentrations of power and wealth. There are vested interests that have disproportionate control and work to maintain and profit from inequality and militarism. These forces need to be challenged and transformed before there can be genuine peace or justice.

In a flash of recognition, I saw that many of the policies of my country and those of other nations are based on the flagrant disregard of the precepts. In fact, much of the evil in the world comes from the systematic—and often societally sanctioned—violation of the precepts by governments, corporations, and other institutions. Let us measure our own society's conduct by the precepts.

The First Precept. Think of the Gulf Massacre in this context and the glorification of the slaughter of over a quarter of a million people, many of them civilians. We live in a war economy fueled by a vast military-industrial complex and billions of dollars of arms sales. Our nuclear policy is based on the threat of mass murder, our foreign policy upon institutionalized violence. Our economy depends on the whole-sale destruction of nature.

The Second Precept. We as Americans comprise six percent of the world's population and consume forty percent of the world's resources. Many of these resources flow to us from countries ruled by dictator-ships that our government has installed, supported, and controlled. In turn they set terms of trade favorable to us, while exploiting and terrorizing their own people, with our government's covert support. This amounts to official theft, not "exchange." Most of our military might is used to control what is not rightly ours.

The Third Precept. Think of the energy and resources our society devotes to stimulating sexual desire unconnected to commitment or love—through advertising, pornography, and popular culture in general.

The Fourth Precept. Governments and politicians lie. The secrecy system exists not so much to keep secrets from the enemy as to keep the truth from the public. Our government routinely resorts to force rather than peaceful means to deal with conflict, while claiming the opposite, as in Panama, Libya, Nicaragua, Grenada, and Iraq.

The Fifth Precept. We are constantly bombarded by advertising for alcohol, cigarettes, caffeine, pharmaceutical drugs. Even more perni-cious, our government, through its covert intelligence apparatus, is secretly but deeply involved in abetting the operators of the drug trade, as became evident in the Iran-Contra scandal.

Suddenly, during the retreat, I saw a way the precepts can be of utmost social relevance. We must hold them as a standard of behavior for nations, institutions, and corporations as well as for individuals. It is essential that we end the double standard that exists between public and private morality. We must ask of our country what we ask of ourselves.

Those of us living in a democracy have a special obligation to do all we can to move our nation along with our own lives in the direction of following the precepts. We must act individually and together to prevent the government that represents us from supporting mass murder and terrorism, stealing, lying, supporting drug traffickers, and raping the Earth. In fact, our survival, in the long run, depends on it.

Likewise, the more fully we follow the precepts, the more powerfully we can act for social change. Indeed, political work is an extension of personal life.

In the spirit of Thây's reformulation of the precepts in positive terms, imagine a world in which individuals and institutions alike act with compassion and loving kindness, where governments as well as the citizens they serve are mindful, cultivate a healthy environment, and truly protect the lives of people, animals, and plants. Imagine a time when the resources of the Earth are redirected away from killing towards the enrichment of life.

What if our President's policies conformed to Buddhist principles, Americans pledged allegiance to the Five Precepts as well as the flag, and we celebrated Interdependence Day along with the Fourth of July? Such thoughts inspire in me a Buddha smile.

STEPHEN BATCHELOR

The Future Is in Our Hands

"WHAT IS YOUR PRACTICE?" Many Buddhist practitioners would assume that this question is about the kind of meditation they do, for they tend to answer, "I practice vipassana," or "dzogchen," or "shikantaza." Such responses reflect a widespread view that practice is essentially a matter of spiritual technique. Ethics, from this perspective, is seen as a set of values and precepts that support one's practice.

The Buddha, however, spoke of practice *(siksa)* as threefold: consisting of ethics, meditation, and wisdom. Yet as Buddhists seek to express themselves in the technocentric culture of the West, they often see what they "do" primarily in terms of the second of these three practices, namely meditation. For this fits a world view in which the solving of problems by means of applying techniques is considered paramount.

The most significant aspect of the emerging engaged Buddhist movement is that of redefining what is meant by "practice." By emphasizing engagement, the focus of practice shifts from an exclusive identification with meditation to an inclusion of ethics. The danger here is that "engaged Buddhists" become subtly (or less than subtly) dismissive of other Buddhists who "only" meditate. As with the technocentrism of meditators, engaged Buddhists are liable to succumb to another Western obsession: the belief that action alone counts.

Ethics as practice begins by including ethical dilemmas in the sphere of meditative awareness—to be mindful of the conflicting impulses that invade consciousness during meditation. Instead of dismissing these as distractions (which would be quite legitimate when

cultivating concentration), one recognizes them as potentials for actions that may result in one's own or others' suffering.

The practice of such mindfulness leads to increasing sensitivity
regarding the moment-to-moment emergence of thoughts and emotions. Often it is not until I find myself taken over by an emotion, such
as anger, that I first become conscious of it. Such meditation trains
me to observe states of mind at their inception.

This does not mean that I suppress or disregard those impulses that
do not conform to my spiritual self-image. Mindfulness is to accept
whatever arises and to recognize it as such. At the root of my practice
of ethics is the ability to accept that I am as much a potential mur-
derer, thief, rapist, liar, and drug-abuser as those convicted of such
offenses in prison. To practice ethics is to be able to accept the reality
of such impulses—and let them go. To let them go means to allow
them to follow their own nature of passing away. For only when I
affirm an impulse ("Yes, I hate that person!"), do I set in motion the
train of events that culminates in verbal or physical action.

As the power of mindfulness increases, it allows me increasing freedom to choose what to do. Mindfulness is empowered, however, not
just by a greater capacity to be mindful—we have probably all had the
experience of mindfully observing ourselves break a precept. Mindfulness is also empowered by its "sister" qualities of faith, enthusiasm,
meditation, and wisdom (the other four of the five powers, *indriya*,
the Buddha spoke of). To the extent that such mindfulness is absent,
the more a choice is liable to be subject to the forces of psychological
habit and social conditioning. Only when mindfulness is fully empowered am I fully free to choose.

What makes me choose one thing as opposed to another? What
makes me believe that this action is right while another is wrong?
Mindfulness can make me aware of what impulses are arising from
moment to moment, but it does not tell me which of these impulses
to let go of and which to follow. To know this, I need to be aware of
my priorities and values. And such awareness lies at the heart of my
Buddhist faith.

The practice of Buddhist ethics is grounded in faith. For I can
neither prove by logic nor observe through the senses what I regard
as right and wrong, good and evil. Even though I may justify my con-

viction of what is right and wrong by appealing to conscience or intuition or Buddha nature, such an appeal is likewise an act of faith in something (such as conscience) that I can neither prove nor observe.

"Buddhist ethics" generally refers to those sets of precepts that I commit myself to as a layperson, a monastic, an aspiring bodhisattva, a Zen practitioner, or a follower of the Vajrayana. Precepts are formal statements of the values I choose, on faith, to live by. It is to those values, enshrined in the precepts, that I refer when making an ethical choice.

When baldly stated (for example, "Do not kill"), a precept may seem merely to dictate what is forbidden. Underlying this precept, however, are values: that life is precious, that the diminishing of suffering is good, that compassion is good, that the protection and enhancement of life is good.

A tension runs through all the Buddhist traditions between those who emphasize the literal meaning of the precepts and those who emphasize the values that underlie them. Common to many traditions is the story of two monks who see a woman drowning in a river. One dives into the water to save her, while the other looks on disapprovingly. When they return to the monastery, the latter accuses the former of breaking the monk's precept of touching a woman's body. His friend responds, "I let go of her on the bank of the river. You are still clinging to her."

Every ethical dilemma presents me with a uniquely complex situation that has never existed before and will never exist again. No number of precepts will ever be able to legislate for the infinite number of possible ethical dilemmas I may face. While precepts can take care of many simple choices, it is the dilemmas in life that cause me to agonize over them that demand the practice of ethics. For they call on me to look deeply at the situation and then choose, with wisdom, what to do. Such wisdom requires that I look beyond the wording of the precepts to the values they enshrine.

Action *(karma)*, declared the Buddha, is intention. To intend to do something is to choose to act in a certain way. Every such choice, however, is a risk; for I can never know the outcome of an action. All I can aspire to is the wisdom of knowing what might be best—a wisdom that requires the humility to acknowledge that I might get it wrong.

So the practice of ethics also entails the practice of meditation and wisdom. The Buddha's Threefold Training is present in any significant ethical act: as the commitment to a set of values embodied in precepts; as the clarity, stillness, and freedom of mindfulness that allows me to be aware of what is taking place at the moment; and as the wisdom to choose what might be the best thing to do.

In the Spring of 1993, I was fortunate to be part of a group of Western Buddhist teachers who met with His Holiness the Dalai Lama to discuss, among other things, Buddhist ethics, especially among teachers. The Dalai Lama is simultaneously a preeminent upholder of the historical Dharma and one of the foremost interpreters of its meaning. He is at once radically liberal in terms of doctrinal interpretation while highly conservative in matters of ethical orthodoxy.

It is the student, the Dalai Lama declares, who ultimately invests the teacher with authority by placing him or her in that role. Why is it that certain teachers in America and Europe have become embroiled in scandals? Why have they been able to exploit and abuse their students? This was an issue about which the Dalai Lama was deeply concerned.

The student, he noted, often fails to examine sufficiently the person's ethical and spiritual qualities before accepting him (it's usually "him") as a teacher. Yet the Tibetan tradition states clearly that one should devote years of close scrutiny before taking such a step. But the fault lies primarily with the teacher. The Dalai Lama observed, "Many friends I knew here [in India and Tibet] were very humble, but in the West they became proud." A simple monk catapulted from an impoverished settlement in India to a city in Europe and America to be revered and showered with wealth would understandably be prone to let such treatment go to his head. "Alcohol," His Holiness commented, "is often at the root of these problems." Of course: a tempting strategy for someone uprooted from his home-culture then thrust into a bewildering and demanding world for which he lacks the necessary social and emotional skills to cope.

That would be all very well except for the fact that most of these Asian teachers, and their Western successors, are supposed to be enlightened. What does "enlightenment" mean if those who have it are still subject to those less than edifying forms of behavior from whose grip we poor unenlightened souls are struggling to be free? At the very least, one would hope, enlightenment would imply a degree of contentment. But if someone were contented, why would he succumb to the conceit of self-importance? Why would he become dependent upon alcohol? Why would he indulge in a series of transient sexual encounters? Even unenlightened, contented people have no need for these things.

If a teacher's actions are unethical, responded the Dalai Lama, then even if they have practiced for many years, their practice has been wrong. Quite simply, they lack a proper understanding of the Dharma. There is a "gap" between the Dharma and their lives. He challenged the idea that once one has insight into the ultimate truth of emptiness, then one is no longer bound by the norms of morality. On the contrary: through revealing the web of relationships that ethically connects all living beings, the understanding of emptiness does not mystically transcend morality but grounds it in experience.

His Holiness expressed some concern that, on occasion, the Zen experience of *satori* is confused with either a deep state of concentration *(samadhi)* or simply a state of nonconceptuality, neither of which in themselves imply transformative understanding. The emphasis in Zen of high levels of enlightenment, he noted, might well entail the danger of leaving lower levels of simple neurotic behavior untouched. He likewise wondered about Buddhists he had met who talked of experiencing emptiness but seemed to lack human warmth, which indicated to him either a meditative lapse into sheer nonconceptuality or mental "sinking" (a subtle form of dullness). "Therefore," he concluded, "I prefer the gradual path."

Someone remarked that our days together "had a bone-deep sense of rightness" about them. The meeting with the Dalai Lama served as a confirmation of something many of us had intuitively known to be true all along, but had found neither the courage nor the words to express. "Past is past," said the Dalai Lama on the last day. "What is important? The future. We are the creators. The future is in our hands. Even if we fail, no regrets—we have to make the effort."

Hope for the Future

I WANT TO SPEAK with you about the importance of kindness and compassion. When I speak about this, I regard myself not as a Buddhist, not as the Dalai Lama, not even as a Tibetan, but as one human being, and I hope that you will think of yourself as a human being rather than just an American, or a Westerner, or a member of a particular group. These things are secondary. If you and I interact as human beings, we can reach this basic level. If I say, "I am a monk; I am a Buddhist," these are, in comparison to my nature as a human being, temporary. To be human is basic. Once you are born as a human being, that cannot change until your death. Other characteristics—whether you are educated or uneducated, rich or poor—are secondary.

Today we face many problems. Some are essentially created by ourselves, based on divisions due to ideology, religion, race, economic status, and other factors. Because of this, the time has come for us to think on a deeper level, on the human being level, and from that level to respect and appreciate the sameness of ourselves and others as human beings. We must build closer relationships of mutual trust, understanding, respect, and help, regardless of differences in culture, philosophy, religion, or faith.

After all, all human beings are made of flesh, bones, and blood, wanting happiness, and not wanting suffering. We all have an equal right to be happy, and it is important to realize our sameness as human beings. We all belong to one human family. We quarrel with each other, but that is due to secondary reasons, and all of this arguing, cheating and suppressing each other is of no use.

Unfortunately, for many centuries, human beings have used all sorts of methods to suppress and hurt one another. Terrible things have been done. We have caused more problems, more suffering, and more mistrust, and created more hatred and more divisions.

Today the world is becoming smaller and smaller. Economically and from many other viewpoints, the different areas of the world are becoming closer and much more interdependent. Because of this, international summits often take place; problems in one remote place are connected with global crises. The situation itself expresses the fact that it is now necessary to think more on a human level rather than on the basis of the matters which divide us. Therefore, I am speaking to you as just a human being, and I earnestly hope that you are also reading with the thought, "I am a human being, and I am here reading the words of another human being."

All of us want happiness. In cities, on farms, even in remote villages, everyone is quite busy. What is the purpose? Everyone is trying to create happiness. To do so is right. However, it is very important to follow a correct method in seeking happiness. Too much involvement with superficialities will not solve the larger problems.

There are all about us many crises, many fears. Through highly developed science and technology, we have reached a very advanced level of material progress, both useful and necessary. Yet if you compare the external progress with our internal progress, it is quite clear that our internal progress falls short. In many countries, crises—terrorism, murders, and so on—are chronic. People complain about the decline in morality and the rise in criminal activity. Although in external matters we are highly developed and continue to progress, at the same time we neglect our inner development.

In ancient times, if there was war, the effect was limited. Today, because of external material progress, the potential for destruction is beyond imagination. When I visited Hiroshima, though I knew something about the nuclear explosion there, I found it very difficult to see it with my own eyes and to meet with people who actually suffered at the moment of the bombing. I was deeply moved. A terrible weapon was used. Though we might regard someone as an enemy, on a deeper level an enemy is also a human being, also wants happiness, also has the right to be happy. Looking at Hiroshima and thinking about this, at that moment I became even more convinced that anger and hatred cannot solve problems.

Anger cannot be overcome by anger. If a person shows anger to you and you respond with anger, the result is a disaster. In contrast, if you control anger and show the opposite attitude—compassion, tolerance, patience—then not only do you yourself remain in peace, but the other person's anger will gradually diminish. World problems also cannot be challenged by anger or hatred. They must be faced with compassion, love, and true kindness. Even with all the terrible weapons we have, the weapons themselves cannot start a war. The button to trigger them is under a human finger, which moves by thought, not under its own power. The responsibility rests in thought.

If you look deeply into such things, the blueprint is found within—in the mind—out of which actions come. Thus, first controlling the mind is very important. I am not talking about controlling the mind in the sense of deep meditation, but rather in the sense of cultivating less anger, more respect for others' rights, more concern for other people, more clear realization of the sameness of human beings. This attitude may not solve problems immediately, but we have to try. We have to begin promoting this understanding through magazines and through television. Rather than just advertising to make money for ourselves, we need to use these media for something more meaningful, more seriously directed towards the welfare of humankind. Not money alone. Money is necessary, but the actual purpose of money is for human beings. Sometimes we forget human beings and become concerned just about money. This is illogical.

After all, we all want happiness, and no one will disagree with the fact that with anger, peace is impossible. With kindness and love, peace of mind can be achieved. No one wants mental unrest, but because of ignorance, depression and so on, these things occur. Bad attitudes arise from the power of ignorance, not of their own accord.

Through anger we lose one of the best human qualities—the power of judgment. We have a good brain, allowing us to judge what is right and what is wrong, not only in terms of today's concerns, but considering ten, twenty, or even a hundred years into the future. Without any precognition, we can use our normal common sense to determine if something is right or wrong. We can decide that if we do such and such, it will lead to such and such an effect. However, once our mind is occupied by anger, we lose this power of judgment. Once lost, it is very sad—physically you are a human being but mentally you are not complete. Given that we have this physical human form, we must safeguard our mental capacity of judgment. For that, we cannot take out insurance. The insurance company is within ourselves: self-discipline, self-awareness, and clear realization of the shortcomings of anger and the positive effects of kindness. Thinking about this again and again, we can become convinced of it; and then with self-awareness, we can control the mind.

For instance, at present you may be a person who, due to small things, gets quickly and easily irritated. With clear understanding and awareness, that can be controlled. If you usually remain angry about ten minutes, try to reduce it to eight minutes. Next week make it five minutes and next month two minutes. Then make it zero. This is the way to develop and train our minds.

This is my feeling and also the sort of practice I myself do. It is quite clear that everyone needs peace of mind; the question is how to achieve it. Through anger we cannot. Through kindness, through love, through compassion, we can achieve peace of mind. The result will be a peaceful family—happiness between parents and children; fewer quarrels between husband and wife; no worries about divorce. Extended to the national level, this attitude can bring unity, harmony, and cooperation with genuine motivation. On the international level, mutual trust, mutual respect, and friendly and frank discussions can lead to joint efforts to solve world problems. All these are possible.

But first we must change within ourselves. Our national leaders try their best to solve our problems, but when one problem is solved, another crops up. Trying to solve that, there is another somewhere else. The time has come to try a different approach. Of course, it is very difficult to achieve a worldwide movement of peace of mind, but it is the only alternative. If there were an easier and more practical method, that would be better, but there is none. If through weapons we could achieve real, lasting peace, all right. Let all factories be turned into weapons factories. Spend every dollar for that, if that will achieve definite, lasting peace. But it is impossible.

Weapons do not remain stockpiled. Once a weapon is developed, sooner or later someone will use it. Someone might feel that if we do not use it, millions of dollars will be wasted, so somehow we should use it—drop a bomb to try it out. The result is that innocent people get killed. A friend told me that in Beirut there is a businessman who deals in weapons solely to make money. Because of him, many poor people in the streets get killed—ten or fifteen, or a hundred every day. This is due to lack of human understanding, lack of mutual respect and trust, not acting on a basis of kindness and love.

Therefore, although attempting to bring about peace through internal transformation is difficult, it is the only way to achieve a lasting world peace. Even if it is not achieved during my own lifetime, that is all right. More human beings will come—the next generation and the one after that—and progress can continue. I feel that despite the practical difficulties and the fact that this is regarded as an unrealistic view, it is worthwhile to make the attempt. So wherever I go, I express this, and I am encouraged that people from many different walks of life receive it well.

Each of us has responsibility for all humankind. It is time for us to think of other people as true brothers and sisters and to be concerned with their welfare, with lessening their suffering. Even if you cannot sacrifice your own benefit entirely, you should not forget the concerns of others. We should think more about the future and the benefit of all humanity.

If you try to subdue your selfish motives—anger, and so forth—and develop more kindness, more compassion for others, ultimately you will benefit more than you would otherwise. So sometimes I say that the wise selfish person should practice this way. Foolish selfish persons always think of themselves, and the results are negative. But a wise, selfish person thinks of others, helps others as much as he or she can, and receives good results.

This is my simple religion. There is no need for complicated philosophies, not even for temples. Our own brain, our own heart is our temple. The philosophy is kindness.

About the Contributors

Robert Aitken
Robert Aitken, Roshi, is the founder and retired director of the Diamond Sangha, a Zen Buddhist community in Honolulu. He is author of *Original Dwelling Place: Zen Buddhist Essays, Taking the Path of Zen, The Mind of Clover: Essays in Zen Buddhist Ethics, The Gateless Barrier: The Wu-Men Kuan (Mumonkan), A Zen Wave: Basho's Haiku and Zen,* and *The Dragon Who Never Sleeps: Verses for Zen Buddhist Practice.*

A. T. Ariyaratne
A. T. Ariyaratne is the founder and leader of the Sarvodaya Shramadana movement in Sri Lanka, which uses the principles of Gandhi and Buddhism to implement programs for the poor among 10,000 villages in education, health care, transportation facilities, agricultural projects, and technologically appropriate energies. He has received international recognition for his work, including the Niwano Peace Prize from Japan in 1991.

Allan Hunt Badiner
Allan Hunt Badiner is a consulting editor for *Tricycle: The Buddhist Review* and editor of *Dharma Gaia: A Harvest of Essays in Buddhism and Ecology.* He is founder of teknozen &ction websites, a World Wide Web design firm. He lives in Big Sur, California, with his wife Marion and daughter, India.

Richard Baker
Richard Baker-roshi is Abbot, Head Teacher, and founder of the
Dharma Sangha centers: Crestone Mountain Zen Center in Colorado,
and the Buddhistisches Studiumzentrum in the Black Forest, Germany. He is the Dharma Successor of Shunryu Suzuki-roshi, and
author of *Original Mind, the Practice of Zen in the West* (forthcoming
from Riverhead Books).

Stephen Batchelor
Stephen Batchelor spent ten years as a Buddhist monk in both the
Tibetan and Zen traditions. He is the author of *The Awakening of the
West: The Encounter of Buddhism and Western Culture, The Faith to
Doubt: Glimpses of Buddhist Uncertainty, Alone with Others: An Exis-
tential Approach to Buddhism,* and *The Tibet Guide* (winner of the
Thomas Cook Guidebook award), and translator of many Buddhist
texts. He is Director of Studies at the Buddhist-based Sharpham
College in Devon, England, where he lives with his wife Martine.

Alan Cutter
Alan Cutter is a Vietnam veteran and Protestant Minister in Duluth,
Minnesota, where he lives with his wife Ann and their three children.
He is the pastor of Lakeside Presbyterian Church and serves as vice-
president for the National Conference of Vietnam Veteran Ministers.

The Dalai Lama
His Holiness, Tenzin Gyatso, the Fourteenth Dalai Lama has been
the spiritual and temporal leader of Tibet since 1951, when he was sixteen years old. Since 1959, he has lived in exile in Dharamsala, India.
In 1989, he was awarded the Nobel Peace Prize. He is author of many
books, including *The Good Heart, Freedom in Exile, Worlds in Harmony:
Dialogues on Compassionate Action, Kindness, Clarity, and Insight,* and
many other books.

Chân Phâp Dâng
Chân Phâp Dâng is a Buddhist monk and core member of the Order
of Interbeing. He lives at Plum Village, Thich Nhat Hanh's retreat
center in Thenac, France.

Bill Devall
Bill Devall has written extensively on the environmental movement
and deep ecology and is the author of *Simple in Means, Rich in Ends*
and coauthor of *Deep Ecology: Living as if Nature Mattered.*

Patricia Marx Ellsberg
Patricia Marx Ellsberg is a social activist, public speaker, and workshop facilitator. Her life's work has been to bridge the political and
spiritual worlds. She works closely with her husband, Daniel Ellsberg.

Maha Ghosananda
Samdech Preah Maha Ghosananda is a meditation master and an
international peacemaker. Often referred to as the "Gandhi of Cambodia," he leads peace marches across war-torn Cambodia. He is author of *Step by Step: Meditations on Wisdom and Compassion.* He has
been nominated for the Nobel Peace Prize three times.

Thich Nhat Hanh
Thich Nhat Hanh was born in Vietnam in 1926, and since the age of
sixteen has been a Zen Buddhist monk. He is founder of Plum Village, a retreat community in southwestern France, and since 1983, he
has been leading retreats throughout the U.S. and Europe on the art
of mindful living. He is author of seventy-five books, including *Living Buddha, Living Christ, Love in Action, Being Peace,* and *Old Path
White Clouds: Walking in the Footsteps of the Buddha.*

Sister Jina van Hengel
Sister Jina van Hengel is a Buddhist nun of Irish and Dutch ancestry
living at Plum Village, Thich Nhat Hanh's retreat center in southwestern France. She travels throughout Europe leading retreats.

Chatsumarn Kabilsingh
Dr. Chatsumarn Kabilsingh, professor of Religion and Philosophy at
Thammasat University in Bangkok, focuses on the historical patterns
of discrimination in Thai society and exclusion in its religious tradition. She has traveled worldwide presenting papers on women and

Buddhism, and Buddhist ecological ethics. She is author of *Thai Women in Buddhism.*

Sister Chân Không

Sister Chân Không (True Emptiness) was born in Vietnam in 1938. She began working in the slums of Saigon as a teenager, distributing food, helping the sick, and teaching children. In 1964, she joined Zen Master Thich Nhat Hanh in founding the School of Youth for Social Service, which grew to an organization of over 10,000 young people organizing medical, educational, and agricultural facilities in rural Vietnam, and rebuilding villages destroyed by the war. Now she lives in exile at Plum Village, Thich Nhat Hanh's community in southwestern France, where she is a Dharma teacher, community leader, and social worker. She is author of *Learning True Love: How I Learned and Practiced Social Change in Vietnam.*

Maxine Hong Kingston

Maxine Hong Kingston, winner of the National Book Award, is author of *The Woman Warrior: Memoirs of a Girlhood among Ghosts, China Men, Hawaii One Summer,* and *Tripmaster Monkey: His Fake Book.* She leads meditation and writing workshops for veterans of war.

Jack Kornfield

Jack Kornfield was trained as a Buddhist monk in Thailand, Burma, and India and has taught meditation worldwide since 1974. He is a husband, father, psychotherapist, and founding teacher of the Insight Meditation Society in Massachusetts and Spirit Rock Meditation Center in northern California. He is coauthor (with Joseph Goldstein) of *Seeking the Heart of Wisdom: The Path of Insight Meditation,* and author of *A Path with Heart, Living Buddhist Masters, A Still Forest Pool, Buddha's Little Instruction Book, Teachings of the Buddha,* and *Stories of the Spirit, Stories of the Heart.*

Arnold Kotler

Arnold Kotler was a monk at the San Francisco and Tassajara Zen Centers for fifteen years. He is a Dharma teacher ordained by Thich Nhat Hanh, and the founding editor of Parallax Press.

Kenneth Kraft

Kenneth Kraft is professor of Japanese religions at Lehigh University. He is author of *Eloquent Zen: Daito and Early Japanese Zen* and editor of *Zen: Tradition and Transition* and *Inner Peace, World Peace: Essays on Buddhism and Nonviolence*. He lives in Philadelphia with his wife, Trudy, and two daughters.

Sister Annabel Laity

Sister Annabel Laity, a Buddhist nun and Dharma teacher in the Tiep Hien tradition, lives at Plum Village in France, where she helps lead the daily practice of mindfulness. She also leads retreats internationally, and is translator of many books by Thich Nhat Hanh, including *Breathe! You Are Alive*, *Our Appointment with Life*, and *The Sun My Heart*.

Joanna Macy

Joanna Macy is a scholar of Buddhism, general systems theory, and deep ecology, and is known in many countries for her workshops and trainings to empower creative, sustained social action. Her books include *Thinking Like a Mountain: Toward a Council of All Beings*, coauthored with John Seed *et al.*, *Mutual Causality in Buddhism and General Systems Theory: The Dharma of Natural Systems*, and *World As Lover, World As Self* (Parallax Press, 1991). She is translator of *Rilke's Book of Hours*.

Peter Matthiessen

Peter Matthiessen (Muryo Sensei) studied Zen with Nakagawa Soen Roshi, Eido Shimano Roshi, Taizan Maezumi Roshi, and received Dharma Transmission from Bernard Tetsugen Glassman Roshi in 1984. He is author of many books, including *The Snow Leopard*, *Nine-Headed Dragon River*, and *East of Lo Monthang*, and is a lifelong environmentalist and worker for social justice.

Svein Myreng

Svein Myreng is a Dharma Teacher in the Order of Interbeing. He works in adult education in Oslo, Norway, where he lives with his wife, Eevi.

Saki Santorelli
Saki F. Santorelli, Ed.D., is an Assistant Professor of Medicine, Associate Director of the Stress Reduction Clinic, and Director of Clinical and Educational Services at the Center for Mindfulness in Medicine, Health Care, and Society at the University of Massachusetts Medical Center. He has written and coauthored a number of articles and book chapters on meditation in both the scientific and popular press. He is currently writing a book about mindfulness in the helping relationship.

Sulak Sivaraksa
Sulak Sivaraksa, leading Thai dissident, is founder of International Network of Engaged Buddhism. He has been a visiting professor at UC Berkeley, University of Hawaii, Cornell, and Swarthmore. He is author of *Seeds of Peace: A Buddhist Vision for Renewing Society*. He won the Right Livelihood Award in 1995.

Gary Snyder
Gary Snyder is a Pulitzer-Prize winning poet and teacher of literature and wilderness thought at the University of California at Davis. He is founder of the Ring of Bone Zendo, and author of *Mountains and Rivers Without End, Axe Handles, Turtle Island, Earth House Hold*, and many other books.

Shunryu Suzuki
Shunryu Suzuki-roshi was founder of the San Francisco and Tassajara Zen Centers. He is author of *Zen Mind, Beginner's Mind*.

Kazuaki Tanahashi
Kazuaki Tanahashi is a peace and environmental worker, painter, writer, and translator. He is a founding member of Plutonium Free Future, coordinator of Ten Millennium Future, and a Fellow of the World Academy of Art and Science. His publications include *Brush Mind, Moon in a Dewdrop: Writings of Zen Master Dogen, Penetrating Laughter: Hakuin's Zen and Art*, and the translation of Morihei Ueshiba's *Aikido*.

Claude Thomas
Claude Thomas is a combat veteran of the Vietnam War. He was ordained a Peacemaker Priest by Roshi Bernard Glassman in 1995. He has two books forthcoming from Parallax Press.

Robert A. F. Thurman
Robert A. F. Thurman is Jey Tsong Khapa Professor of Indo-Tibetan Studies at Columbia University. In addition to a number of important translations, his published works include *Wisdom and Compassion: The Sacred Art of Tibet* and *Tsong Khapa's Speech of Gold in the Essence of True Eloquence: Reason and Enlightenment in the Central Philosophy of Tibet*. With His Holiness the Dalai Lama, he is currently writing *The Tibetan Book of Inner Science*.

Marci Thurston-Shaine
Marci Thurston-Shaine is a member of the Order of Interbeing living in McCarthy, Alaska, with her husband and two daughters. She practices mindfulness through yoga, gardening, meditation, and mediation within her small community.

Sources

PART I—BEING PEACE

"Cultivating Altruism" is from *Worlds in Harmony* (1992), pp. 3–10.

"Suffering Is Not Enough" is from *Being Peace* (1987), pp. 3–9.

"Letting Go of Suffering" is from *Step by Step* (1992), meditation selections from the text.

"The Art of Life" is from *Brush Mind* (1990), selected statements from the text.

"Spiritual Practice and Social Action" is from *The Path of Compassion* (1988), pp. 24–30.

PART II—TOUCHING PEACE

"Life Is a Miracle" is from *Touching Peace* (1992), pp. 1–9.

"The Dragon Who Never Sleeps" is from *The Dragon Who Never Sleeps* (1992), pp. XIII–XXII and selected verses from the text. Poems originally published in the fine-press limited edition (Monterey, Kentucky, Gray Zeitz, Larkspur Press, 1990).

"Practicing in the World" is from *Mindfulness and Meaningful Work* (1994), pp. 109–110.

"Mindfulness and Mastery" is from *Mindfulness and Meaningful Work* (1994), pp. 231–235.

"Walking Meditation" is from *The Long Road Turns to Joy* (1996), meditation selections from the text.

"Staggering Meditation" is from *A Joyful Path* (1994), pp. 64–65.

"The Good News" is from *A Joyful Path* (1994), p.1.

"More Good News" is from *A Joyful Path* (1994), p.121.

PART III—COMPASSION IN ACTION

"Love in Action" is from *Love in Action* (1993), pp. 39–47.

"Engaged Buddhism" is from *The Path of Compassion* (1988), pp. XI–XVIII.

"Buddhism in a World of Change" is from *The Path of Compassion* (1988), pp. 9–18.

"Nagarjuna's Guidelines for Buddhist Social Action" is from *The Path of Compassion* (1988), pp. 120–121 and 130–144.

"Waking Everybody Up" is from *In the Footsteps of Gandhi* (1990), pp. 123–139.

"Finding Peace after a Lifetime of War" is from *A Joyful Path* (1994), pp. 59–62.

"Call Me by My True Names" is from *The Path of Compassion* (1988), pp. 31–39.

"Days and Months" is from *Learning True Love* (1993), pp. 96–108.

"Buddhism and the Possibilities of a Planetary Culture" is from *The Path of Compassion*, (1988), pp. 82–85.

"Genuine Compassion" is from *Worlds in Harmony* (1992), pp. 131–139.

PART IV—THE GREENING OF THE SELF

"Dharma Gaia" is from *Dharma Gaia* (1990), pp. XIII–XVIII.

"Early Buddhist Views on Nature" is from *Dharma Gaia* (1990), pp. 8–13.

"Watering the Seed of Mindfulness" is from *A Joyful Path* (1994), pp. 66–69.

"World As Lover, World As Self" is from *World As Lover, World As Self* (1991), pp. 3–14.

"The Sun My Heart" is from *Love in Action* (1993), pp. 127–138.

"The Greening of the Self" is from *World As Lover, World As Self* (1991), pp. 183–192.

"Ecocentric Sangha" is from *Dharma Gaia* (1990), pp. 155–164.

PART V—COMMUNITY

"Building Sangha" is from *A Joyful Path* (1994), p. 115.

"Community As a Resource" is from *A Joyful Path* (1994), pp. 5–22.

"The Six Principles of Harmony" is from *A Joyful Path* (1994), pp. 87–90.

"Precious Jewel" is from *A Joyful Path* (1994), pp. 91–92.

"Acceptance" is from *A Joyful Path* (1994), pp. 106–108.

"Smiling" is from *A Joyful Path* (1994), pp. 110–111.

PART VI—FOR A FUTURE TO BE POSSIBLE

"Diet for a Mindful Society" is from *For a Future To Be Possible* (1993), pp. 62–79.

"Precepts and Responsible Practice" is from *For a Future To Be Possible* (1993), pp. 101–105.

"Precepts for the Twenty-First Century" is from *For a Future To Be Possible* (1993), pp. 90–92.

"The Five Precepts and Social Change" is from *For a Future To Be Possible* (1993), pp. 106–109.

"The Future Is in Our Hands is from *For a Future To Be Possible* (1993), pp. 136–142.

"Hope for the Future" is from *The Path of Compassion* (1988), pp. 3–8.

Parallax Press publishes books and tapes on mindful awareness and social responsibility, "making peace right in the moment we are alive." For a copy of our free catalog, please write to:

Parallax Press
P.O. Box 7355
Berkeley, California 94707

E-mail: parapress@aol.com
World Wide Web: http://www.parallax.org